Dyslexia in Adults: Education and Employment

Dyslexia in Adults: Education and Employment

Gavin Reid and Jane Kirk

University of Edinburgh, Scotland, UK

JOHN WILEY & SONS, LTD

Chichester · New York · Weinheim · Brisbane · Singapore · Toronto

Other Wiley Editorial Offices

John Wiley & Sons, Inc., 605 Third Avenue,
New York, NY 10158-0012, USA

WILEY-VCH Verlag GmbH, Pappelallee 3,
D-69469 Weinheim, Germany

Jacaranda Wiley Ltd, 33 Park Road, Milton,
Queensland 4064, Australia

John Wiley & Sons (Asia) Pte Ltd, 2 Clementi Loop #02-01,
Jin Xing Distripark, Singapore 129809

John Wiley & Sons (Canada) Ltd, 22 Worcester Road,
Rexdale, Ontario M9W 1L1, Canada

Library of Congress Cataloging-in-Publication Data

Reid, Gavin.
    Dyslexia in adults : education and employment / Gavin Reid and Jane Kirk.
      p. cm.
    Includes bibliographical references and index.
    ISBN 0-471-85205-8 (pbk.)
      1. Dyslexics—Services for—United States. 2. Dyslexics—Education—United States. 3.
    Dyslexics—Employment—United States. I. Kirk, Jane. II. Title.

    HV1570.5.U6 R44 2000
    362.1''968553086'0973—dc21

                                                                                    00-051320

British Library Cataloguing in Publication Data

A catalogue record for this book is available from the British Library

ISBN 0-471-85205-8

Typeset in 12/14pt Times New Roman by Saxon Graphics Ltd, Derby
Printed and bound in Great Britain by Biddles Ltd, Guildford and King's Lynn
This book is printed on acid-free paper responsibly manufactured from sustainable forestry,
in which at least two trees are planted for each one used for paper production.

Contents

About the authors

Dr Gavin Reid, MA, MEd, MAppSci, PhD, AMBDA, AFBPsS, is a senior lecturer in the Department of Equity Studies and Special Education, Faculty of Education, University of Edinburgh, UK. He has substantial experience as a teacher, lecturer, educational psychologist and researcher. He has presented over 150 seminar and conference papers throughout the UK, the United States, Eastern and Western Europe, Hong Kong and New Zealand. He is the author of *Dyslexia: A Practitioner's Handbook*, editor of *Dimensions of Dyslexia* and co-editor of *Multilingualism, Literacy and Dyslexia*. He is also co-author of books for teachers and parents on learning styles and dyslexia and a group listening and literacy test.

He has current research interests in adult dyslexia, metacognition, learning styles and assessment. He has contributed to a number of journal articles, participated in national and international consultancy and working groups, and has appeared in television and radio documentaries in the UK, Hong Kong and New Zealand. Gavin is currently active in the university's assessment and support provision for students with dyslexia. He was responsible for the development of the first masters course in dyslexia in Scotland and holds a number of university external examiner appointments.

Jane Kirk, BA, DipCE, AMBDA, is Dyslexia Study Adviser at the University of Edinburgh where she has developed and implemented innovative assessment and support procedures for students and staff. She has considerable experience in secondary school teaching, in working with adult voluntary organisations, in lecturing in higher education and in research involving employers, adults with dyslexia, voluntary organisations and government departments.

In addition, Jane took part, with Gavin Reid, in a national TV documentary based on their research on dyslexia and offending – a programme which generated considerable national interest. Jane and Gavin have developed courses for professionals who are working with adults with dyslexia, and Jane was the joint project leader for a government-funded investigation into best practice in assessment, support and training for adults with dyslexia.

A particular feature of her work has been to pioneer study skills courses for senior school pupils and adults.

Preface

This book has arisen from a need – the need for all adults with dyslexia to be respected and their rights to be recognised as legislation, and even litigation, can only lay a foundation. If effective practices are to emerge, resources need to be provided, attitudes need to change and information needs to be available.

There are many promising areas of progress both in employment and education due to the energies and insights of individuals and groups from independent and voluntary organisations, government services, colleges and universities and dyslexic adults themselves. The purpose of this book is to highlight these areas and ensure that the benefits are known to all.

Despite this progress, the field of dyslexia is still riddled with controversy, conflict and confusion. This book identifies many of these issues and attempts to deal with them in a manner that can be helpful to professionals and adults with dyslexia.

The need for this book has arisen from our experiences, which include (a) assessing and providing support for adults with dyslexia in employment, unemployment and those undertaking study, (b) discussing the needs of employers and government employment agencies, (c) working co-operatively with independent and voluntary organisations, (d) liaising with schools and training organisations and (e) researching activities which identified the widespread nature of these issues and needs in the UK and the USA and indeed in many other countries. We have found these issues to be of world-wide significance and hope that this book will impact on the practices and perceptions of professionals dealing with dyslexia throughout the world.

We are indebted to all with whom we have consulted for their support. They have encouraged us to write this book in which we highlight the need to initiate change and draw attention to good practices within the field of dyslexia.

We also appreciate the self-revelations volunteered by adults with dyslexia throughout our research and consultations for this book. We have listened to their anguish, been exhilarated by their successes and uplifted by their hopes, and it is to them that we dedicate this book.

Gavin Reid and Jane Kirk
University of Edinburgh, UK

Chapter 1

Education and employment: issues for adults with dyslexia

Education and employment can make or break an adult with dyslexia. If identification, acceptance and support are present then education, workplace training and employment can provide opportunities to help adults with dyslexia to develop their skills and fulfil their potential. This, however, presents considerable challenges to colleges, universities, vocational training providers, careers advisers, employers and those who work with employment agencies and provide employment services.

It is important to ensure that those who are responsible for providing training, both academic and vocational, in the workplace and in educational establishments, are aware of the needs of dyslexic adults. Colleges and universities in particular need to take this into account in the development and review of courses, and particularly in the assessment criteria for academic and work-related courses. It has been noted that accommodating to dyslexic people's needs can help to develop good practices that can benefit all students and employees. Employers must consider the needs and the value of dyslexic people in the workforce. There is a great deal of evidence to support the view that dyslexic people can be a considerable asset through their potential creativity, social skills and problem-solving strategies.

Overview of this book

It is the purpose of this book to highlight these needs and challenges and provide strategies and direction on how they can be met. The overriding theme of this book is that post-school success is not entirely in the hands of the dyslexic individual but is in fact the product of a combination of the dyslexic person's endeavours and the accommodations and awareness of those in educational establishments and the workplace. The first chapter of this book will establish this theme and provide an explanation of dyslexia, the range of difficulties and strengths, the implications of these and how they relate to current research in the field.

The subsequent chapters will examine key issues, including assessment and particularly how the assessment can be linked to course design and workplace training (Chapter 2). It is important that dyslexic adults are aware of the strategies and resources they can utilise. It is also important that self-sufficiency in learning is encouraged and that a balance is provided between support and autonomy in learning. These issues are discussed in Chapters 3 and 4, which follow assessment. These chapters will deal, respectively, with (a) course design, course delivery, training needs of staff and employers and (b) the needs of the dyslexic person in the workplace.

There is a delicate balance between providing support and developing autonomy – a balance that is acknowledged in Chapter 5 and throughout this book – and it is important that this is understood in training courses for further education and in workplace training. Unfortunately, sometimes the right type of support is not available when needed and this can result in some dyslexic people becoming disaffected with the system, their difficulties and themselves. Chapter 6 – disaffection, defiance and depression – may sound negative and gloomy but for some dyslexic people that is the reality of their situation. That chapter examines these aspects and provides a message of prevention and support. The chapter is to an extent balanced by Chapter 7, which highlights the positive aspects of dyslexia and, in particular, the global, holistic processing style of many dyslexic people.

The chapter following this (Chapter 8) provides an opportunity for dyslexic people to speak for themselves. It describes the life and work of dyslexic adults in a variety of settings, showing how the strengths can be used to help to overcome difficulties and, additionally, focus on the need to achieve autonomy, as well as informed advice presented in Chapter 9.

Helping dyslexic adults is a shared responsibility and it is crucial that employers, managers and course tutors have an understanding of dyslexia, its characteristics and how it can affect individuals, their families and the community. The remainder of this chapter will therefore provide some definitions of dyslexia and highlight the range of difficulties which can be associated with dyslexia.

What is dyslexia?

Although a number of widely used and accepted definitions of dyslexia are currently being used (Reid, 1998) there are some common strands which can be seen in most definitions. There is also a tendency for definitions of dyslexia to reflect a broader conceptual framework and acknowledge the individuality of dyslexic learners. One of the key issues, therefore, is that people with dyslexia will not all exhibit the same characteristics, nor to the same degree.

Some of the difficulties often experienced by dyslexic adults are:

- difficulties in reading accuracy
- speed of reading difficulty
- persistent spelling errors
- difficulties with grammatical structure
- sequencing difficulties in words and in ideas
- need to re-read text
- difficulties planning and organising written work
- difficulty memorising facts
- difficulty memorising formulae
- following a number of instructions if given at the same time
- taking notes – for example, in lectures
- planning study and general study skills
- transferring learning from one situation to another
- noting inferences in text
- written examinations, particularly if timed.

These are some of the more obvious difficulties experienced by dyslexic people and the degree of difficulties can vary from individual to individual. It is also important to note the strengths of dyslexic adults which can usually compensate for their weaknesses. Some of these strengths include:

- good comprehension skills
- good problem-solving skills

- (occasionally) good visual skills
- ability to process information holistically
- good oral skills
- acute awareness of their difficulties and can quite readily utilise compensatory strategies.

Although not all dyslexic adults fit into the pattern above, the research does indicate that generally dyslexic people have more enhanced right-than left-hemisphere skills (Galaburda, 1993; West, 1999). This means that some tasks will be easier to accomplish than others and they are able to utilise different types of skill to complete tasks.

Dyslexia can be more than a difficulty with reading and spelling. Essentially it is a difficulty with information processing and this affects other aspects such as speed of processing and organisational difficulties. Dyslexic adults can display difficulties and differences at all stages in the information-processing cycle. This has implications for how material is presented, learnt and recalled.

Definitions

It is important that clear definitions of dyslexia are available and understood by all. The British Dyslexia Association suggests a broad definition which clearly displays the range of difficulties which can be experienced by dyslexic people. This is described by Peer (1999: 61):

> as a combination of abilities and difficulties which affect the learning process in one or more of reading, spelling and writing. Accompanying weaknesses may be identified in areas of speed of processing, short term memory, sequencing, auditory and /or visual perception, spoken language and motor skills. It is particularly related to mastering and using written language, which may include alphabetic, numeric and musical notation.

The Adult Dyslexia Organisation in the UK, which is also a registered charity, suggest that

> dyslexia may be caused by a combination of phonological, visual and auditory processing deficits. Word retrieval and speed of processing difficulties may also be present. A number of possible underlying

biological causes of these cognitive deficits have been identified and it is probable that in any one individual there may be several causes. Whilst the dyslexic individual may experience difficulties in the acquisition of reading, writing and spelling they can be taught strategies and alternative learning methods to overcome most of these and other difficulties. Every dyslexic person is different and should be treated as an individual. Many show talents actively sought by employers and the same factors that cause literacy difficulties may also be responsible for highlighting positive attributes – such as problem solving which can tap resources which lead to more originality and creativity. (Schloss, 1999, personal communication)

Issues

A report produced by a working party of psychologists, *Dyslexia, Literacy and Psychological Assessment* (BPS, 1999a) opted for a *working definition* of dyslexia because they felt that a working definition did not require any causal explanation. The working definition they opted for is broadly similar to that developed by a Committee of the Health Council of the Netherlands which focuses on the difficulty at the word-reading level. The BPS working party definition is: 'Dyslexia is evident when accurate and fluent word reading and/or spelling develops very incompletely or with great difficulty' (BPS, 1999a: 18). This definition has met with some critical comment but the authors of the report indicate that the working definition should be applied within the framework, recommendations and purpose of the report and should not be taken out of that context. Joanne Rule of the BDA (BDA press release, BPS report, 29 October 1999) suggests in response to the report that 'dyslexia is greater than the sum of reading and spelling problems'. This is a very valid comment in our opinion, and particularly in relation to adults. The value, however, of the BPS report is that it separates working definition from causal definition and this helps to embrace different theoretical explanations in relation to a causal framework for dyslexia. The report suggests a number of hypotheses associated with dyslexia, which include:

- phonological deficit hypothesis
- temporal processing hypothesis
- skill automatisation hypothesis

- working memory hypothesis
- visual processing hypothesis
- syndrome hypothesis
- intelligence and cognitive profiles hypothesis
- subtype hypothesis
- learning opportunities hypothesis
- emotional factors hypothesis.

Each of these hypotheses refers to different or overlapping theoretical approaches described by academic researchers to explain dyslexia from a causal perspective. The authors of the report suggest that the phonological deficit hypothesis provides the main focus because of the "broad empirical support that it commands' (p. 44) and because of the impact of phonology on the other hypothesis, particularly temporal order hypothesis, skill automatisation and the syndrome hypothesis. We feel that, in the case of adults, the phonological deficit hypothesis may be less important than some other factors, and suggest that dyslexia should in the case of adults be viewed in a functional and situational manner, which includes literacy, communication skills, visual skills, processing speed and self-esteem.

There are many different issues associated with dyslexia and the remainder of this chapter will outline some of these issues relating to adult dyslexia both in the workplace and in further education. These issues will also be discussed in some detail in subsequent chapters of this book.

The use and misuse of labels

Rightly or wrongly it appears that a label is a necessary prerequisite for obtaining the type of help which can be beneficial. But quite apart from that, the existence of a label can offer to the person with dyslexia a useful explanation of the nature of his or her difficulty. Often labels attract funding and support – but that should represent the beginning not the end of the process. Acquiring support should not be the goal of a label but rather a signpost. The type of support necessary does not depend on the label but on a description of the difficulty and the strengths of the individual – in other words the learning characteristics and the needs of the person.

Yet a label can be accompanied by some drawbacks. Just as it might lay open the path for support, it could also impose barriers. Luecking (1997) suggests that a label could inadvertently stigmatise the job seeker and make them dependent on the goodwill of the employer to 'give them a chance'. Although there is little available evidence on employers' perception of dyslexia and how that may interfere with opportunities for successful employment, it has been suggested that employers may be less sensitive to dyslexic type disabilities than they are to other, more visible disabilities (Minskoff et al., 1987). In the UK some advances have been made in this respect by organisations such as the Employers Forum on Disability, and individual initiatives from some large companies who are represented in such groups.

In our UK study (Kirk and Reid, 1999) one of the most contentious issues to be discussed in the focus groups, from the viewpoint of arousing strong and often conflicting views, was in fact the issue of labelling and how this relates to the assessment. It was clear, at least, that a label should not be used for the sake of it, although on some occasions merely having the knowledge that they are dyslexic was helpful to some adults, particularly those who had failed quite significantly at school and subsequently had low self-esteem. At the same time it was noted that providing someone with a diagnosis and a label can, and perhaps quite rightly does, raise one's expectations of the hope of effective support and the desire to redress the effect of previous experiences of failure.

The research showed that if a diagnosis is to take place then the person's emotional needs should be taken into account and a detailed explanation of what dyslexia is, and how it may effect them, was seen as essential – more essential than the actual label.

Some of the concerns about labelling related to the lack of knowledge, confidence and training among professionals involved with dyslexic adults. This situation did vary considerably from area to area but generally the difficulty surrounded the possibility of mis-diagnosis or missed diagnosis. One of the main issues cited in relation to this was the lack of an agreed working definition for dyslexia. It was acknowledged that, in the general literature, a number of different definitions exist but it was quite strongly felt by participants of our study that there should be an agreed definition for those working in employment services and in training provision. This would provide some uniformity and direction for staff, particularly those involved in training programmes.

Links with school, further education and the workplace

This is a crucial area as preparing the dyslexic person for the workplace should begin at school. This preparation is not a one-way process as it should also prepare employers for working with adults with dyslexia in the workplace. There are implications here for links between school careers personnel and employers. In our UK study we found that although many careers professionals had a desire to find out about dyslexia, few had any substantial training.

The relevance of the mainstream school curriculum to employment skills, therefore, should be seen as a key factor to success in adult life. Research findings have provided striking conclusions concerning the transitional period of dyslexic adults to successful employment. It was reported that more than 50% of dyslexic graduates from US high schools did not gain successful employment (Will, 1984). This seems to support the speculation that either the training they received in the high schools did not help them to prepare for employability (failing to match their qualities with job requirements) or they did not receive adequate training despite the proven use of such training (Gerber et al., 1992). This was further supported by Hoffmann et al.'s (1987) study which identified a mismatch between curricular and employment needs. In order to improve this situation, it would be useful to examine the curriculum provided by various institutions (e.g. secondary, post-secondary and vocational) and to assess whether or not such employment training needs were indeed being at least partly, if not fully, met. This would ensure that adults with dyslexia were prepared for successful employment at an earlier stage in their career. Additionally, it may also reduce the economic and resource burdens of the employment agencies or training organisations.

A multi-disciplinary approach to vocational training in schools should therefore be emphasised. The successful completion of secondary school does offer some platform for success in adulthood (Blackorby and Wagner, 1997) as is a vocationally relevant environment within the school and community (Grayson et al., 1997). The integration of the diagnosis and treatment aspects within training programmes can be demonstrated in the training of job-seeking skills, job interest, working habits and practical work skills such as filling in job applications and following directions (Hoffmann et al., 1987). It will only be when such vocational aspects of training have been integrated into the school programmes, that dyslexic people will be able to enter the world of work pre-equipped with both competence and performance. In addition, school professionals should also be informed about the significance of the drop-out rates in relation to unsuccessful employment life (Blackorby and Wagner, 1997; Grayson et al., 1997). In a UK study of over 100 institutions, 43% of the total dyslexic student population were diagnosed as dyslexic after admission to university (Singleton, 1999a). There is a need to ensure that the two-way process of diagnosis and liaison with employers is in place, as it is just as important to prepare the employer as it is the student.

Support

This is a crucial factor because, as the evidence above shows, the dyslexic person may not be diagnosed at school and therefore will not have been able to develop compensatory strategies. The issues relate to who provides the support and what would be the best type of support available. In the UK there are a number of independent organisations and government-funded agencies dedicated to providing support to adults in employment and those unemployed. The Employment Service, a government-funded body, has a range of initiatives and groups which can support adults with dyslexia, such as the Training and Enterprise Councils (TECs), Local Enterprise Councils (LECs), the Basic Skills Agency, the New Deal initiatives such as the Gateway programme, supported employment programmes, training for work programmes and youth training schemes. It is crucial that those responsible for co-ordinating these schemes have effective links with Further Education Colleges. Indeed, many FE colleges in fact operate job training schemes.

Similarly in the United States a wide range of job preparation programmes are available, many of which commence early in secondary schools (Grayson et al., 1997). Disappointingly, however, many follow-up studies on students with learning disabilities still show a 'period of floundering' after leaving school and commencing employment (Halpern, 1992). According to Grayson et al., most secondary school programmes in the United States that serve individuals with learning disabilities tend to focus on remedial academic instruction, which has little impact on post-school adjustment. Edgar

(1987) suggests that it is crucial to shift the secondary curriculum from academic to functional and vocational. Both in the USA and the UK the issues are the same: support for students with dyslexia should commence as early as possible. In secondary school this support should be relevant to students' potential post-school experiences and effective links should be made with employers as early as possible in the secondary school.

The process of identification and assessment

Chapter 2 highlights the range of strategies that can be used for assessment. There is, however, considerable lack of agreement among professionals on the most appropriate strategies for assessment. A survey of 105 psychologists identified 11 different tests and strategies as being the principal assessment tool (Kirk and Reid, 1999). Indeed, one of the conclusions from this survey was the desire for psychologists to have clearer guidelines on what constituted dyslexia and clearer guidelines on assessment. In the UK, the Division of Educational and Child Psychology of the British Psychological Society published a working party report on *Dyslexia, Literacy and Psychological Assessment* (BPS, 1999a) which included an evaluation of commercially available tests. The report concluded that no one test could be considered obligatory in educational psychology assessments for dyslexia and, additionally, that no particular pattern of sub-tests scores could be regarded as necessary or sufficient in deciding whether or to what extent dyslexia is present. The precise battery of tests which could be used to identify dyslexia is very much at the discretion of the individual psychologist who must then use some form of clinical judgement. This selection will be influenced by whatever definition of dyslexia is favoured. Identification and assessment are therefore closely linked to definitions and form an area which has many ambiguous factors.

Work and course support

Work preparation courses vary considerably. There can be a lack of guidelines for support and training. Some training providers deliver the programmes they want to, irrespective of the individual needs of the group, while other work preparation providers who are contracted to provide training are usually given fairly fixed guidelines for programmes which are sometimes too rigid. As a result, because of the funding mechanism, those providers who are contracted to provide support often become locked into inappropriate provision. There is a greater need for liaison between those who are providing the services and those who require it. Support for adults with dyslexia cannot readily be pre-packaged but should be individually tailored to the adults' actual needs in relation to their situation at work or college.

Disability – the term

Dyslexia is a formal category of disability in legislation and for other such practical purposes. Yet one must consider the issues relating to the term 'disability' and in particular against the views and research which highlight the positive side of dyslexia and the abilities of dyslexic people (Reid, 1996; West, 1997b; Davis, 1997). In some cases the word 'disability' is no more than a 'rubber stamp', as in the case of a student whose examination paper is stamped 'Disability' to alert examiners to a processing difficulty. But the use of the word is very emotive and can be very meaningful to the dyslexic person, especially since that person, as is the case with most 'disabled' people, has considerable ability and potential. Whether the term is used or not, it is important that the message relating to the abilities of dyslexic people is heard and understood. In the absence of such sensitivity, the notion of disability can become exaggerated and misunderstood.

Disability legislation in the UK and the USA

Disability legislation is essential but often does not go far enough and may not be altogether effective. In the UK the Disability Discrimination Act (1995) impacts on a wide range of groups in education and in employment. Each education institution must have a disability statement. In employment it is unlawful for employers with 20 or more employees not to make 'reasonable adjustment' for adults with dyslexia. It is estimated that 25% of disabled employees are not catered for under the terms of the Act. So although legislation is important, it primarily categorises the person in terms of the negative connotations of disability.

The effectiveness of the legislation relies to a great extent on the willingness and the acceptance of employers to uphold the Act in spirit and in deed.

Similarly, in the USA the Americans with Disabilities Act, which was fully implemented in 1994, should provide greater opportunities for accommodations for employees who come under the categories of the Act. Gerber et al. (1997) assert that in resolving work disputes neither the spirit nor the letter of the legislation is being smoothly implemented. Yet, while legislation offers the promise of normalisation and is a necessary step in the process, it is by no means the end product.

Assessment availability

In the UK, and indeed the USA, obtaining a full assessment can be costly. Students attending a higher or further education college in the UK can obtain an assessment but this is likely to be related to their course. The assessment will need to be comprehensive enough to obtain some form of diagnosis of dyslexia in order for accommodations and additional resources to be made.

The Employment Service in the UK provide an assessment for those who are unemployed and seeking employment and for those whose employment is at risk on account of suspected dyslexia.

Special allowances

In the USA, the Americans with Disabilities Act indicates that employment testing is discriminatory if they screen out an individual with a disability due to the effects of the disability. Certainly in relation to dyslexia this would mean that if extra time was not permitted then the test may be discriminatory. This is a complex issue. It is necessary to ensure that the design of employment tests do have a cognitive component and one where speed of information processing is a factor, as this can relate to dyslexia. For example, the dyslexic people should perform to their real abilities in the cognitive aspect provided that sufficient time is available; if not, then the degree of extra time necessary would need to be judged. The point of concern is, that by providing extra time which has been decided arbitrarily, this may invalidate the standardisation of the test (Biller, 1993). As a result, the assessment may over-predict the ability of the individual and the employee may then fail to fulfil the expectations and the demands of the employment. In this situation both employer and employee suffer: the latter through work-related anxiety or stress and the former by inappropriate selection of personnel. Biller (1997) describes the outcomes of a number of litigations in which the issue of extra time is the central issue. Some outcomes from these court cases are in favour of the individual who is seeking the additional considerations. For example, Biller describes the outcome of a case in the USA in which a law student pursued a court action in order to obtain extra time – the exam over a four-day period instead of two, a quiet place to take the exam and the use of a word processor and spellcheck. The court refused to uphold the individual claim stating that any underachiever could be termed learning disabled and all could benefit from these concessions irrespective of the causes of the under-achievement. The statement also mentioned the other factors which can cause poor exam performance such as lack of motivation and stress. This judgement seems to highlight a complete lack of understanding of the nature and effects of dyslexia and learning disabilities.

Woods and Reason (1999) comment of the dearth of information used to determine the assessment needs of individual dyslexic students for GCSE examinations in the UK, and this is linked to the ongoing debate as to who should provide assessments that entitle candidates to special examination arrangements. They make a crucial point when they assert that the person who conducts the assessment is less important than the form of the assessment. It could be suggested that the actual nature of the examination should be investigated. It may be possible to provide alternative forms of assessment of competences in a manner which would make special arrangements redundant – for example, oral examinations, untimed open book assessment or portfolio assessment.

The screening process

The issue of screening will be discussed in detail in Chapter 2, but it is widely recognised that screening is an essential first step in the process.

In some cases, the use of a comprehensive and valid screening measure may be sufficient to decide on the accommodations necessary. Recently there has been considerable progress in the area of computer screening and pencil and paper screening measures. The value of the screening approach is that it can be implemented relatively quickly and can be used without lengthy training – often the results of screening tests can be interpreted easily, and very importantly can be easily understood by the dyslexic person. A survey (Singleton et al., 1998) on screening in relation to higher education found a wide variety of screening techniques in use. Almost all respondents in their study used a dyslexia check-list and gave students some form of interview. Around half of the sample used various standardised tests of reading and spelling while the rest did not. Clearly if the screening is carried out by an experienced professional this could add considerably to the value of the exercise. An extended interview can yield information of considerable importance towards an eventual diagnosis.

Additional support and tuition

This is an important area because many people are under the misapprehension that dyslexic people need basic literacy skills when this type of tuition can be demoralising and inappropriate. Indeed, a course in basic literacy skills would highlight the areas in which the person with dyslexia has had unpleasant and unsuccessful experiences. Yet many of the support programmes for dyslexic adults which we have examined were little more than courses in basic literacy skills which utilised methods more appropriate for young children than for adults. Often the term 'remedial help' is used to describe the nature of the programmes for dyslexic adults. There are some very fundamental issues regarding the implications of using this term and it is felt strongly that the term 'support' should be used rather than 'remedial help' to describe the programmes for dyslexic adults. Remediation has deficit connotations and alludes to a dependency culture where the adult with dyslexia is essentially in the hands of others who can provide the necessary 'remediation'. We feel that one should be striving to achieve autonomy in learning and that responsibility should shift from the trainer to the client as soon as the support programme is established. This will be discussed in some detail later in the book, but there are some excellent examples of training programmes utilising these principles such as that implemented by Klein and Sunderland (1998) which focus on the relevance of the programme to the individuals needs, directed towards success and some form of achievement and should eventually lead to the person taking charge of his or her own learning. Similarly, McLaughlin et al. (1994) suggest three main principles of support – literacy, life skills and coping strategies – which should also provide an overarching framework for support to achieve autonomy in learning. Support, therefore, should have a work preparation ethos if the individual is in or seeking employment and a course-focused ethos if attending a tertiary education course.

The report by a Working Party of the Division of Educational and Child Psychology of the British Psychological Society (BPS, 1999a), referred to earlier in this chapter, recommends that for older learners (secondary school and further education) direct teaching to address word reading and spelling problems usually plays a secondary role to consideration of the continuing impact of dyslexia on the individual. This implies that equality of opportunity and full curriculum access focusing on the educational, social and cognitive needs of the person is of greater importance than any remedial type programme in literacy.

Use and overuse of technology

There have been considerable developments in software packages suitable to support dyslexic adults, and developments in this area are ongoing. The British Dyslexia Association have a computer committee to monitor developments and provide advice on all matters relating to computers and dyslexia. There have also been many studies looking at the impact of assistive technology on the individual with dyslexia. Raskind et al. (1997), in reviewing the American studies, suggests however that most of these studies have been from the *outside* and few have gained the *insider's* perspective. Reid and Button (1995) stress the importance of focusing on the insider's perspective in order to prevent investigators from imposing their preconceived views on how individuals should utilise technology. In a study of five interview vignettes, Raskind and colleagues found a range of views in relation to the use and benefits of technology. The researchers felt, although it was not explicitly indicated by the respondents, that technology had enhanced their ability to function independently. Two of the informants in the study indicated that technology actually enabled them to turn their weaknesses into greatest strengths. While it should be acknowledged that technology can be beneficial to the dyslexic adult, attention should be paid to the risk of extreme reliance on technology for all types of situations. To some individuals dyslexia support has been equated with 'computer', but this should only be part of the package. Following lengthy studies, Healy (1998) has already indicated the dangers of computer misuse in the learning situation. This makes it of vital importance that the individual needs of the person is the major determining factor in the provision of support.

Holistic needs

It is important to view the dyslexic person in a holistic way and to appreciate the importance of self-concept and, perhaps, the counselling needs of the individual.

This is crucial, because it is too easy to focus on, and deal with, the person's difficulties but ignore the individual's holistic needs. Indeed, Hoffmann et al. (1987), in examining the factors identified by trainers which they felt were crucial in determining the successful outcome of any intervention programme, ranked self-concept as the most important. We suggest that literacy skills are only important in conjunction with other real-life skills and that training should integrate both these factors. McLaughlin et al. (1994) suggest that dyslexia is a life-span disabling phenomenon, but one which individuals can control if the self-concept is positive and their holistic needs are identified.

The needs of adults with dyslexia are situational and can vary at different points throughout life and work challenges. For that reason it is important that those who provide initial and subsequent assessment and support should be trained, knowledgeable about dyslexia and possess some skills in counselling. It is also important that the dyslexic individuals appreciate exactly what dyslexia means as far as their strengths and difficulties are concerned and have a notion of acceptance and optimism in relation to the future, whether it be in study or in the workplace.

Employment awareness

It is important that this aspect is seen as a priority. Employers have a key position in relation to the selection of dyslexic people and in ensuring that their skills are fully utilised in employment. Dyslexic adults often live under the constant pressure of satisfying expectations derived from a variety of sources, even once secure in their jobs they have to ensure that they fulfil the expectations of their employers. It is important, therefore, that employers are fully aware of the needs and skills of dyslexic people and utilise their skills appropriately in the workplace. It should also be considered that some dyslexic people may feel apprehensive about their difficulties being revealed. Every effort should be made to minimise any stigma and one of the most effective means of achieving this is through awareness campaigns and liaison between dyslexia groups and employers. In the UK, groups such as the Employers Forum have made some headway in this direction and have the potential to achieve much, not only with the major employers, but also with small-scale companies. This type of dissemination is also the focus of the British Dyslexia Association training courses for trainers and employers (Myers, personal communication). This course, called *Dyslexia: Working with and for Dyslexic Adults,* comprises sessions on an introduction to dyslexia; dyslexia friendliness and signposting (that is, where and how to find information on dyslexia).

From the US perspective, Luecking (1997) suggests that the message to employers should be 'reframed and that direct inquiry into the needs of the employer should replace charitable appeals.' Each job, and each individual, offers a distinct pattern of needs and support. It is crucial that the employer is central to meeting the individuals needs, job development needs and the needs of the company. A partnership between job preparation programmes and employers is therefore paramount.

Contextualising the assessment

This is extremely important because an assessment should provide more than a diagnosis; it should also provide some guidance in relation to how the individuals can deal with their dyslexic difficulties and use their strengths in the workplace or at college. It is crucial that the assessor has information on the type of work or course difficulties the person may experience. An assessment should not be done in isolation and needs to be contextualised for course or work demands.

The requirements of training in speech therapy will be quite different from those experienced in a law or medical degree. Similarly, in the workplace, attention should be paid to the type of employment in addition to obtaining a diagnosis. Payne (1997) suggests that such aspects as knowledge of learning styles, understanding job descriptions, knowledge of strategies which have already been developed, and views on disclosure, should all be discussed with the dyslexic person at the time of the assessment and certainly be part of the feedback process. In the UK, a study by Kirk and Reid (1999) also revealed the need to focus on metacognitive skills through asking individuals how a task was performed. Both studies found that in many instances the dyslexic individuals had compensated for their difficulty exceptionally well and, while this is very positive for those concerned, it does make it more difficult to make a diagnosis. The assessor therefore needs to be aware of this factor. Other factors, such as English being a second language or a history of failure, need to be considered in formulating an assessment strategy and an outcome.

Feedback

It is important that following an assessment the dyslexic person receives clear and jargon-free feedback. This feedback should be relevant to the person's particular course or employment as well as providing some form of general diagnosis of his or her dyslexic difficulty.

Directory of services

There is a significant need for a directory to inform people of where to go and who to see when seeking help. There are an increasing number of organisations involved in providing services to dyslexic people in job training, access to college courses or help with locating and using resources. These resources are described in Chapter 9. It is important that this help should be readily accessible.

Similarly, in the USA a number of projects have been funded by grants from the US Department of Education Office of Special Education and Rehabilitative Services (OSERS). Some of these are described by Rapp (1997) but often projects which can investigate and recommend good practices are not sufficiently disseminated to be known to many dyslexic adults. However, the internet can offer readily available information on relevant websites. Certainly helplines are extremely useful for this purpose, but much of the benefits of these rest on the goodwill of volunteers.

Learning style

The importance of identifying the learning style of the adult with dyslexia and to provide feedback on the most effective means of processing information for that person cannot be emphasised enough. This is often a neglected area of an assessment and subsequent accommodations, yet is a vital one in relation to assisting the individual to achieve some success and gain some pleasure from work tasks. This is discussed in some detail later in this book, but it is a significant factor and should be considered in recommendation for accommodations in the workplace. Acknowledging learning styles can help the employer to gain maximum benefit from the dyslexic employee and can prove to be cost effective.

Training

The need to initiate informed, consistent and accredited training for all individuals involved in dealing with dyslexic people, irrespective of the extent or level of their contact, is of considerable importance.

The implementation and acceptance of all the points discussed above rely to a great extent on the level and extent of training of the professionals who have some form of contact with dyslexic people. Chapter 3 outlines a proposal for training in order to support adults with dyslexia. Professionals should have some access to training, even if it is only at an awareness level.

Summary

All the above points are important and will therefore be addressed in some form in later chapters. It is worth noting in this introductory chapter that some particular aspects of the dyslexic profile have extremely significant importance for the eventual employment success of dyslexic adults, such as, the process of identification and assessment. It is important that this process should be clearly defined and that professionals involved feel confident of the outcome. Additionally, it is important that the information from the assessment is communicated in a clear and sensitive manner to the dyslexic person. Some people may well feel some stigma attached to the label *dyslexic*, and although this should not be the case, the individual's feelings and views need to be sought and dealt with sensitively. It is necessary to help dispel any unfortunate stigma which the individual may associate with being dyslexic. Often this can be dealt with by emphasising that dyslexia is a difference and not a disability. This 'difference' is the manner in which information is processed. This is why it is important to identify particular styles of processing and skills so that these can be used effectively to learn and retain new information.

It is also important that assessment should link to support and not become an isolated piece of information which provides little useful information to the dyslexic person. This will be dealt with in Chapter 2.

The following issues were identified and formed the basis of an investigation (Kirk and Reid, 1999). The context of our study was employment and dyslexia and the working practices of employment service staff engaged with dyslexic clients and indeed other independent groups who provide services to adults with dyslexia.

The focus, therefore, was;

- What is dyslexia?
- How can it be most effectively assessed?
- What is the rationale and theoretical support for such an assessment?
- How does a dyslexia diagnosis differ from a workplace assessment; and are their any common elements?
- How can the dyslexic person be most effectively supported following an assessment?
- Considering the time constraints and the range of expertise required from staff engaged by the employment service, how can dyslexia assessment be both efficient and cost effective?
- What are the training implications of staff involved with interviewing, screening, assessing, tutoring and supporting dyslexic adults in employment?

These questions are addressed in this book and were touched on in the issues identified in this chapter.

Without doubt there is much progress still to be made in the area of adult dyslexia. There has been promising progress in the area of children with dyslexia and this, together with the disability legislation, offers considerable hope for adults.

This introductory chapter has set the scene for this book and identified some of the key issues in dyslexia in adults, at college, in employment and those unemployed who may require some form of job training. All the issues mentioned are of importance. Communication and enhanced awareness of dyslexia among professionals is of overriding importance as this can have an impact on the quality and provision of services for dyslexic people. The training of professionals involved with dyslexic people is also vital as it is through training and awareness that staff in colleges, employers and work-related personnel can develop an understanding of dyslexia and of the needs of dyslexic individuals.

Chapter 2

Screening, assessment and support

One of the principal purposes of assessment is to identify support strategies which can be utilised by the dyslexic individual. The nature of the actual dyslexic difficulties and the strengths and weaknesses should relate to support and strategies. This will not only benefit the dyslexic person but the employers, course tutors and others involved in training programmes for dyslexic people.

Background factors

Labelling

One of the most contentious issues, certainly from the viewpoint of arousing strong, and often conflicting views, is the issue of labelling and how it relates to the actual assessment (Kirk and Reid, 1999). It is clear that a label should not be used for the sake of it, although on some occasions merely having the knowledge that they are dyslexic is helpful to some adults, particularly those who have failed quite significantly at school and subsequently have low self-esteem. At the same time it should be noted that providing someone with a diagnosis and a label can – and perhaps quite rightly does – raise one's expectations of the hope of effective support and the desire to redress the effect of previous experiences of failure.

Follow-up

It appears that the follow-up to a diagnosis depends on a considerable number of factors, which could mean that the adult is provided with effective and appropriate support or, alternatively, further periods of frustration and anxieties. If a diagnosis is to take place, then sufficient attention should be paid to providing feedback to the individual. This should take into account the person's emotional needs and a detailed explanation of what dyslexia is and what the effect may be.

Perspectives: difficulties and strengths

It is important to understand and appreciate that many people have different perspectives of dyslexia and this can have some influence on the conduct and the outcome of an assessment. In our discussions with professionals and employers we always feel it is necessary to begin with a definition of dyslexia. Even then a number of misunderstandings may still emerge.

The range of factors which need to be considered in order to obtain information which can lead to a diagnosis are:

- sequencing of information
- organisation of work
- cognitive aspects such as memory and learning
- metacognitive aspects including transferring learning to new situations
- visual aspects in relation to acuity, tracking and visual distortion in some circumstances
- motor difficulties in relation to co-ordination
- processing speed
- literacy areas
- workplace-related factors.

Not all adults assessed as having a dyslexic difficulty will require the same degree of input and support, nor will they experience the same degree of difficulties in the workplace as some other dyslexic people. Therefore, the work context and awareness of dyslexia among employers is important.

Additionally, of course, it should be noted that dyslexic adults could display considerable abilities (West, 1997b), particularly in problem solving and creativity. The manner in which information is processed may be random rather than sequential. To harness the skills of dyslexic people it is necessary for employers and support providers to appreciate this factor. These factors have implications for the assessment.

Some dyslexic people experience difficulty in the workplace. Performance in the workplace may become impaired to the extent that it results in loss of confidence and threat of job loss. Additionally, dyslexic people who are unemployed may have difficulty in obtaining employment because of their diagnosed or indeed undiagnosed dyslexia.

Often there may also be some apprehension in pursuing advancement at work which can put employment under threat. Dyslexic adults will have difficulty in learning new tasks in the time usually allocated for retraining and this may also put employment under threat. These factors should be considered in an assessment since any combination of these factors can result in distress on the part of the dyslexic adult which can further exacerbate the difficulty.

Work-related difficulties

Moody (1999) explains that the weaknesses of dyslexic people affect efficiency at work in a number of ways, for example:

- *Literacy skills*: following a technical manual, reading reports quickly and writing memos in clear English;
- *Memory*: remembering telephone numbers, recalling what was said at meetings;
- *Sequencing ability*: difficulty in filing documents in correct place and looking up entries in dictionaries and directories;
- *Visual orientation*: may have difficulty dealing with maps;
- *Hand/eye co-ordination*: can result in poor presentation of written work and figures;
- *Speech*: may talk in a disorganised way, especially at meetings and on the telephone;
- *Organisational skills*: may miss appointments and their work area can look disorganised;
- *Emotional factors*: may display anger, embarrassment and anxieties.

On a positive note Moody also describes the manner in which dyslexic people can process information holistically, which means they can be creative and innovative in the workplace.

Klein and Sunderland (1998) describe dyslexia as an invisible disability and describe the type of difficulties outlined by Moody above. They suggest that approximately 4–10% of the general population are estimated to be dyslexic, although they point out that the figure is likely to be much higher among those who failed or did poorly at school.

Support

It is important to consider support throughout the assessment. Sometimes basic skills courses are offered to unemployed people with dyslexia and this can perpetuate a cycle of failure because these courses continue to focus on areas in which the dyslexic person has failed. As Klein and Sunderland point out, recruitment and selection for schemes such as Modern Apprenticeship rely partly or mainly on performance in written tests and often the level of Non-Vocational Training is also determined by literacy skills. Some dyslexic people may be excluded from entry to schemes that could develop their strengths because their specific difficulty is undiagnosed or perpetuated.

Higher education

It is not as unusual for young adults to obtain a dyslexia diagnosis after leaving school. In the Higher Education Sector in the UK (Singleton, 1999a) a survey of over 100 Institutions indicated that on average 51 students per Institution (range 0–225) declared themselves to be dyslexic on their application form (1.5% of the total student population) yet 43% of the total dyslexic student population group were identified as dyslexic after admission to university (range 0–375). Given that dyslexic students who achieve entry to higher education may have more accomplished compensatory strategies than those who fail at school, the figure for undiagnosed dyslexic young adults would likely be well in excess of 1% of the school leaving population. The common threads running through the experiences of dyslexic students as identified in the report are similar to that noted earlier in this chapter as being generally characteristic of dyslexia:

- difficulty adapting past learning to new experiences
- difficulty prioritising information
- difficulty organising themselves
- time management difficulties.

Compensatory strategies

Dyslexia in adults can be more difficult to identify than in children. Adults have often developed compensatory strategies and can therefore conceal many of the dyslexic characteristics. Usually a crisis time occurs when unemployed and undiagnosed dyslexic adults commence some form of work that exposes their dyslexic difficulties. At the same time the dyslexic characteristics will have prevented the person from achieving both in education and in work and confidence will be low and work experience success minimal. For example, the shop assistant in a picture-framing shop whose responsibility is to take orders, measure picture frames, convert customers' 'inch' measurements to 'centimetres', and work out cost, which may be costed per square foot, has functions to perform which will prove difficult for unsupported dyslexic people. This can lead to a series of mistakes and, eventually, reluctance to deal with customers. This can be misinterpreted by colleagues and managerial staff as laziness.

Professional competence

It is essential that those conducting an assessment are fully trained and experienced with the adult population and particularly in relation to work demands. Many educational psychologists who have an enhanced training in assessments for dyslexia, are usually experienced in assessing children, not adults. Care should be taken to ensure that if an assessment is undertaken by an educational psychologist, he or she has experience and knowledge of adult dyslexia and the workplace. Being a chartered educational psychologist in itself does not necessarily equip one to conduct an adult assessment. Indeed, an examination of *The*

Directory of Chartered Psychologists (BPS, 1999b) shows that only 27% of those providing educational psychology services indicated that they can perform dyslexia assessments on adults.

Assessment process

We suggest that a structured system of identification and assessment represents good practice. This structure should include:

- initial screening, interview
- cognitive assessment
- diagnostic assessment
- workplace assessment/or implications for the workplace and recommendations for support
- a user friendly report which should have a clear summary attached.

Klein and Sunderland (1998) suggest that a good assessment will:

- have a clear purpose;
- test the skills the person will need to succeed in the workplace and/or the course of study;
- be contextually based in the vocational area;
- be clearly laid out and printed;
- have unambiguous instructions;
- state the criteria for assessment.

Role of IQ

Although an IQ measure can be a good general guide to the person's cognitive abilities it should be treated with caution in relation to a dyslexia as this may not accurately reflect the real ability of the dyslexic person (Miles, 1996). The nature of the conventional IQ test means that some sub-tests will be challenging for dyslexic people and the aggregate score may not represent the individual's real intellectual ability. This is particularly the case with the memory dependent sub-tests (Singleton, 1999a).

Following a study of 160 dyslexic people, Congdon (1989) reported that the anomalies were such that 'attention should be given to the nature of each subject's profile of results rather than to global IQ scores'. Miles (1996) reports with astonishment how some take the concept of global IQ for granted and uncritically cite IQ figures without any consideration of the sub-skills of which the IQ figure is composed. He does, however, concede that traditional intelligence tests such as the Wechsler Adult Intelligence Scale (WAIS) do have an important role to play in the assessment of dyslexic people and argues that the central factor is the fact that dyslexic people perform effectively on a large number of intelligence test items while, in other items, score lower than control subjects. It is important to understand that some adults fail a particular intelligence test item not through lack of understanding but because they have a difficulty in dealing with symbolic material at speed, fail to remember instructions, or have difficulty in recalling facts from long-term memory (Miles, 1996). Similarly, Nicolson (1996) suggests that IQ scores should not be central to diagnosis and support and suggests that if a suitable screening–support–assessment–support system were in place at all developmental stages and ages then the notion of IQ scores would have less importance.

Several studies from the Yale, Connecticut, longitudinal investigation conclude that dyslexia is dimensional rather than categorical because no qualitative differences can be noted between low-achieving and under-achieving poor readers (Shaywitz et al., 1997).

Turner (1997) suggests that the WAIS is 'encrusted' with a wealth of research findings accumulated over many years and of the 11 sub-tests in the WAIS-R, seven sub-tests load on an unrotated first factor (the *g* component) at 0.70 or above. Turner suggests even shorter forms of the WAIS, although providing less profile information, preserve unusually high validity and reliability while offering significant economy.

There has also been some debate regarding the relationship between IQ, reading ability and the reading process (Turner, 1997; Stanovich, 1991, 1996). The British Psychological Society Working Party Report, *Dyslexia, Literacy and Psychological Assessment* (BPS, 1999a) suggests that the relationship between intelligence and reading is complex and more likely to be multi-faceted rather than linear. General cognitive abilities, the report suggests, are influential in the access of semantic and syntactic information, particularly with increasing text complexity and also in the ease of which dyslexic learners can utilise compensatory strategies.

The IQ test can be extremely useful not only as a general indicator of cognitive abilities but because it provides a profile of abilities. In the case of dyslexia this profile is usually uneven, highlighting strengths and difficulties. The views of many experienced psychologists working in this field suggest that there is usually a significant discrepancy between skills involved in verbal reasoning, oral comprehension and non-verbal problem solving on the one hand and skills which depend heavily on working memory on the other (Singleton, 1999a).

This view is supported by Moody (1999) who suggests that a commonly found dyslexic profile shows high scores on tests of verbal reasoning, but poor scores on tests of short-term memory and visuo-motor tasks. She suggests that the psychologist may wish to supplement the IQ test with more specialised tests particularly relating to memory.

Range of screening and assessment strategies

There is an increasing number of tests and other assessment procedures which can be suitable for adult assessment. Some descriptive comment of these procedures will be made below to identify the main uses of particular tests and assessment strategies and to highlight how these may be linked to support.

Wechsler Adult Intelligence Scale

The Wechsler Adult Intelligence Scale (WAIS) is widely used by psychologists and a number of updated versions have been produced. The most recent WAIS-III (Wechsler, 1999) extends the range of sub-tests in its predecessor (WAIS-R).

The WAIS-III is divided into two parts or 'scales'. The verbal scale consists of seven sub-tests and assesses the development of language skills. It includes tests of expressive vocabulary, comprehension, reasoning, general knowledge, mental arithmetic, attention and short-term memory.

The performance scale consists of seven sub-tests and assesses the development of visual (perceptual) and motor (manual) skills. There are tests of observation, constructing patterns, jigsaws, sequencing and copying symbols giving information in relation to visual perception, reasoning, spatial and sequencing skills, short-term memory and speed of information processing.

A brief description of each WAIS-III sub-test is shown below:

- *Information*: General knowledge, long-term memory.
- *Digit span*: Recall of information (numbers), short-term auditory memory, concentration.
- *Vocabulary*: The ability to express ideas verbally, word knowledge and long-term memory.
- *Arithmetic*: Attention, concentration, short-term auditory memory numerical reasoning.
- *Comprehension*: Interpret social situations, make practical judgements, reasoning.
- *Similarities*: Concrete and abstract reasoning skills, conceptual understanding.
- *Picture completion*: Visual perception.
- *Picture arrangement*: Sequencing of information.
- *Block design*: Spatial ability.
- *Object assembly*: Analysis of parts into a whole.
- *Digit symbol*: Paper and pencil task, visual motor integration, speed of information processing.
- *Symbol search*: Visual motor integration, visual memory.
- *Matrix reasoning*: Abstract reasoning skills.
- *Letter–number sequencing*: Working memory and attention.

The WAIS is essentially a cognitive assessment which provides an IQ score and verbal and performance intelligence quotients. The sub-tests comprise a cognitive profile which can reveal a pattern of strengths and weaknesses. The time taken to administer the WAIS can be lengthy. Although the WAIS can be very useful it may not be necessary to use it in every assessment.

It is important to be aware of the type of information which administration of the WAIS can yield, and particularly the specific sub-tests which can provide useful data to help in the diagnosis of dyslexia. Research which involved analysing over 100 WAIS profiles from the WAIS-R and collaboration with a psychologist experienced in adult assessment (Lannen, personal communication) showed that three specific sub-tests yielded information which considerably aided the eventual diagnosis. These sub-tests were digit symbol, digit span and arithmetic. Usually, though not always, dyslexic students would have difficulty with these sub-tests because they focus on short-term memory processing and speed of processing. At the same time it was noted that dyslexic adults usually do well in comprehension and similarities sub-tests in the verbal scales and the object assembly and block design in the performance scale.

It is interesting to note in relation to the Wechsler Intelligence Scale for Children (WISC) that there is conflicting evidence regarding the use of sub-test profiles to identify a dyslexic cognitive profile. Frederickson (1999) studied the diagnostic value of the arithmetic, coding, information and digit span sub-tests which are usually linked to dyslexia in what has become known as the ACID profile. She found that although the profile was statistically more prevalent in dyslexic samples it still only accounted for 4–5% of a dyslexic sample, and she concludes that the low incidence offers little diagnostic value. This seems to concur with a study in the USA (Watkins et al., 1997) who found, on examining the profiles of all dyslexic children in one school year in three south-western suburb districts, that the ACID profile accounted for 4.1% of the SpLD group.

On the other hand, Turner (1997) argues in favour of identifying and understanding dyslexia through the use of cognitive profile analysis. He also suggests that the deficit in phonological working memory among dyslexic learners could be influential in the eventual cognitive profile. The manual for the WISC-III UK (Wechsler, 1992) outlines the procedure for identifying the ACID profile.

It should be noted, however, that not all dyslexic adults will perform to this pattern in the assessment as many have developed effective compensatory strategies to overcome some of their weaknesses such as short-term memory. So although the WAIS can offer many insights into the adult's cognitive functioning it needs to be supplemented by other forms of assessment.

The most recent version of the WAIS, the WAIS-III (Wechsler, 1999a) offers considerable promise that it too will prove useful in an assessment for dyslexia. It is more user-friendly than the WAIS-R and offers a richer potential for more informed data due to the inclusion of additional sub-tests. Lannen (personal communication) suggests that the additional sub-tests in both the verbal and performance scales can be beneficial, particularly the additional memory tests, which look at attention, memory process and recall. In the performance scale of the

WAIS-III one of the additional sub-tests – matrix reasoning – can be particularly useful when assessing people in the older age range. This is because, unlike block design, it does not have a timed element and therefore will not discriminate against older people who may need more time to complete this type of processing task.

The Wechsler Memory Scale (WMS-III)

This test is co-normed with the WAIS-III described above. It can provide useful information on three main aspects of memory: immediate memory, both auditory and visual; general memory, delayed; and working memory, which involves letter number and spatial span. Moody (1999) suggests that this test can supplement the memory data obtained from the WAIS as often more sophisticated information on the person's memory processes are required than that which can be obtained from the WAIS.

Screening questionnaires and checklists

A great deal of information can be gleaned from questionnaires and checklists and there are a number of commercially available screening materials which can be suitable for initial identification. Some customised screening materials have also been developed by professionals involved in dealing with dyslexic adults, for example staff in further education colleges and universities (Wales, 1998; Bertram, 1998; Kirk, 1998) and disability employment advisers and occupational psychologists (Kirk and Reid, 1999).

An example of an effective interview schedule that helps to establish work goals and explore current difficulties in the workplace is used by York and Humberside Disability Service in the UK (YHDS, 1999). This is essentially an interview guide rather than a blanket checklist and is an example of good practice. The interview guide is divided into five areas:

- Current skills
- Work training
- Education
- Developmental history
- Employment aspiration.

An initial interview should obtain information about coping and compensatory strategies of the individual. This type of schedule that provides details and informative responses is preferable to a typical checklist which usually allows only for yes/no responses. These checklists, however, can often misinform and mislead the individual.

Additionally yes/no checklists can be administered without assistance from qualified professionals and, given the implications of finding out that one is dyslexic, this is not a desirable practice. It is important that only professionally qualified and experienced people administer screening and interview schedules.

The interview should conclude with a summary and possible action. One such action, for example, may well be referral to an experienced psychologist for further assessment. It also provides a list of recommendations in relation to workplace adjustments which the individual could negotiate with the employer.

The following section will describe some of the most useful commercially available screening and other types of tests.

Dyslexia Adult Screening Test (DAST)

This test (Fawcett and Nicolson, 1998) consists of 11 sub-tests. These are: rapid naming; one-minute reading; postural stability; phonemic segmentation; two-minute spelling; backward span; nonsense passage; non-verbal reasoning, one-minute writing; verbal fluency; and semantic fluency. The test is easy to administer and has been influenced by the most recent research in dyslexia, particularly relating to the role of the cerebellum in relation to dyslexia and phonological processing. Verbal fluency and semantic fluency can be useful and can relate more directly to some forms of occupation. As well as articulation these tests call for a degree of recall from long-term memory and organisational skills – these factors can easily relate to the workplace. Similarly, backward span is a test of short-term memory and this also can relate to some workplace demands. The screening takes around 30 minutes to administer and yields a substantial amount of data. The data it provides is more than one would expect from a screening test and therefore can also be used for diagnostic assessment. In fact the DAST, in conjunction with a workplace needs assessment, can provide sufficient information which can help to identify appropriate workplace accommodations.

Bangor Dyslexia Test

This screening test (Miles, 1991) is designed for people up to 18 years of age. It consists of 10 sub-tests which provide information on cognitive aspects of memory and the person's abilities to repeat polysyllabic words and some questions relating to directional confusion. It is short and easy to administer and can lead to a discussion of the person's difficulties. It is essentially a useful starting point and has been used in a number of countries.

Computer screening

This method offers some potential for quick and accurate screening of adults. Computer screening can minimise clinical judgement, is quick and easy to administer, requires little training, can be self-administered and can provide useful informative feedback to the individual. There are several computer screening programmes available, including the following:

'Study Scan' (Zdzienski, 1997) is a computerised assessment programme which also incorporates a screening test, 'QuickScan', which consists of 100 questions and takes around 15 minutes to administer. The responses to the yes/no questions provide information on whether the adult has dyslexic characteristics and how these may be overcome in relation to utilising the dyslexic person's learning style. Although developed for the student population, it has shown potential to be adapted for a more general population (Kirk, 1999).

An investigation of screening methods for dyslexia in higher education has been carried out by psychologists at the University of Hull on behalf of the Higher Education Funding Council for England. A report by Singleton, Trotter and Smart in 1998 examined a wide variety of screening techniques, including checklists and interview methods, use of standardised tests, quantitative approaches and computerised programmes. This data provides strong evidence to support a two-tiered approach.

There is undoubtedly a need for a valid and reliable screening system for adults with suspected dyslexia that can be used speedily and by personnel without a great deal of training. Such a system would need a high degree of confidentiality and not be perceived by the adult as threatening in any way. It would also need to be able to be completed independent of support staff. Computerised assessment offers an attractive solution to these problems.

Singleton (personal communication), together with the Dyslexia Research Group at the University of Hull, pioneered the Cognitive Profiling System (CoPS: Singleton et al., 1996/97) which is now used in over 2,500 UK schools. The Hull researchers have developed a computerised adult screening and assessment system. At present the programme is only available in Swedish and is known as RVT, which stands for ReLS Vuxen Test (*vuxen* means adult in Swedish). It comprises tests of reading and spelling, phonological processing, sound discrimination and memory (Ohlis et al., 1999). The RVT is self-administered and takes 20 minutes for an adult to complete. Results are available immediately and are easily interpretable. They are also developing an *intelligent interpretation* system which will provide recommendations for teaching which will be appropriate for adults with reading or writing difficulties. The Hull research group are also in the process of developing a similar computer test in English which would offer possibilities for the employment service in the UK. In general, the potential advantages of computer-based assessment are considerable. Financially they can be cost effective, particularly in the longer term (Singleton, 1999b). Although many such developments are in their infancy, further trials and development will result in enhanced reliability.

While it is important that the person conducting or overseeing the screening has some training in dyslexia, this does not have to be administered by a psychologist. Clearly, then, the advantages of this form of assessment – that it can be less time-consuming and is self-administered – means that it places less time demands on professionals than conventional individually administered tests.

Attainment tests

It is usually necessary to obtain some information on the individual's level of reading and spelling. The Wide Range Achievement Test (WRAT-3) is a standardised assessment for use between the ages of 5 and 75 years and provides a reading and spelling level and a percentile score. There is an alternative form for re-test purposes and the complete battery can be administered in around 30 minutes. The norms are based on US samples and show good validity and reliability (Singleton, 1999a, McLoughlin et al., 1994).

Woodcock Reading Mastery Test

This battery of tests includes non-word reading, single oral word reading, single word comprehension, and a comprehension passage. It offers a good source of information which can help to identify discrepancies between decoding, as in non-words, and comprehension of text and is suggested to be a good diagnostic indicator of dyslexia (Aaron, 1989). This test has also good standards of reliability and validity; the norms are standardised in the USA.

Spadafore Diagnostic Reading Test

The Spadafore Diagnostic Reading Test (1983) consists of tests of single word oral reading, prose reading, reading comprehension and listening comprehension. McLoughlin et al. (1994) suggests that this test provides a very comprehensive picture. It has graded norms but is also criterion referenced, indicating whether an individual has reached independence, instructional or frustrational levels for each section. This test also provides information about the level of reading skill required for specific occupations, and could therefore be useful in discussing work-related factors. Also, as McLoughlin suggests, it could be useful in career counselling.

The Basic Skills Test

This test (Smith and Whetton, 1988) may be included in a test battery particularly because it is a group test and requires the examinee to read a newspaper and answer questions in a test booklet.

Workplace assessment

In the USA, Payne (1997) has developed a Workplace Accommodations Assessment Model which involves a four-phase process – assessment, planning, implementation and evaluation. Payne suggests that an effective assessment should involve workplace factors such as the work environment, management of the company or organisation, the performance and the needs of the employee. In this model the employee's assessment involves a disability diagnosis such as the strengths and weaknesses of the individual, their processing style, their job responsibilities and a site review. The assessment should also involve an assessment of the organisational environment, looking at aspects such as essential functions of the workplace, the learning culture and resources. Payne develops the suggested workplace accommodations from these two elements – the disability diagnosis and the organisational environment. This model is appropriate for dyslexia assessment in the workplace. It is comprehensive and has a cohesiveness which suggests that assessment is a process which begins and ends in the workplace. It is important that the person conducting the assessment should obtain an overall view of the individual not only from a clinical and cognitive perspective but also from a workplace and environmental one. The workplace environment can in fact hold the key to the suggested accommodations and the potential success of the intervention. Some workplace factors which should be taken into account include the noise in the workplace, rate of disturbances, opportunities to work alone or in groups, size of the workplace and the pace of work. In a factory shop floor, for example, dyslexic people may be easily distracted by the range of stimuli around them. This may be suitable when conducting some tasks, but if the task requires merchandise to be arranged by size, colour or counting, then the dyslexic person can easily become disorientated. Space within the work environment should be made available for certain tasks and one could assess any difference in the dyslexic employee's performance when carrying out the task in a different environment. For that reason, learning styles assessment is important because that form of assessment incorporates both the person's learning preferences and the effect of the workplace environment. Often, as Payne points out, the work environment can change to meet new product or service demands and it is not unusual for employers to overlook the needs of employees with specific disabilities. For that reason Payne includes site review in her model, which includes an examination of the layout of the workplace, and even for dyslexic people this can be important to enable them to process information effectively without too many disturbances. Payne also suggests that it is important to consider workplace patterns of communication. Dyslexic people may not be able to articulate their needs fluently and often in fact internalise their feelings in relation to workplace stresses. This seemed to be the situation with a number of the dyslexic people interviewed for a later chapter in this book. Harry and Alex (see Chapter 8) both indicated that they 'kept things to themselves' and perhaps that is the reason why we found a considerable number of undiagnosed dyslexic people. Often they were doing a job under unnecessary stress or coping with changing workplace demands without the recognition and support they may have qualified for if their dyslexic difficulties had been known.

It is important to consider the form of communication within the workplace and whether or not it is conducive to open dialogue and discussion of difficulties without any stigma being attached. Payne talks about the learning culture of the workplace. This is a crucial factor for dyslexic people as many workplaces have a print culture – more so now with many employees communicating via e-mail even from within the same office. The dyslexic person may miss out on important memoranda because of this. It is preferable, therefore, to ensure that workplace communication is multi-perceptual with scope for meetings, large notices and individual reminders as well as more conventional means of communication.

Although there are quite sophisticated screening and questionnaire instruments for identifying adult learning styles (Dunn et al., 1996) some fairly basic questions about how the individual prefers to learn can often be sufficient to obtain some indication of the person's style. Questions can be asked relating to how the individual takes in information, how information is stored and memorised and how the person prefers to record that information. Kaufman (1994) describes an information-processing model in relation to interpretation of the individual's cognitive profile of input, integration, storage and output – questions can therefore be directed to the person in relation to these factors. The integration aspect is how the person assimilates the information his or her existing body of knowledge or understanding of a concept. This essentially refers to metacognitive assessment and will be discussed later in this chapter.

The importance of focusing the assessment on workplace needs is crucial. Payne provides some examples of a delivery driver who was dyslexic and had difficulty processing customers calls, but by installing a portable printer and voice mail the driver was able to obtain a printout of the calls so that he could re-refer to the addresses and details several times. Similarly, the person with visual discrimination and sequencing difficulties may have problems working with columns of figures and particularly if working under time demands. A simple technique using colour coding could have prevented the employee making repeated mistakes. This type of information should become apparent if workplace factors are considered in the assessment.

In the UK a survey revealed that workplace assessment is the key factor in a dyslexia assessment because many of the difficulties are situational (Kirk and Reid, 1999). Dyslexic difficulties can be exacerbated by inappropriate employment or course choice. This part of the assessment has implications for career counselling which is seen as an extremely key factor in any assessment which has implications for employment. Only a few careers counsellors had an adequate knowledge and understanding of dyslexia.

McLoughlin et al. (1994) suggest that one must also be aware of the secondary symptoms which can be displayed by dyslexic people such as low self-esteem, negativity, poor motivation and seemingly unrealistic anxieties. This, according to McLoughlin et al., can become a cycle of distress and further diminishes the confidence of dyslexic people and the opportunities for them to experience social and work-related success.

Informal assessment

Informal assessment can be conducted in conjunction with standardised assessment, and test results can be examined diagnostically by an experienced assessor by looking at patterns of errors in reading and spelling (Klein, 1993). Factors such as those discussed under miscue analysis, omissions of letters, substitution of words, semantic confusion and sound confusion can all be helpful in identifying a pattern of difficulties.

Alm (1997), in a Swedish study for the Employability Institute of Uppsala, suggests that a diagnostic procedure should include a free writing exercise where people write 10–20 sentences about themselves. This can reveal the extent of the person's everyday writing skills and also show discrepancies between those and oral communication.

It can also be useful to look at the individual's learning style and relate this to support programmes and to the workplace. We have found the Dunn and Dunn *Learning Styles Inventory* (*1975–1996*) to be a useful guide in this respect (Dunn et al., 1996) which is in questionnaire form. This inventory focuses on environmental, emotional, sociological, physiological and psychological factors and can be useful in helping the individual to become more aware of people learning preferences and working context (Reid, 1998; Given and Reid, 1999; Alm, 1997).

Diagnostic information

This is an extremely important part of the assessment process and the information gathered from the assessment should also be used diagnostically. This can be done by looking for further indicators of dyslexia and areas of strengths and weaknesses. These can be utilised and integrated into support programmes and workplace adjustments. The type of tests which can be used diagnostically include:

- single-word reading tests
- non-word reading tests
- reading comprehension
- listening comprehension
- analysis of spelling errors
- in-depth analysis of reading using, for example, miscue analysis
- additional tasks of short-term memory, sequencing activities
- visual assessment.

Diagnostic assessment should be integrated with both the cognitive and the workplace assessments unless specific aspects relating to literacy are to be identified. The system known as miscue analysis (Arnold, 1992) can be used to identify a pattern of reading and spelling difficulties, and although this is used mainly with children it is also very appropriate for adults.

It can be seen from this system whether, for example, the person is revealing a pattern of omissions which may expose some visual difficulties. This was the case with one of the people interviewed in Chapter 8 who reported that when the person he was reading to inadvertently turned over two pages, he intentionally continued the story line as though he was actually reading the words when in fact he was reading for meaning.

Many of these strategies can be administered informally by experienced dyslexia specialists but some can be incorporated into some of the standardised instruments discussed in this chapter and also shown in Appendix 1 (p. 208).

Strengths

As well as identifying the individual's weaknesses, the assessment will obtain information on the person's strengths. It is through these strengths that the dyslexic person will develop self-sufficiency in learning. These strategies will be described in detail in a subsequent chapter of this book, but a summary of these will be shown below:

Visual strengths

Some dyslexic people may prefer to process information visually, which can have implications for learning in the workplace and for learning through lectures at college.

Problem solving

This can be a strength for dyslexic adults. They can possess excellent problem-solving skills which may not be obvious due to the random way they normally process information. They usually can be described as divergent thinkers, which means that they may not process information linearly or logically but may solve problems in a divergent and creative manner (West, 1997b)

Motivation

Dyslexic people are usually highly motivated despite their obvious difficulties, history of difficulties and even failure. It is perhaps because of these difficulties that dyslexic people feel they have to try harder, and therefore expend more effort than others to complete similar tasks. This should perhaps be taken into account when tasks which require new learning are being set for dyslexic people.

Reading strategies

Dyslexic people usually have difficulty with pace and accuracy when reading. These factors can restrict advancement in college courses and in work training but can be overcome using compensatory strategies including the use of context to obtain meaning, skimming and scanning, and, through skilful reading strategies, obtaining the main points of an article or book. A summary of key points should be presented to the person with dyslexia. This would apply whether the material to be read was a work manual or a reader for a college course. It is not necessary to read every word in a passage to obtain full meaning but skimming text does require practice and this type of reading should be recognised as legitimate by tutors and employers. Underlining or highlighting key words should be encouraged, as there is much to be gained by dyslexic adults undertaking the highlighting of key words by themselves. This could help to develop understanding and retention.

Process and issues

Process

A multi-dimensional approach has been suggested to identify adult dyslexia. Anderson (1994) places emphasis upon the importance of obtaining detailed information about the clients concerning their educational history, cognitive ability assessment, thorough reading diagnosis, written expression, spelling and mathematics. This identification information has important implications for the design of any appropriate training programme, flexible enough to provide a combination of training methods for particular dyslexic individuals.

Objectivity, contextual factors and clear structure should be emphasised for effective investigation and interpretation. In so doing, professionals would be required to have the knowledge and skills to enable them to provide information, support, advice and guidance (McLoughlin et al., 1994).

McLoughlin and colleagues suggested a four-step process:

1. Identification.
2. Information gathering.

3. Psychological testing and diagnosis.
4. Developing an understanding of dyslexia and taking action.

Screening tests should provide basic information about education, training, qualifications, work experience, present occupation, family history, medical information and coping strategies (Scarborough, 1984).

There is a general agreement on the formal model of diagnosis comprising psychological testing, objective observation and qualitative analysis, and clinical judgement (McLoughlin et al., 1994; Rack, 1997) and many practitioners in the field of adult dyslexia have placed emphasis on a multi-disciplinary approach to diagnosis and support (Pumfrey, 1996; Wright et al., 1996; Hoffmann et al., 1987).

Screening tests should be appropriate for use with dyslexic adults and should include background information as well as information which can inform clinical judgement.

McLoughlin et al. (1994) emphasised the measurement of general abilities, working memory, and verbal and non-verbal skills in addition to spelling and reading performance, and the results of these tests may have important implications for training and teaching. This process should be conducted by trained professionals, and evaluation, diagnosis and recommendation should be provided by their services (Anderson, 1994).

Issues

Predictive value of tests

A more specific investigation concerning the validity of a widely used test battery was conducted by Faas and D'Alonozo (1990) in a study which set out to investigate the WAIS-R scores as an instrument of predicting employment success and failure. A group of 86 dyslexic adults aged from 18 to 59 years were categorised into two success levels, determined according to their employment history (i.e. successfully employed and not successfully employed). The subjects were drawn from three advocacy groups specialising in supporting adults with learning disabilities in the USA.

WAIS-R was targeted because it was frequently used by educationalists and remedial agencies for dyslexic adults for the purpose of diagnosis and training.

An exhaustive statistical analysis (mean score, two group discriminant analysis) was conducted using the WAIS-R sub-test scores in comparison to the success level of the subjects. Results demonstrated that there was a significant difference between the abilities measured by WAIS-R test and employment success. It was further shown that the comprehension clusters of the WAIS-R comprehension sub-test was the best predictor of a successful transition from school to employment, and the verbal ability of adults with learning difficulties was identified as playing a major role in their employment success (Faas and D'Alonzo, 1990). Visual organisation and sequencing skills were also claimed to be important factors. Comprehension sub-tests purportedly measure the ability to listen to an orally presented question or direction, understand what is said, and to formulate and deliver an appropriate verbal or motor response. Low scores on this sub-test would be taken to indicate that the subject may not be performing with responses an employer would expect. Such verbal abilities tasks further involve assessment of the abilities to memorise factual information and to use well-developed vocabularies appropriately.

Pumfrey (1991) further drew attention to the potential points at issue when making decisions based upon test scores. His contentions are three-fold: (1) it is difficult to detect errors of measurement; (2) multiple test scores are not necessarily used in making decisions; and (3) labelling and criteria are externally imposed. For example, in a study by Wright et al. (1996), a fixed percentage was used instead of a more common approach to a cut-off score.

Key points

Key points which can provide a summing up to this chapter on assessment are:

- Identification and assessment have been characterised by ongoing controversy and anxieties, from many areas – schools, psychologists, parents and dyslexic adults themselves.
- These issues, which have caused anxieties, result from factors relating to some key questions in the administration and interpretation of assessment.

- Issues include: What is the purpose of the assessment? How is the assessment to be carried out? What tools are to be used? What is the effect of the assessment? Some of the implications stemming from these questions are shown below.

Why?

This question asks why an assessment should take place. It implies that there should be a clear purpose when undertaking an assessment and, more importantly, a clear outcome so that the results of the assessment can and will be used to benefit the dyslexic person. If this question is not thoroughly considered, the dyslexic person may be left with unfulfilled expectations.

How?

How an assessment is to be conducted can generate some uncertainties. There are many tests that can be used in dyslexia assessment, but only a few *dyslexia* tests. Even the tests designed to screen and assess for dyslexia are not free from criticism. Some feel a range of strategies should be used, depending on the criteria which is set for the assessment. Interview and observation techniques can supplement, to a greater or lesser extent, psychometric measures.

Who?

Labelling a person's difficulties is a considerable responsibility that should not be taken lightly, and it is important that the assessor has a higher level of training.

There is some debate as to which professional group should have the main responsibility in relation to dyslexia assessment. Traditionally, psychologists – educational and occupational and sometimes clinical – have been viewed as the appropriate professionals to do this on the grounds that they can access 'closed tests' restricted to psychologists. It is *not* because those psychologists have a more detailed and advanced training in dyslexia and dyslexia assessment than other professional groups, because this may not necessarily be the case. These two aspects require further elaboration. The 'closed test' is particularly interesting as the tests referred to are mainly the Wechsler Adult Intelligence Scale and the Wechsler Intelligence Scale for Children. As indicated earlier in this chapter, these tests can be used to identify the intellectual level of the person undertaking the test and as a diagnostic tool to identify the cognitive profile of the individual. To an experienced and trained psychologist such information, together with other tests and information from interviews and observations, can help towards a diagnosis of dyslexia. Yet some professionals, usually teachers with an AMBDA status (UK), or advanced training in dyslexia in the USA, have more detailed knowledge and more specific training in dyslexia assessment than some psychologists. At university and college level it is still the expectation that psychologists undertake formal assessments and provide recommendations for any special course considerations. This practice is reinforced by the higher education working party report (Singleton, 1999a).

A point worthy of note is the disparity among psychologists in relation to their expertise in dyslexia assessments. Initial training courses may have a minor element in dyslexia but many psychologists may have had little or no experience in undertaking dyslexia assessments. This is an important point, merely being able to access closed tests does not in itself provide the expertise necessary for a diagnosis of dyslexia, particularly as the closed tests are not dyslexia tests *per se* but require considerable interpretation and clinical judgement.

What?

The question of what constitutes dyslexia is one which needs to be considered throughout the assessment. The nature of dyslexia and the debate regarding the range of difficulties is discussed in Chapter 1 of this book, but clearly the assessor would need to have clear criteria in relation to what constitutes dyslexia and whether the data accrued from the evidence is consistent with the criteria for dyslexia. One would need therefore to identify what one is looking for before conducting an assessment.

Effect

It is important to consider the effect of the assessment on the individual. There are issues regarding disclosure, and the opinions of the client need to be fully considered. One of the important aspects of conducting an assessment is the reporting back, particularly to the dyslexic person. This needs to be done sensitively and effectively, which means that the assessment should have a positive effect on the person and therefore follow-up is important. If feedback and follow-up are not carried out effectively then the person can be left feeling inadequate.

Conclusion

In summing up this chapter on assessment and support it is important to note that initial screening is important and should be done together with an interview. These should include background information and the person's current coping strategies and should not merely be a checklist of symptoms. The assessment should include standardised and diagnostic information, and that information should, as far as possible, be related to the workplace. An actual workplace assessment and guidance on choice of career are important factors in an assessment and the individual's workplace aspirations should also be discussed.

Computer screening techniques can also be useful as these are usually easy and quick to administer and can minimise the variations which sometimes arise from clinical judgement. It is also important that the individual conducting the assessment has knowledge and experience of dyslexia in adults. Since it is acknowledged that many of the difficulties associated with dyslexia in adults are situational, the actual work context is of crucial importance as difficulties can vary according to the workplace. Dyslexic adults vary considerably in their learning style and use of compensatory strategies and these factors, together with metacognitive factors relating to how an individual prefers to learn, must be considered. Finally it is important to acknowledge the positive aspects and the skills and strengths displayed by the individual. These should be clearly indicated to the dyslexic person so that a positive course of action can be formulated from the results of the assessment.

Chapter 3

Training for training

It has been established in Chapters 1 and 2 that dyslexia can be a disabling condition that affects how people learn and work. Those who show some of the signs of dyslexia nevertheless have qualities that make them valued members of a workforce. However, they can make an even more effective contribution in the workplace if they receive appropriate support, and this chapter considers how that support can be provided. It begins by offering two perspectives on dyslexia and seeks to derive from these a number of pointers to good workplace practice in regard to dyslexia. It then outlines three levels of courses that might be made available in a wide variety of work settings to enable those with dyslexia to become valued members of a working community. The chapter concludes by discussing other courses which personnel, training and other managers might access in their attempt to ensure that those with dyslexia are adequately supported.

Dyslexia: two models

The 'individual' model of dyslexia (Figure 3.1) portrays the individual beset with difficulties and incapacities that derive from the condition. It is a picture of a worker who displays a range of deficits which make him or her a problem in the workplace.

By contrast the 'social' model (Figure 3.2) portrays the various kinds of support and accommodations which integrate the person with dyslexia fully into the workplace.

How can a difference be made in the life of the adult with dyslexia? How can all the personal deficits identified in Figure 3.1 be turned into a collective attempt to provide support of the kinds identified in Figure 3.2?

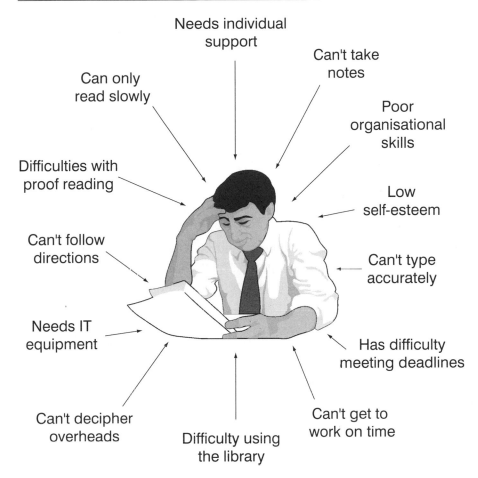

Needs individual
support

Can't take
notes

Can only
read slowly

Poor
organisational
skills

Difficulties with
proof reading

Low
self-esteem

Can't follow
directions

Can't type
accurately

Needs IT
equipment

Has difficulty
meeting deadlines

Can't decipher
overheads

Difficulty using
the library

Can't get to
work on time

Figure 3.1 Individual model of dyslexia (adapted with permission – Scottish Equality Awareness Trainers in Disability, Glasgow)

Although the objective of any support programme will be to make adults with dyslexia independent, this aim cannot be realised without collective action. Figure 3.1 attempts to illustrate the frustrations and limitations experienced by adults with dyslexia. However well motivated and hard working they may be, they are constantly confronted by obstacles which prevent them achieving their best potential. Among the difficulties encountered are:

- employers who issue unfair deadlines;
- important documents and articles produced in a small and difficult-to-read typeface;

- no support person identified in the workplace or educational institution;
- limited availability of appropriate IT equipment, including voice-to-text software;
- inflexible working hours – dyslexic people may process slowly and need extra time to cope with complex tasks.

In addition, there may be the hidden difficulty of poor attitudes in the peer group. University and college students often experience similar difficulties:

- lecturers may not provide structured notes or paper copies of overhead transparencies;
- extensive reading lists can be provided in dense, small print;
- assistance with the planning and structuring of written assignments or with accurate recording of laboratory experiments may not be provided.

In contrast, Figure 3.2 represents how the adult with dyslexia can become independent and successful. The strengths of the adult with dyslexia can be extensive and include: good people skills; highly developed creative ability and high versatility in problem solving. Society cannot afford to ignore the specific needs of this important sector of our community and various measures are already acknowledged to be of help. For example, our public facilities could be made more accessible by use of appropriate signage; by stopping the use of capital letters in bold type, and replacing the writing with letters in upper and lower case the life of an adult with dyslexia could be made easier; by adopting oral assessment we could enable adults with dyslexia, who are often very articulate and confident when presenting information orally, to display their abilities and suitability for promotion.

Groups like the BDA, ADO or IDA lobby continuously for such changes to be introduced to make the lives of adults with dyslexia less complicated. However, society in general has a responsibility to provide the forms of support advocated in Figure 3.2.

The starting point must be to raise awareness of dyslexia among a wide range of the population: among educators; trainers; employers; services and prison officers and families. Misunderstandings of the concepts of dyslexia must be minimised and replaced with knowledge of the processing difficulties encountered by people with dyslexia.

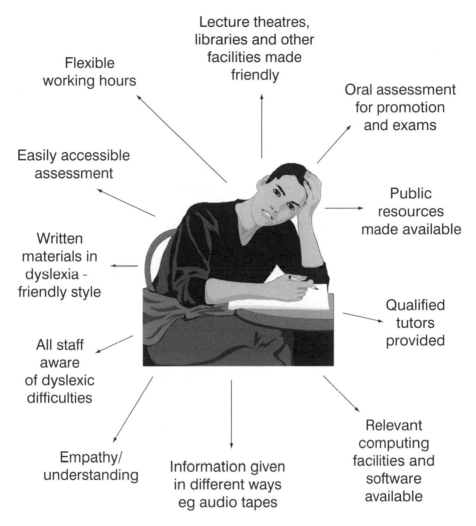

Flexible working hours

Lecture theatres, libraries and other facilities made friendly

Oral assessment for promotion and exams

Easily accessible assessment

Public resources made available

Written materials in dyslexia - friendly style

Qualified tutors provided

All staff aware of dyslexic difficulties

Empathy/ understanding

Information given in different ways eg audio tapes

Relevant computing facilities and software available

Figure 3.2 Social model of dyslexia (adapted with permission – Scottish Equality Awareness Trainers in Disability, Glasgow)

At the level of the individual workplace, provision needs to be made so that the working environment can be modified to accommodate people with dyslexia. Those who regularly come in contact with adults with dyslexia need to be sensitive to the difficulties and encouraged to play their part in creating a supportive working environment for such people. Three groups of people can be identified. Firstly, there are key staff who are likely to have dealings with people with dyslexia. Included in this group are front-line and reception staff, who are usually the first contact with the organisation; management staff, who would interview candidates; and any other interested members of the workforce. The second group are those who have a supervisory or management role within the workplace, who regularly present courses to trainees and offer ongoing staff development. Finally, the third group are specialist support workers who might be asked to support adults with dyslexia on a one-to-one basis. This group might include social workers, army or prison officers or personnel officers in large organisations.

These three groups have different training needs and three types of course are proposed. Course A, for the first group, would be an awareness-raising exercise lasting up to one day but, if necessary, could be presented in a few hours. For the second group, Course B would include the identification of adults with dyslexia, how to provide support for them and how to implement that support. To cater for the more specific needs of the third group Course C is proposed. It would be offered in two parts. Part 1 would develop the concepts introduced in Course B; part 2 would provide the participant with the opportunity to undertake a research project, a staff development programme or a detailed analysis of an issue relating to dyslexia in the workplace. The end product would be presented to colleagues and provide further awareness-raising or some other improvements in the workplace to make it more acceptable to those with dyslexia.

Some suggestions about the content and delivery of these three courses are provided in the next section of this chapter. Course A is described in some detail, including samples of overhead transparencies, to illustrate possible approaches. Courses B and C are outlined using the same structure. The other chapters of this book will inform the presenters of courses B and C and provide a basis for any discussion.

Course A: Awareness-raising

Target group

Front-line and reception staff, members of management team, any interested staff.

Aim

The objective of the course is to raise awareness of dyslexia in a particular workplace.

Key learning outcomes

By the end of the course the participants should be able to:

- recognise the principal features of dyslexia;
- know how dyslexia can interfere with effective performance at work;
- understand that changes in the work environment can minimise the problems encountered by adults with dyslexia.

Method

The workshop presenter will offer a short explanation of dyslexia and how it affects people. There will then be two workshops: the first will focus on the implications for an adult with dyslexia in the particular context of the participants; the second will attempt to provide support strategies in their particular situation.

Activities

1. Divide the participants into groups of 5 or 6 people. Ask them to discuss the main implications for adults who have just been diagnosed as having dyslexia in their place of work. Each group should list the difficulties the dyslexic person might face and determine the two primary difficulties. One person should be appointed to report back.
2. The whole group should select the two most common difficulties.
3. Different small groups should then be formed to determine the procedures that could be put in place to best support their colleagues who are dyslexic. Again one person from each group should report back at the plenary session.

Resources

- Overhead projector
- Set of slides
- Flipchart or similar
- Pens.

Evaluation

Feedback from the course is important for ongoing improvement and modification. Ideally questions should cover: the administrative organisation of the course; the effectiveness of the presenters; the relevance to the work situation; and, finally, the general usefulness of the session. In addition, the participants should always be invited to offer suggestions for improvements to any aspect of the course. An example can be found in Appendix 2.

Content of the presentation

Slide 1   Overview
Slide 2   Dyslexia
Slide 3   Difficulties
Slide 4   Discrepancies
Slide 5   Differences
Slide 6   Workshop 1
Slide 7   Workshop 2

Suggested duration: Between 3 hours and one day.

Qualifications for entry: No formal qualifications, an interest in dyslexia.

Slide 1: Overview

Supporting adults with dyslexia

- ■ What is dyslexia?
- ■ How does it affect our colleagues?
- ■ What are implications for our workplace?
- ■ What procedures could be put in place to make a difference?

Notes

It is important to begin the session by outlining the structure of the course. The presenter should give approximate timings. It should be emphasised that the objective is to raise awareness of the difficulties faced by adults with dyslexia in the workplace. It is also important to focus the group on their particular situation. The presenter should direct attention away from the parents who want to discuss their child's experience at school.

Slide 2: Dyslexia

Dyslexia

- ■ Distinctive pattern of difficulties
- ■ Relates to processing information
- ■ Can be seen within a continuum
- ■ Can lead to discrepancies in performance

Notes

It is important to talk about the variety of difficulties an adult with dyslexia can experience, examples of which can be found in Chapter 1. The myth that the **only** difficulty connected to dyslexia is bizarre spelling should be dispelled. The concept of the condition being within a continuum is also worth emphasising. At one end the processing difficulties can be very slight and, with appropriate support strategies, can be overcome. At the other end of the continuum the condition can be totally debilitating and very difficult to cope with. At this level of severity the condition can be complicated by extremely low self-esteem and, sometimes even, mental health problems. State that dyslexia can be defined in terms of difficulties, discrepancies and differences. Then continue by dealing with each term separately.

Slide 3: Difficulties

Difficulties

- Speed of processing
- Word recognition
- Memory
- Automaticity
- Organisation
- Semantic confusion
- Syntax
- Visual/motor

Notes: Points to highlight

- The pace at which adults with dyslexia process can be very slow. It is not that they cannot read or write but they have to proceed at their own rate. This makes working to tight deadlines very stressful, which, in turn, leads to mistakes.
- Poor word recognition is linked to poor short-term memory.
- Automaticity — Some dyslexic people never achieve full automaticity in using written language. Automaticity can be explained by using learning to ride a bicycle as an analogy. When you master the skill of riding a bike you never need to go back to first stages. Dyslexic people never usually become fully automatic readers: they often have to revert to first principles.
- Organisational skills affect all life skills, particularly with lateness. Dyslexic people cannot be dismissed because they are dyslexic but they can be dismissed for poor time-keeping.

Slide 4: Discrepancies

Discrepancies

- Oral/written
- Different subject areas
- Reading accuracy/comprehension
- Performance/abilities

Notes

The most common discrepancy is between oral presentation and written report. This can cause confusion in the workplace when an employee gives a stunning oral presentation then is asked to record it in writing. The poor quality of the written account can be interpreted as laziness by the management.

Discrepancies in different areas emphasises the need for appropriate careers advice. For example, there is little point in training a person with poor spacial awareness to be a mechanical engineer.

Slide 5: Differences

Differences

- **Processing style**
- **Learning style**
- **Strategies for learning and study**
- **Speed of processing**
- **Learning experiences**

Notes

Dyslexic people do process differently from non-dyslexics. This can be seen as one of their strengths: they often excel in problem-solving situations because of their different way of thinking. Companies are beginning to realise that having dyslexic people in their teams is a great advantage. Identification of learning style is extremely important for adults with dyslexia so that they can acquire appropriate strategies to deal with their difficulties.

Slide 6: Workshop 1

Supporting adults with dyslexia

■ What are the implications for adults with dyslexia in your workplace?

■ Discuss the question with your group and decide which are the two greatest obstacles.

Slide 7: Workshop 2

Supporting adults with dyslexia

■ What procedures could be introduced to make life easier for adults with dyslexia in your workplace?

■ Discuss the question with your group and provide two support strategies.

Course B: Training in dyslexia

Target group

Supervisory staff, trainers, staff development officers.

Aim

To provide training in dyslexia for supervisory staff to enable them to offer effective support in the workplace to adults with dyslexia.

Key learning outcomes

At the end of the course the participant should be able to:

- identify individual adults with dyslexia;
- plan and implement appropriate support programmes for adults with dyslexia within staff development provision;
- use the findings from their own reading and current research to plan and implement programmes for adults with dyslexia.

Method

The course will be presented in seven units. The course will be delivered by lectures, seminars and workshops. It will offer opportunities to analyse practice issues collectively and relate these to various contexts in which they work.

Unit 1   Introduction to course
Revision of Course 1   definitions, continuum

An examination of different
perspectives   neurological
psychological
educational

Issues related to theory and practice

Unit 2   Discover range of resources
          within the field of dyslexia

Unit3   Assessment strategies   rationale for assessment
                                                interview procedures
                                                screening tools

Unit 4   Dyslexia and literacy   acquiring functional literacy
                                                appropriate materials

Unit 5   Support strategies in context   variety of approach

Unit 6   Study skills   organisational factors
          Learning styles
          Self-concept   interpersonal skills

Unit 7   policy, practice and provision   in own company
                                                Nationally
                                                Careers service

Evaluation: See Appendix 2.

Suggested duration: 3 days or 21 hours flexible delivery.

Qualifications for entry: Some involvement in supporting staff.

Course C: Advanced training

Target group

Specialist support workers within the armed services, social work,
prison services and personnel officers in large organisations.

Aim

To provide advanced training in dyslexia to specialist support workers
to enable them to identify and provide specific support programmes in
the workplace for adults with dyslexia.

Key learning outcomes

At the end of Course C the participant should be able to display:

- a knowledge of a range of assessment procedures that can be used to identify and assess adults with dyslexia;
- an awareness of practical considerations and implications of assessment for the adult with dyslexia;
- competence in developing suitable programmes for adults with dyslexia;
- an ability to conduct an investigation, with reference to relevant literature, related to one aspect of their work with adults with dyslexia.

Method

Course C is divided into two parts. Part 1 is delivered by lectures, seminars and workshops that are intended to give participants the opportunity to collectively analyse practice and policy issues and relate those to the various contexts in which they work.

Part 1

Unit 1	Assessment, post-screening	discrepancy phonological diagnostic
Unit 2	Motor and visual factors	
Unit 3	Processing	input > cognition > output identifying strengths and weaknesses learning styles
Unit 4	Impact of assessment	workplace adjustments social and emotional factors provision of support

Part 2

Part 2 provides the course participant with the opportunity to develop a research project, staff development project or a detailed analysis of an issue related to dyslexia. The outcome will be presented to colleagues in a seminar presentation. This part of the course will be presented as an open learning experience so that much of the work will be done in the workplace. It is suggested that the group meet on three occasions:

Day 1

- Short presentation of research techniques based on (Lewis and Munn, 1987):
  What information do I want?
  Why do I want it?
  When do I need it?
  How do I collect it?
  Where can I find it?
  From whom do I get it?
- Brainstorming of difficulties and problems arising in professional practice and, deriving from these, issues that are researchable.
- Consideration of possible lines of inquiry and investigation.
- Discussion of previous studies.
- Development of research plan.
- Brief presentation by an adult with dyslexia.

Day 2

- Review of progress.
- Presentation by course members of interim reports.
- Discussion of reporting and presentation strategies.

Day 3

- Seminar presentation and discussion.

Evaluation: See Appendix 2.

Suggested duration: Part 1, 2 days or 14 hours used flexibly; Part 2, 3 days' contact plus personal study.

Qualifications for entry: Specialist interest in working with adults with dyslexia.

Training programmes

Throughout the UK and the USA there are pockets of good practice in the provision of training for adults with dyslexia. Klein and Sunderland (1998) suggest that a successful learning programme for dyslexic adults should:

- be completely relevant to the individual needs and goals of the person;
- give people immediate, or almost immediate, experience of success;
- enable people to eventually take charge of their own learning.

Specific support programmes

The JET (Joint Efforts in Training) project in Crosett, Arkansas, developed a 7-step plan for working with adults who have learning disabilities. This innovative approach assists instructors, involved in training in the workplace, to work with employees in order to identify specific needs and help them to acquire strategies to be successful in the workplace.

DARC in Birmingham, England (Ribbon Courses; Rose et al., 1997), have developed a programme that focuses on improving the self-esteem of the person. The main objective is to provide strategies to cope with situations and tasks in daily life and work.

The whole area of support is one that should be developed by moving away from the intensive remedial type help to a more independent, resource-based learning environment which offers the adult an opportunity to develop learning skills which can be transferred to other situations.

Fulcrum (McDowell, 1999) and the *Ribbon Course* (Rose et al., 1997) place a heavy focus on helping adults to understand their dyslexic difficulties and aim to change the perception of the adult through this enhanced understanding. The key should be related to self-knowledge and self-esteem. Both support programmes focus on positive attributes as well as on developing an understanding of work-related situations.

The 'three strands of provision' outlined in the Birmingham and Solihull Pact document and developed by McLoughlin (McLoughlin et al., 1994) provide an example of a comprehensive and relevant support package. These strands are:

1. *Structured language programme.* This involves a literacy programme within a framework, which is both multi-sensory and cumulative.
2. *Life skills.* This would be unique to each individual and would be essentially functional in nature, involving forms, letters, reports and functional reading.
3. *Coping strategies.* This includes support systems, awareness of difficulty and learning style, self-esteem raising and the use of support aids.

The principle of 'three strands of provision' – 'Literacy', 'Life skills' and 'Coping strategies' – should provide an overarching framework for support to achieve autonomy in learning. The support should be underpinned by a work preparation ethos. Emphasis should be placed in helping people with dyslexia to gain an understanding of their difficulties. The aim should be to develop their self-perception and so lead to increased confidence to deal with their day-to-day challenges.

Right to Write (UK) Ltd. indicates that support should be seen within a 'work preparation ethos' and should be offered in a non-educational environment and in a non-educationally focused way. *Right to Write* highlight the differences between educational type support and employment focused support and recognise that

> *many clients have negative associations with traditional teaching and need more realistic short-term assistance than longer-term remedial teaching*

and

> *a client's dependence on the tutor is kept to a minimum when support forms a basis for training and then monitoring and 'trouble shooting' rather than continual intensive support.* (Personal Communication, 1999)

The aim of support is to provide the means for the individual to take responsibility for his or her own learning, and view the support as a cushion rather than a need.

Specific features of support

Language

Many of the commercially produced language programmes for dyslexic people are inappropriate for adults. These, however, may be adapted and certain components may be used in a support programme. The actual nature of the language focused on would depend on the individual assessment and the specific nature of the person's literacy difficulty.

Many of the language approaches for use with dyslexic people are outlined in Reid (1998). Essentially these are described as 'bottom-up' approaches, which include the following;

- phonological awareness
- letter recognition
- word recognition
- word meaning
- use of word in language.

This approach is a sequential and cumulative process and one that can be arduous and lengthy for many dyslexic people. It is also inappropriate for adults as much of the teaching content replicates a situation in which the person has previously failed.

While it is appreciated that an element of basic literacy is necessary it should not be the mainstay of the available support time.

A top-down approach to reading for adults is advocated. This involves:

- word and language experience as the starting point
- help to promote prediction of words and key phrases.

Consequently, this will help individuals to become better readers.

This is preferable to lengthy and arduous immersion in the sub-skills of reading which most of the bottom-up programmes promote (Reid,

1998). A support programme should focus on the context and the language aspects rather than the print components. Life skills will be unique to every adult with dyslexia. Examples of this will include form filling, writing messages, making notes and completing applications. Mackie (1996) begins a support programme by establishing the personal interests, routines and lifestyles of the dyslexic person. A learning plan relevant to the personal life and work goals of the person is then developed. He suggests that learning objectives should be short-term, achievable and practical.

Compensatory strategies

It is important to emphasise that coping strategies, or compensatory strategies, are not excuses for failure. Everyone has conscious or unconscious coping strategies that are part of their everyday routine. People with dyslexia sometimes find it difficult to develop such coping strategies, though some actually do and become quite accomplished in their use. It is important, therefore, that this should follow on from an assessment, which focuses on learning styles and learning preferences.

Identification of learning style

Perhaps the most individual of the strategies for learning and coping is that of recognition and utilisation of an individual person's learning style. Given and Reid (1999) suggest that there are five domains to learning styles;

● Emotional
● Sociological
● Environmental
● Physiological
● Psychological.

These relate to the environmental model of learning styles developed by Dunn and Dunn, which are widely used in education and learning in the USA and many other countries.

Dunn and Dunn's model (Reid, 1998) identifies five principal characteristics and 21 elements, all of which affect the learning of students. This, in turn, will affect how successful dyslexic people are at accepting and retaining new learning (Reid, 1998).

General strategies

Klein and Sunderland (1998) provide a list of general strategies and resources which can be adapted for use by the dyslexic person, such as how to use diaries and wall charts, coloured overlays and highlighters. For example, they describe how 'one employee had three colour-coded diaries – at work, at home and in her car – and a watch with an alarm on it to ensure she got where she was supposed to be on time'. This emphasises the need to view coping strategies in an individual way as the above would not be successful for all dyslexic people.

Information and communications technology

Compensatory strategies should include information and communications technology (ICT). Word processors can eliminate writing difficulties and recent software includes help with presentation of documents, grammar, spell-checkers, structure and sequencing – indeed many of the areas that cause considerable difficulties for dyslexic people. There are also developments of spell-checkers aimed specifically for dyslexic people (Andersson, 1999). The British Dyslexia Association has a computer committee who can be consulted on these matters. Information on ICT that will help support adults with dyslexia is included in Chapter 9.

Computer skills training for people of all ages with dyslexia should include:

- Word processing
- Voice recognition software
- Use of the Internet
- Touch-type read and spell (TTRS).

Funding of individuals

Approaches could be made to employers to fund innovative initiatives. Increasingly the private sector is becoming involved in the funding of projects in education, as are independent and voluntary bodies. In addition, Fulcrum has successfully negotiated contracts with large employers such as Cadbury's and British Telecom. This type of initiative of dealing with dyslexia support in the actual workplace context is commendable. Not only is it more relevant to the individual but it also engages employers in the issues relating to dyslexia in the workplace. The practice introduced in 1998 by the Rover Group, of allocating funds for self-development to individuals, was also commendable as this allows those people with dyslexia to be responsible for their own learning.

Conclusion

This chapter has recommended that people with dyslexia can be supported in a way that enables them to make a full contribution in the workplace. What is required is a commitment on the part of managers and others to provide that support. Suggestions have been made about the range of courses that might be provided for different categories of staff. Reference has been made to commercially available training opportunities. No doubt the provision of support for adults with dyslexia will call for the investment of additional resources. The most important change, however, costs nothing: it involves a change of attitude.

Chapter 4

Dyslexia and the workplace

The nature of the difficulties

'When you are dyslexic, you grab things as you go along. You develop things in a step-ladder kind of way' (Osmond, 1993). The above comment illustrates the manner in which adults with dyslexia cope with the demands of employment and indeed life. It appears almost as though every situation presents new challenges and therefore continual demands, which may at times exceed the person's resources. This can result in work stress (Reid and Hinton, 1999) and perhaps health-related absence and unemployment.

It has been suggested (Hoffmann et al., 1987) that adults with dyslexia live under constant pressure of satisfying expectations from a variety of sources, particularly relating to gaining and retaining employment. Even once they are secured in their jobs they have to ensure that they still fulfil the expectations of their employers. Rapp (1997) suggests that aspects such as organisational and leadership skills, goal setting, learning strategies and generalisation skills often need to be developed on the job, perhaps in the step-ladder-like way suggested in the comment above.

Hoffmann et al. (1987), in a US study of almost 400 adults with dyslexia and 1,000 service providers, found that specific job training was one of the most crucial needs identified by the group. Hoffmann's study also suggested that dyslexic adults may not have a full understanding about themselves – that is, their strengths and weaknesses – yet such knowledge is in many cases crucial to selecting appropriate employment and developing skills to maximise job training.

What are the workplace difficulties?

Clearly there can be many difficulties and challenges for the dyslexic adult in employment. Essentially these can be summarised into three areas;

- Finding employment
- Maintaining employment
- Enjoying employment.

In relation to finding employment, aspects such as reading advertisements, completing application forms and performing well at interviews can present difficulties. There are many aspects within employment itself which can pose problems like time management, repetitive mistakes, speed of completing tasks, attention span, not enough time to learn job skills and the need for extended feedback.

At the same time it is important that the particular job should be satisfying and enjoyable. We are time and again quite staggered at the number of adults with dyslexia who find themselves in employment which is inappropriate for their skills and the specific demands of the job puts them under almost daily pressure. This type of situation clearly removes much of the pleasure and self-satisfaction from work. Feelings of frustration and lack of self-confidence can prevent the person with dyslexia from enjoying employment.

Academic skills

Many adults with dyslexia have not fulfilled their potential at school and may still have an inadequate level of literacy skills which will impede their opportunities for employment. Literacy skills are not only referring to the ability to read and write but also include a variety of other skills. Literacy skills cannot be isolated from the wider context of learning and poor literacy skills can have an effect on other aspects such as verbal communication, problem solving and the development of general knowledge.

It is important that the person with dyslexia obtains a degree of academic success as this will provide a springboard for further training and often the necessary academic skills which may be a prerequisite for some workplace training programmes. Many leave school with little or no academic qualification but many of these people enrol for courses later in life and often perform exceptionally well. At that stage they are usually highly motivated and may have a more detailed knowledge of their dyslexic difficulties and the most appropriate coping and compensatory strategies. Essentially they become better learners. It is our view that people with dyslexia have poor metacognitive awareness, which means that they often need to be shown the most effective way to learn. They are unable to do this as children but in adulthood they have the self-knowledge and more experience in learning and are able to become better learners. This view is supported by Mackie (1996) who suggests that while a support programme for dyslexic adults may help to improve their skills in reading and writing it should also help them to learn about their own abilities to learn – in other words, they should become better learners. For example, a person can learn to spell a few crucial words which will help that person to take on a new task, but more importantly the person can appreciate that he or she has developed skills in learning which in this example has made him or her an autonomous learner in this particular task. For that reason it is important to develop and discuss with the dyslexic person how – that is, by what rules – a certain word should be spelt the way it is; this understanding of the nature of the task and the learning process helps with the generalisation of new learning to other situations. It is the acquisition of these skills which will most benefit the person with dyslexia.

Self-advocacy in the workplace

One of the important aspects relating to assessment, as indicated in Chapter 2, concerns the effectiveness of feedback to the person with dyslexia following an assessment. Effective feedback should enable the person to have a realistic perception of their abilities as well as the nature of their dyslexic difficulties. The person with dyslexia should be satisfied with no less than that, and should expect this information following an assessment. Similarly, in the workplace, opportunities for self-advocacy should exist. In other words the person with dyslexia should be able to approach their employer easily and with the confidence that they can provide a clear outline of the strengths and difficulties in relation to their dyslexic profile. Nosek (1997) suggests that the key to self-reliance and opportunities for adults with dyslexia is a practical knowledge of basic life skills. The examples in Chapter 8 ('Speak for yourself') offer some insights into the benefit of acquiring basic life skills for the dyslexic people interviewed.

Much still needs to be done to educate employers about what dyslexia is and how it can affect individual workers. Kirk and Reid (1999) found that the issue of employer awareness and support for dyslexic adults was among the most prevalent of the issues discussed among the 200 professionals who participated in our group discussions. In the UK the initiatives stemming from the New Deal legislation have done much to help and there are pockets of good practice, but much has still to be achieved in this area. Also in the USA the Americans with Disabilities Act 1994 promotes an end to discrimination regarding most employment-related activities, including incidental job functions as well as core ones, but also has some loopholes – for example, the employer is not obliged to ask the applicant about the nature or severity of the disability at the interview. This is all the more reason why the adult with dyslexia should be encouraged to develop self-advocacy strategies as he or she may well be in the best position to help to educate employers.

In our study of professionals involved with adults with dyslexia we found that one of the most contentious issues was related to labelling. While some felt that a label could be counter-productive, many felt that it could be extremely helpful. At the same time it is emphasised that a label should not be used just for the sake of it. We suggest that having the knowledge that they **are** dyslexic can be extremely helpful to some adults, particularly those who had failed quite significantly at school and consequently have low self-esteem. Certainly those we interviewed for the chapter 'Speak for Yourself' all found the label beneficial.

Working it out: strengths and abilities in the workplace

Some of the strengths and abilities of adults with dyslexia are shown below, but more often than not dyslexic people have to work things out for themselves in order to be able to use these skills. Often that is exactly the problem – they have particular strengths which could be advantageous in employment but are not able to appreciate how to use these strengths and how to apply them to the workplace.

It is important to realise that not all dyslexic people will have all the characteristics shown below, but many have some or all of them and others have to apply the skills they do possess in order to resolve a work problem. The main characteristics are:

- good visual and spatial skills in creative areas such as mathematics, engineering and the physical sciences (West, 1997a);
- abilities to recognise patterns of information and to represent three-dimensional images in work with computers;
- a special facility for mentally rearranging designs and information which would have a contribution to creative and novel design – as demonstrated, for example, by Leonardo da Vinci, Auguste Rodin and Albert Einstein (Osmond, 1993);
- a more holistic way of viewing the world, which aids the discovery of solutions to problems (Osmond, 1993)
- rich colour memory and the ability to use fast multi-sensorial combinations;
- willing to meet expectations and have high regard in work (Plata and Bone, 1989).

Preparation for employment: Job choice and careers advice

This is not an unusual scenario:

> *The student arrives at the door of the dyslexia adviser or the disability adviser at the college or university mid-way through the course of study and indicates that he or she is experiencing considerable difficulties. An assessment reveals that the principal difficulty relates to visual–spatial skills. The student is doing a mechanical engineering course!*

It is not uncommon for dyslexic students to find themselves in a course which highlights their weaknesses and further undermines their confidence.

It is important that dyslexic students obtain effective careers advice and it is crucial that the demands of the course are made clear to them at the outset. The three implications to stem from this are;

1. The need to make careers personnel aware of dyslexia.
2. To ensure that open days and course introductions are user friendly in terms of the demands of the course, that this can be fully appreciated by the student, and that the student's dyslexic difficulties are acknowledged and appreciated by the course director.
3. To ensure that those people with dyslexia are fully aware of the extent of their dyslexic difficulties.

There are also implications here for employers as often jobs require retraining and sometimes the full nature of a job is not made clear to the applicant at the interview stage. The employer has a role to play in helping dyslexic people to select appropriate jobs to match their skills and not jobs that would highlight their difficulties. If this situation does arise the difficulties inherent in this situation can be minimised through knowledge and use of learning styles (discussed later in this chapter).

Careers staff, therefore, have a key role to play and should consider the following:

- How to obtain at least an awareness training in the area of dyslexia.
- To recognise that not all dyslexic people will display the same strengths and difficulties.
- To obtain information on the assessment which will clearly indicate the person's strengths and weaknesses.
- The need to consider the dyslexic person as an individual and his or her needs and ambitions and preferences should be acknowledged. This may mean the dyslexic person does pursue a course or profession which may not be the most suitable, if this is the case attempts should be made with employers and course directors to ensure that support can be available.

Liaison between education and work

In the study conducted by Kirk and Reid (1999) this aspect was raised as being of crucial importance. The relevance of the mainstream school curriculum to employment skills is a key factor to the success of adult life. Research findings have provided striking conclusions concerning the transitional period of dyslexic adults to successful employment. Hoffmann et al.'s (1987) study identified a mismatch between curricular and employment needs. According to Nosek (1997), two of the top determinants for work success are: work experience during secondary school and vocational education during secondary school. There is little doubt that these factors are prevalent in both the UK and the USA but it is important to also use those opportunities to inform the employer and the dyslexic student about dyslexia and reasonable adjustments in the workplace.

In order to improve this situation, it is necessary to reappraise the curriculum priorities provided by various institutions (e.g. secondary, post-secondary and vocational) and to assess whether or not such employment training needs were indeed being at least partly, if not fully, met. This would help to ensure that adults with dyslexia are prepared for successful employment at an earlier stage in their career. In the long term this would also reduce the economic and resource burdens of the employment agencies and training organisations.

A multi-disciplinary approach to vocational training in schools has already been emphasised. The successful completion of secondary school does offer some platform for success in adulthood (Blackorby and Wagner, 1997). If work skill training programmes are indeed to be introduced at the school level, it would be advisable to adopt a multi-disciplinary or multi-faceted approach to integrating both the diagnosis and treatment aspects of vocational training with a more integrated, vocational relevant environment within the school and community (Grayson et al., 1997). A technical report prepared by the National Joint Comitteee on Learning Disabilities in the USA (NJCLD, 1994) suggested that careful planning is essential in the transition from secondary to post-secondary education and such planning involves contributions from four groups – the student, the parent(s), and secondary and post-secondary professionals. The report outlines specific roles for each of these groups; for example, the student should have an understanding of his or her specific disability and have realistic work goals; the secondary school personnel should form a transition team and develop an appropriate packet of materials to record the students' progress and to facilitate service delivery to the post-secondary school; the post-secondary staff should be responsible for negotiating reasonable adjustments within the faculty. This report is clearly far reaching and the many recommendations and suggestions highlight the importance of this transition period for the young person with learning disabilities including dyslexia.

The integration of the diagnosis and treatment aspects within training programmes can be demonstrated in the training of job-seeking skills, job interest, working habits and practical work skills such as filling in job applications and following directions (Hoffmann et al., 1987; NJCLD, 1987). It will be only when such vocational aspects of training have been integrated into the school programmes that dyslexic people will be able to enter the world of work equipped to deal with the varying demands of the workplace. In addition, school professionals should also be informed about the significance of the drop-out rates in relation to unsuccessful employment life (Blackorby and Wagner, 1997; Grayson et al., 1997).

A multi-disciplinary approach to vocational training in schools is therefore advocated. If work-skill training programmes are indeed to be introduced at the school level, it would be advisable to adopt a multi-disciplinary or multi-faceted approach to integrating both the diagnosis and support aspects of vocational training with a more integrated, vocationally relevant environment within the school and community (Grayson et al., 1997).

Due to the greater understanding of dyslexia and the need to ensure wider access to further and higher education in both the USA and the UK, the number of students with dyslexia entering post-school education is increasing. In the UK an increasing number of disability support centres in higher education have been established (Singleton, personal communication). This has been accompanied by an increase in the number of students with dyslexia entering university courses. Additionally in the UK funding has been made available from the Higher Education Funding Council and other bodies for projects to help students with disabilities.

In the USA, 8.4% of graduate students reported a disability (Brinckerhoff, 1997). In 1994 the National Board of Medical Examiners received 400 requests for alternative assessment and three-fold increases have been noted in law faculties for special admission considerations.

It is important, therefore, that university and college personnel make themselves available to school staff and to potential recruits before any student decides on a particular course. It is also important for staff and students to know the types of support that are available for different courses.

Matching jobs and skills

The matching of an occupation or course of training to a particular student can depend on a combination of good judgement and appropriate advice. But, realistically, in many cases even the best matched occupation can still require some special consideration by employers and the use of compensatory strategies by the adult with dyslexia. In these situations the use of learning styles can be an important factor for both the dyslexic person and the employer.

Learning styles

Learning styles are essentially 'characteristic cognitive, affective and physiological behaviours that serve as relatively stable indicators of how learners perceive, interact with, and respond to the learning environment' (Keefe, 1993). Many models of learning styles take into account both environmental and cognitive factors. Therefore the workplace as well as the person's learning preferences are important.

Workplace factors

The Dunn and Dunn learning styles model offers a well-researched example of a learning styles model which gives considerable focus to environmental factors. Many research studies using this model have shown that environmental as well as cognitive factors can affect learning and ultimate success. Some of the factors in the Dunn and Dunn model relate to

Sound

Some people can work and learn more effectively in certain sound conditions. Usually a global type of learner prefers music or at least some form of auditory stimulation.

Light

Again some people prefer dim light while others prefer brighter lights. The Dunn and Dunn research studies show that lighting can affect learning and therefore would be an important consideration in the workplace, especially if new or demanding learning is to take place.

Design

The research has indicated that many global learners prefer an informal learning situation and particularly one which utilises visual and kinaesthetic processing. A formal classroom type of situation is not usually the most effective learning environment for global learners.

Group learning or learning alone

Some people can learn most effectively if working on a task alone; global learners, and many people with dyslexia are global learners, usually prefer working in groups. This allows social interaction from which global people usually benefit, and group discussion which also is one of their preferences for learning.

Perceptual preference

Instructions for work tasks can be provided to employees in a number of ways. Usually this would involve either visual, auditory, kinaesthetic or tactile learning. It is important that the instructions are provided in a variety of ways because if they are given purely orally, the learner is then relying on the auditory modality. Many dyslexic learners are stronger in other modalities and may indeed have a weakness in the auditory modality. Many are in fact stronger in the visual modality so they should be allowed to make visual images or mind maps as they are learning, or indeed the information should be provided visually.

Time of day

It is interesting that many employees, when training on the job, may remark to their boss that they will take home the new information that is to be learnt. This may be because they prefer the informal setting of their home for learning but it may also be due to the time of day preference. Many prefer to learn in the evening as opposed to the morning and this is the case for many with a global learning style (Dunn and Dunn, 1993).

Mobility

The Dunn and Dunn research also highlights the importance of mobility for some people in relation to effective learning. This suggests that some people have a learning style that requires them to be fairly active when learning and can only really remain in one learning position for a short period of time. It is important therefore that trainers are aware of this and that classroom learning takes account of the need for some learners to be mobile. Sometimes group discussion can help to bring in a certain amount of mobility into a learning situation.

Structure

Learners who have a global preference need a structure. Often they have difficulty imposing their own structure and it is important for the manager to ensure that job instructions and new learning tasks are presented in a structured way. This helps the learner in relation to what has been achieved and what else has to be completed. The structured activity can act almost like a checklist and helps to keep the learner on task.

Global and analytical

Many dyslexic people have a global learning preference and this means that they prefer simultaneous processing of information as opposed to sequential. They can therefore work on several tasks at the same time.

- Global learners benefit from a context for learning and need to see the purpose of the task. Therefore, it is beneficial if this is explained to them at the outset.
- They also need clear expectations and should know how and if their learning is to be monitored.
- They would benefit from an overview of the new material to be learnt before embarking on the actual task of learning. This overview may be in the form of talking through the task and identifying what is already known to the learner.
- They also benefit from making connections.

It is also helpful to assist the learner to make connections among the different content areas of the new learning. To focus on patterns and to link different aspects of the information to be learnt. The use of sub-headings and the identification of concepts are important in this respect.

Personal and meaningful

Certainly frequent use of illustrations will make the information more meaningful to learners with a global learning style. Biographical information when appropriate and the use of situations personally familiar to the learner can help to personalise the content and also make it more meaningful to the learner.

Cognitive and environmental aspects

It is important to consider cognitive and environmental aspects of learning in the workplace. Not only will this benefit people with dyslexia but also others in the workforce. The research shows that recognising an individual's learning preferences can enhance learning and success.

For example, Ingham (1991) showed how the results of an experimental study showed that truck drivers, truck mechanics and their managers learned significantly more when their individual learning style perceptual preferences are matched with the appropriate instructional method. Additionally, the study showed that these employees expressed significantly more positive attitudes towards company-sponsored training programmes when instruction complements their individual learning style preferences. She argues that the message from this study is clear: employers and trainers must analyse a person's perceptual strength and training materials should be designed to complement these preferences. This is confirmed by a two-year joint study for the American Society for Training and Development and the United States Department of Labor (Carnevale et al., 1988) which stated 'trainers should attempt to identify the type of sensory stimulus – whether visual, auditory or tactile – that helps each employee learn best, and then design multiple use training that addresses all preferences'.

Training and retraining

Effective training in relation to job skills either at college or in the workplace is important because often the learner has to obtain the skills in a fairly short space of time. In some situations in the workplace induction training may be limited or non-existent. While this can place demands on many people, those with dyslexia are at a greater disadvantage because, in addition to their dyslexic difficulties relating to short-term memory, sequencing and literacy, they also may not be aware of how to learn effectively and efficiently. This is the metacognitive aspect of learning and essentially relates to being aware of how one learns.

Metacognition

Three important aspects of metacognition are:

- self-direction
- self-monitoring
- self-assessment.

When the learner acquires competence in these aspects then learning can be efficient and successful. By efficient we mean learning the maximum information in the shortest time span, but learning it in such a manner that the information is meaningful and can be transferred to other new learning situations. These are key aspects of metacognition.

Self-direction essentially involves such questions as:

- What is my goal?
- What do I want to accomplish ?
- What do I need?
- What is my deadline?

It is important that these basic questions are addressed by the dyslexic learner. This will help with keeping on task and make learning more efficient.

Similarly with *self-monitoring*, it is important that questions such as those below are addressed;

- How am I doing?
- Do I need other resources?
- What else can I do?

This should lead to *self-assessment,* when the learner should ask such questions as:

- Did I accomplish my goal?
- Was I efficient?
- What worked?
- What did not work?
- Why did it not work?

Raising these questions will highlight to the learner how efficient or otherwise the learning was and how the process could be improved for a subsequent learning situation.

The metacognitive process could be summed up in the following four stages;

1. **Understanding** – that is, questions relating to the task. It is essential to focus on this before embarking on the task and, importantly, this should lead to a plan of action. An example is of a worker who has to reorganise a storeroom. She will need to know exactly what that means. Is it to make it easier to find information? Should the materials be stored in a certain way? In other words, what is the purpose of the activity? Answers to the questions should help the person to decide how to go about the task.
2. **Sequence of learning** – What will be the different stages of learning? Should this be written down and planned?
3. **Monitoring** – Is the plan working? Do you have to change anything? Will you reach your learning target?
4. **Checking** – Have you succeeded? How do you know you have reached your goal? Can you describe how you did it?

In general, metacognition involves the ability to transfer previous learning to new learning. The learner should focus as much on the 'how' as the 'what', therefore the process is important. If possible this process should be recorded and evaluated by the learner so that it can be used again for new learning.

Training and support

Evidence from the literature highlights the improvement that can be made when appropriate support is provided (Nicolson and Fawcett, 1997; Frith, 1995; Hill, 1991). Moreover, some researchers further emphasised the quantity and quality of support (Lundberg, 1985) and the provision of a positive teaching and learning environment (Hill, 1991).

The use of multi-sensory techniques in learning has long been established as the most suitable approach for those with dyslexia (Pumfrey and Reason, 1991). Due to the variation in the nature of individual patterns of difficulties, however, it seems reasonable that teaching programmes would require the use of a wide range of techniques. Common principles can be identified for use in training programmes. For example, these should be designed to address the following:

- individual needs;
- provide immediate experience of success (Presland, 1991; Hill, 1991);
- encourage individuals to participate and take responsibility for their learning (Klein, 1993);
- establish a rapport with the dyslexic adults to help building confidence and trust;
- handle with great sensitivity (McLoughlin et al., 1994); for example, when arranging group work, it would be more appropriate to group the adults with more or less the same level of literary skills;
- respond to each individual's needs and learning style;
- require a great deal of flexibility;
- establish why an individual needs training and help set realistic goals and course content;
- use appropriate materials (e.g. books with a high level of interest but low readability level); and
- the development of efficient learning skills such as comprehension, listening skills, note taking, checking and proof-reading and preparing for examinations.

The main components of programmes relating to support and occupational guidance described by McLaughlin et al. (1994) are:

- initial assessment;
- self-understanding;
- generating alternatives;
- obtaining occupation information;
- making choices;
- implementing plans.

We feel it is important to have some guiding principles or models to help direct the professional and the dyslexic person through the process of assessment, support, careers guidance and workplace adaptations. But perhaps the overriding factor should relate to the individual needs of the dyslexic person – these needs will vary from individual to individual.

Social and personal factors

Social skills and interpersonal skills are important to help the individuals with dyslexia to communicate the extent of their difficulty to employers and to help to give them the social confidence necessary to compensate for their difficulty. Social skills training is therefore important and should be part of work preparation programmes for dyslexic adults.

Social skills training should focus on controlling words and actions in order to overcome impulsive behaviours; assertiveness training should promote independence; conversational skills training, and training to promote understanding of social interactions, should be taught for the purpose of establishing friendships. This could be conducted either individually or with adult groups (Hoffmann et al., 1987; Brown, 1997). This can also help the dyslexic individual to develop self-advocacy skills.

Employers and employment programmes

There are a number of workplace factors which are crucial to a person's job performance (for example, increasing work pace, changing equipment, managerial styles, team size). However, an appropriate and planned policy of accommodation and support would help dyslexic adults to overcome expected and unexpected problems. Employers should be encouraged to take an integrative and problem-solving approach to working collaboratively with dyslexic employees. This will assist the identification and implementation of any potential individualised modifications to the working environment which may benefit the dyslexic person.

In the UK there are a number of employment programmes aimed to help young people or the unemployed to return to work. Some of these are described briefly below.

Access to Work

This programme is provided by the Disability Services (DS) division within the Employment Service – a centralised government body with responsibility for employment and the unemployed. The DS sets out to provide help for people with disabilities in securing or retaining employment through practical support such as the provision of special aids and equipment, adaptations to premises, support workers and other assistance in meeting personal needs. It will also meet all the approved costs with travel to work or communicator support at interview. In some circumstances this could be applicable to those with dyslexia.

Training for work

This is an initiative which helps individuals to update or gain new skills. It is sponsored by the local government, via the Training Enterprise Companies (TECs) or Local Enterprise Companies (LECs). It aims to provide either an in-house training or work placement for a period from 6 weeks to 6 months, dependent upon individual needs. Training for Work was replaced by Work-Based Training for Adults in 1998–99.

Supported employment programme

The Supported Employment Programme is a programme designed to help severely disabled people into work through placement in a workshop, factory or, increasingly, within open employment with a host employer and at a pace most suitable to the individual. A subsidy is given by the Employment Service to cover the shortfall in productivity levels at the beginning of the programme.

Employment rehabilitation/work preparation

This specialist programme aims to help people with disabilities to return to work. It is provided by selected local organisation by the Employment Service on either a part-time or a full-time basis, ranging from a few days to a few weeks, dependent upon individual needs.

Work-based learning

A flexible scheme receiving support from the European Social Fund provides special accommodation and special help for people with disabilities through equipment adaptations, residential training and Special Local Training (training closer to home). It is available locally through TECs, LECs and their training providers.

Other training opportunities

A wide range of training, information and support services are provided from the TECs and LECs for learning new skills and improving career prospects. Moreover, pre-vocational training or work-related skills training (e.g. basic skills training or training in English) is available for people who need extra help in reading, writing and arithmetic skills. A Career Development Loan (CDL) is available to assist with fees for training.

   For people under the age of 25, a number of training programmes are available through Youth Training in England and Wales and Skillseekers in Scotland; there are also Modern Apprenticeships and National Traineeships.

Job Introduction Scheme

The Job Introduction Scheme provides a financial contribution or grant towards the employer's costs for the first six weeks of employment where the employer or the disabled person has some doubts or reservations about whether the job is within the individual's capabilities. A job trial can be arranged under this scheme for people with a disability.

Employment needs

Employers and employees need to work collaboratively to create a work environment which suits both (Sauter and McPeek, 1993). Due to the specific characteristics of dyslexic people in relation to the workplace demands, appropriate task and work modifications could help them to work more efficiently and effectively. Employers should also be patient when employees are trying to adapt to new facilities (McLoughlin et al., 1994). However, according to the sample of employed dyslexic adults surveyed in Hoffmann et al.'s (1987) study, only 24% of the employers who had been informed about the dyslexic conditions of their employees had made job modifications according to the dyslexic employees' specific needs. With a view to the poor response, there remains a need for the employers to be taking a more participatory role in support issues. Some clear guidelines for employers in the accommodation of employees with dyslexia would be useful and helpful when implementing the policy of accommodation in the work environment.

It is important that special consideration and planning should precede the employment of adults with dyslexia. Success in employment should not be a hit or miss affair but should be the product of planning and consideration, taking account of the specific needs and the abilities of dyslexic people. There is clearly much to be done before trainers and employers are fully aware of the potential, as well as the specific difficulties, of dyslexic people, but beginning at school and developed by careers counsellors and workplace trainers, much can still be accomplished.

Disability Discrimination Act

The Disability Discrimination Act was established in the UK in 1995. The definition of disability covers a broad range, including dyslexia. In order to be included in legislation the dyslexic difficulties would need to have an impact on the day-to-day activities of the individual. The Act provides the disabled person with the right not to be discriminated against in any aspect of employment, including interview arrangements, recruitment, terms and conditions, workplace arrangements, training, promotion and dismissal. In addition to these civil rights, the Act aimed to help more people with disabilities to acquire and keep jobs, and to develop career prospects.

Who is affected by the Act?

The Act was designed to impact upon a wide range of groups, including disabled individuals, further education (FE) and higher education (HE), their employers, trade associations, advisers and service providers. Further and higher education institutions are required to recognise the needs of disabled people who wish to study, and to provide information to parents, pupils and students. Moreover, each institution is required to produce a disability statement describing their current provision and future developments in supporting students with disabilities.

Provisions under the Act

Under the Act it is unlawful for employers with 20 or more employees to treat disabled people less favourably than any other employee for reasons related to their disability, unless there is a good reason. Within the Act, employers will have to make appropriate (e.g. need factor) and reasonable (e.g. cost factor) measures to accommodate the job needs of dyslexic employees in the workplace.

It can be noted that, to date, 95% of employers (with 4.5 million employees, including a quarter of all disabled employees) are not obligated by these conditions stated above because they have less than 20 employees. In response to this a consultation exercise has been introduced concerning the potential effects of not including this group of employers within the Act.

Similarly, it will be unlawful for trade associations to treat people with disabilities less favourably than their non-disabled peers without good cause. This also applies to the advisers and training providers. Thus they have to take account of the requirements of the Act when providing services to disabled people – for example, when they are getting advice about job seeking and getting job-related training.

Appeal

Unfair discrimination cases can be reported to a civil court or an industrial tribunal. Alternatively, they could be brought to the Advisory Conciliation and Arbitration Service (ACAS) or the Labour Relations Agency (LRA) in the case of Northern Ireland. Cases could also be dealt with and resolved at a local level without going through the court thus shortening the processing time.

Advisory

A number of groups have advisory roles in the existing civil system. Two councils were set up in particular to advise the Government on the discrimination of disabled people: the National Disability Council and the Northern Ireland Disability Council. In addition, a separate group, the National Advisory Council on Employment of People with Disabilities (NACEPD), targets the provision of advice to the Government on the Act generally, and for employment issues in particular.

In December 1997 the Disability Rights Taskforce (DRT) was set up with the aim of reporting to the Government on how best to secure the civil rights of disabled people.

Disability Rights Commission

The purpose of the Disability Rights Commission is to network the existing disability organisations, including employers and businesses. It also works collaboratively with public and statutory bodies on issues concerning discrimination. Its aims are seven-fold:

- to make recommendations about civil rights for disabled people (based upon the Disability Discrimination Act 1995, Human Rights Bill);
- to work towards the elimination of discrimination against disabled people in England, Scotland and Wales (similar arrangements will be organised in Northern Ireland);
- to promote the equalisation of opportunities;
- to offer advice and information to both disabled people and organisations representing employers and business;
- to promote good practice among employers and service providers;
- to function as a central source of advice for employers and business;
- to promote conciliation services for disabled employees and the employers and service providers.

The work context of the Employment Service

The services of the Employment Service are delivered mainly via Jobcentres. To date, there are approximately 1,008 Jobcentres throughout the UK. Jobcentres adopt locally based approaches to which a range of programmes and services are provided and designed, in particular to help people to find work (e.g. Jobsearch, Jobfinder Plus (25+), Jobclubs, Job Interview Guarantee, Work Trials, Work-Based Learning, Pre-Vocational Training and Travel to Interview Scheme).

A wide range of job-seeking leaflets and booklets are also available from the Jobcentres. A homepage is available at

http: //www.employmentservice.gov.uk

In recent years, the Employment Service has been taking active initiatives in introducing both up-to-date and cost-effective services and programmes to help job seekers (e.g. the introduction of the New Deal programmes).

Professionals dealing with disability

In the UK the Employment Service has a number of professionals who deal with disability and disability issues. Some of these are described below.

Disability Services managers

The Disability Services (DS) division is one of the many divisions in the Employment Service. Disability Service managers are responsible for the overall running of a variety of groups, such as the Disability Employment Services Team, which provide services for disabled people in employment. These groups are involved in training and research work.

Local Occupational Psychologists

The Local Occupational Psychologists (LOPs) are senior managers within the Local Occupational Psychologist Service. They supervise the Occupational Psychologists (OPs) within the region. The Local Occupational Psychologist Service is a sub-division of the Occupational Psychology Division within the Employment Service. Their service works with the DS locally to enable people with disabilities to obtain or retain employment through effective assessment, work preparation and placing action.

Occupational Psychologists

The Occupational Psychologists (OPs) report to the LOPs managers in their region. Some of them also work within the PACT teams under the Disability Services division. They specialise in work with individuals who have a disability, offer specialist help and advice to people with disabilities, and may help them to either gain or retain employment.

Disability Employment Advisers

Disability Employment Advisers (DEAs) aim to help and give advice to individuals with severe or complex disabilities who are encountering employment barriers in obtaining or retaining employment. They are mainly based in Jobcentres with support from the PACT teams (supervised by the PACT managers) or the regional business centre. They draw on the professional expertise of OPs. They work under the DSD (supervised by the DSD managers) and there are now more than 1,000 DEAs.

New Deal and New Deal for Disabled People

The idea to help people to get work was initiated by the UK Government in May 1997. The New Deal programme is part of the Government's programme of welfare reform which sets out to help unemployed people to get employment.

There are four general options for New Deal clients: a subsidised job with an employer; full-time education and training; work with a voluntary sector organisation lasting for six months; and work with the Environment Task Force lasting six months.

Role of employers

It is important that employers have some awareness of dyslexia and that they are aware of the needs and abilities of dyslexic people. Klein and Sunderland (1998) suggest that employees can help by:

- being aware that dyslexic difficulties do not indicate incompetence;
- recognising the dyslexic person's strengths and encouraging creative solutions to difficulties;
- accepting that there are alternative ways of doing things and exploring these with dyslexic employees;
- giving the employee opportunities to explain what is difficult and to ask for resources that may help;
- providing the appropriate support and resources as is practicable.

Klein and Sunderland (1998), therefore, suggest that employers should be informed on how dyslexia can affect people in the workplace, for example:

- taking down a telephone message accurately;
- reading memos accurately, particularly at speed;
- filing in alphabetical order;
- remembering verbal instructions;
- filling out forms;
- giving information clearly in writing;
- time keeping;
- organising and prioritising a workload.

While these are general points and may not apply to all dyslexic people, they featured in our discussions and interviews with dyslexic adults. Much seems to depend on the awareness of employers, the support offered and accepted and the perceptions and awareness of the adult with dyslexia.

We suggest, therefore, that employers should:

- Ask their dyslexic employees how their dyslexic difficulties affect their job. This should be done with empathy and trust.
- Find out if further assessment is required from an occupational psychologist or educational psychologist, ensuring that the person who conducts the assessment is familiar with dyslexia in adults and work-related difficulties associated with dyslexia.
- Discuss with the dyslexic employees the types of accommodations that can be made to the workplace.
- Find out about their strengths and how they themselves feel about being dyslexic. Are they, for example, comfortable for the knowledge that they are dyslexic to be freely available to colleagues and managers?

- Monitor and review the accommodations which have been made and discuss this with the dyslexic person

Dyslexic people can help themselves by:

- understanding and accepting their dyslexic difficulties;
- utilising their strengths;
- talking to their employer about their dyslexic difficulties – do not hold this back;
- ensuring that they have access to all the help that is available should they need it – from the employer, trade union, government bodies and voluntary associations, friends and colleagues.

It is informative to gain insights from dyslexic people themselves about the type of difficulties they have experienced in employment and how employers and workplace considerations can minimise these difficulties. These insights are described in Chapter 8 ('Speak for Yourself'), but here it is sufficient to suggest that the workplace, legislation, professionals and employers have a considerable function to ensure that the workplace offers productive and fulfilling opportunities for dyslexic people to maximise their abilities.

Chapter 5

Strategies for learning

Whose responsibility?

In the previous two chapters an attempt was made to describe a number of ways in which adults with dyslexia could be supported by employers, course tutors and others with responsibility for training and support. It was emphasised that in order for society to reap the benefits that this very able section of the community could contribute, if appropriately supported, there had to be a collective effort to offer that support.

However, adults with dyslexia have a responsibility to themselves to become familiar with their condition; to understand how they process information; to devise strategies to cope with what for them is a different way of thinking; and to deploy tactics to deal with day-to-day living. This chapter will describe some of these strategies and link them to situations in the workplace and in study in further and higher education. It will deal briefly with learning styles and consider their importance for students with dyslexia. The major thrust of the chapter will be concerned with study skills, and the following will be discussed:

- Organisation
- Reading strategies
- Note taking
- Lectures, talks and seminars
- Essays and reports
- Presentations
- Examinations: revision and techniques.

The overall aim is to present, in non-technical language and in a practical way, how the adult with dyslexia may be helped to acquire the skills and aptitudes of the autonomous learner and to help him or her to become more self-sufficient.

Learning styles

It is important for students, employers, employees and course tutors to be aware of the role of learning styles for study and work. This important feature of learning is highlighted elsewhere in this book, particularly in Chapter 4. Many adults with dyslexia are not aware of how they learn and perpetuate the same inappropriate learning pattern throughout their life. Learning styles are comparatively easy to identify through questionnaires (Dunn and Dunn, 1996: Lashley, 1995: Hobson et al., 1998). The QuickScan Screening Test (Zdzienski, 1997) provides a learning styles profile. Learning styles can also be identified through observation and reflection. After a task is completed it is important for the adult with dyslexia to reflect on the manner in which it was accomplished. It is extremely important to consider the process of learning as well as the outcome. It is only by doing this that an individual can identify which components of the task were easy and which were difficult, and why. Asking and answering these questions can inform the learner about subsequent learning.

It is important that the employer and the course tutor are aware of how learning styles can affect job performance or course success as work procedures and course teaching can influence the quality of the experience for the learner. For example, a visual learner may have difficulty in following auditory instructions or a person with a kinaesthetic preference may require a 'hands on' learning experience rather than being shown what to do.

Study skills

Organisation

A learning difference that affects most adults with dyslexia is a difficulty in organising their work. They want to learn, they are keen to write, they wish to achieve, but they cannot easily organise a programme of study. They need to be able to process ideas more efficiently so that answers to questions will 'flow', dissertations can be completed and reports or books will be digested. Effective organisation is essential in any context that involves processing written materials. Indeed, it is more important for such learners, especially if they are not full-time students, to be thoroughly organised and systematic in their study habits.

There are four aspects of organisation that need to be addressed:

- Target setting
- Time management
- Finding a place to study
- Using aids to support learning.

Target setting

It is important to set realistic targets. Study is only part of a wider range of responsibilities. Family commitments, social and sporting activities and work-related responsibilities all have to be considered when planning a study programme. The first thing that has to be determined is how much time will be available for study. One approach is to take a blank table divided into days and hours. Using different coloured pens the following information can be entered:

- *Designated work time* – e.g. either lectures or office hours (red)
- *Personal time* – eating, shopping, child care (blue)
- *Regular commitments* – sports, church, music (green)

It is only after this review has been completed that a realistic study plan can be devised. The number of hours to be allocated to different learning tasks can then be calculated in order to fit into a particular lifestyle. If this task is completed in reverse order – that is, if the number of hours of study has to fit into a pattern of living – it could lead to pressures and conflicts of interest. It is always easier to watch a film or take part in the office football match than to apply oneself to study. If a plan has been adopted it will be easier to refuse spontaneous invitations and derive satisfaction from achieving learning goals.

When the number of hours that are to be devoted to study is determined, then a study plan can be prepared. A useful starting point is to list all the tasks required by the programme of study. For example, the list might include:

- write up notes
- read relevant articles
- revise for examination
- compose an essay
- record lab work.

Having formed a list it is necessary to prioritise the tasks to be addressed. A certain amount of satisfaction will be gained from adhering to a structured plan, for that can motivate a person to persevere with further study. It is less stressful to plan in advance what you intend to study and not make ad hoc arrangements when you happen to wake up on a Saturday morning!

Time management

Once a work-plan has been established time-management should be considered so that the plan will be used efficiently. Dyslexic difficulties are exacerbated by pressures of time. If there are deadlines to be met it is essential to begin studying well in advance. Thus, as soon as the date of the examination is known, it is essential to prepare a revision plan. In addition to a weekly schedule, it is useful to have a monthly, or yearly, calendar highlighted with the main study events.

In the words of Scotland's bard, '*the best laid schemes gang aft agley*' and sometimes factors outwith one's control will impinge on the study plan. This feature of study planning should be recognised and contingency plans set. 'Catch-up' time can be found in a cancelled social event, from flexi-time that has to be used up, and from the extra time gained from not having a lie-in. If life is ordered in this way panic situations will be avoided and it will be possible to relax and maximise learning potential. It is important to avoid using vacation time for emergency study time. Family and friends have expectations at such times and everyone will be put under unnecessary pressure if study is allowed to interrupt holiday activities. Friends and family cannot be expected to co-operate with a person's study habits if they do not know what the study plan is. Close members of the family have a right to know when they can make contact and when they will be interrupting study. Clear communication can avoid potential conflict and ease some of the tensions and pressures associated with study. It is also essential to be aware of time-wasting and task-avoidance strategies. Is it really necessary to make that phone call now? Must the dog be taken to the vet for his annual injection at this precise moment?

Finding a place to study

The ideal place to study is a warm, well-ventilated, quiet room equipped with a large table, accessible bookshelves, efficient, tungsten lighting, a power point for a computer, and a comfortable but supporting chair. However, not everyone can afford such luxuries. The most important single item would be a table where work can be set up, and materials left undisturbed. This can save the time and effort of setting-up every time you wish to study. It is worth making an effort to be comfortable, otherwise discomfort can easily be used as a study-avoidance tactic.

Using aids to support learning

There are several electronic aids and types of software to support the learning of adults with dyslexia (a list is provided in Chapter 9). A computer with word-processing facilities is virtually indispensable for producing accurately presented work. However, the following are also useful and less expensive aids for studying:

- coloured writing pens
- coloured highlighting pens
- 'Post-it' notes in different shapes and colours
- paper in different colours
- a wall chart
- cork board for checklists
- Blu Tack for attaching *aide-memoires* to visible objects
- index cards and box for notes.

For most people an important aspect of study is planning, but for adults with dyslexia good organisation is even more essential.

Reading strategies

Adults with dyslexia often have difficulty, not with understanding the content of texts, but with the pace at which they process the written word. It is essential that they acquire strategies to support them with the essential skill of reading.

Ann Arbor (1987a,b,c) provides a course of tracking in three parts which strengthens eye co-ordination and, therefore, increases the speed of reading. In Part 1 the student has to identify the letters of the alphabet in sequence from a passage of random letters under timed conditions. A record is kept of the improvement in the rate of completion of each passage. There are 60 short passages. When a plateau is reached, the student graduates to Part 2. Part 2 consists of a number of passages of non-words grouped in sentences. Each passage includes commonly used words such as *then, but* or *and.* Again, under timed conditions, the student identifies and highlights the prescribed word or words. Passages are worked through systematically until the time plateau is reached. The student then graduates to Part 3, where they are asked to identify full sentences from nonsense passages. Improvement to the speed of reading occurs when the exercises are done regularly. Three or four exercises every day of the week is better than 20 on a single day. Significant improvements to the reading speed and confidence of adults with dyslexia have been reported after persevering with this course. One mature student claimed that she had even started reading novels for pleasure because she could now get to the end before she had forgotten the beginning!

Adults with dyslexia must acquire their own strategies for reading. They have to recognise that lack of automaticity means that it is extremely important that they become active readers. They must know what they want to obtain from the text: in advance, they must note key words and issues, list any people or places needed, and make a rough outline of the text so that they know the geography of the book. It is advisable to look at different sections before reading the main body of the book. The contents and the index can provide a good overview of the content of the book. Reading the introductions and summaries of the chapters, if available, will also be found helpful. The headings in a chapter will help to build up a picture of the content. It is important to prepare for reading a book, particularly if specific information or ideas are needed. A variety of approaches should be tried until suitable strategies are identified.

Many methods of reading have been identified: skimming; scanning; reading for detail; reading for revision and learning; and reading for entertainment. **Scanning** is adopted when it is necessary to find a specific item in a passage. Since the aim is to focus on trying to find key words only, the remainder of the text can be ignored. **Skimming** is useful when it is necessary to find out what a passage is about: it provides a rough idea before beginning to read in detail. **Reading for detail** is used when we have to read short complicated pieces of text – for example, to identify unfamiliar technical words or complex formulae. A method of **reading for study** is SQ3R (Survey, Question, Read, Recall, Review). This method provides a structure for reading; and it is particularly valuable for the adult with dyslexia since it helps such learners to establish specific routines in their reading. It is important to be able to relax with a good novel and simply **read for pleasure**.

Reading difficulties might be so significant that dyslexic people have to use other ways of coping. Information Communication Technology can help in a number of ways. Firstly, any book or article can be read by a scanner. In order to read back text the computer needs to have a sound card, speakers or headphones and have text-reading software loaded, such as TextHelp. A sophisticated, but expensive, piece of equipment is the Kurzweil 3000 scanner. This scanner 'is a combination of scanning software and text to voice software, making the scanning and reading of material accessible with one click of a button and because of its multi-sensory approach to reading provides both visual and auditory feedback.' (http://dyslexic.com/kurzweil3000.htm). Many talking CD-ROMs are now available. Alternatively, ordinary CD-ROMs can be used with text-reading software. Less expensive, but sometimes effective, coping strategies involve: the use of highlighter pens to focus attention while reading; the use of a book mark or ruler to help to follow the text down the page; or the use of your finger to trace the words across the page.

As with all aspects of study, the adult with dyslexia who wishes to become an efficient reader must be organised and know how to process the text. An efficient approach to reading might be summarised in the following way:

Stage 1   Scan the texts
           Skim the material
           Look at contents and index
           Examine the structure of the book
Stage 2   Read introductions and summaries
           Look at diagrams and illustrations
           Find key words

Stage 3 Read more carefully
        Pay more attention to detail
        Ask yourself questions about the content
        Try to write down the key point(s) at end of the chapter.

Note taking

Taking accurate notes from whatever source is not only a key study skill but also a life skill. Notes can be made from two main sources:

- from written materials – textbooks, reports, articles
- from spoken sources – lectures, talks and seminars.

For each source adults with dyslexia need to think about their strengths and weaknesses so that they can use appropriate coping strategies. Learning styles also play an important role in acquiring efficient note-taking skills. People with dyslexia need to know how to process information in whatever form.

The following are hints for taking notes from a listening source:

- Prepare in advance
- Try to establish the structure of the talk or lecture.
- Fold one-third of the page lengthwise and leave it blank to enter key points later.
- Listen for clues, for example, repetition of points or emphasis.
- Remember anecdotes as a way of memorising.
- If lecture notes/overheads come from an electronic source print them off in triple spacing so that notes can be placed in the appropriate space.
- Keep thinking about the topic.

The following are hints for taking notes from the written word

- Avoid simply noting down the words of the author. One of the key tests of understanding is that we can paraphrase what we read into our own words.
- Do not begin taking notes too early: wait until the main points emerge.
- Assess whether or not a point is noteworthy.

Notes can be made in either diagrammatic or linear form. People with good spacial awareness should practise using 'spider' diagrams and mind maps. Those with strong visual perception are advised to use the linear note form. Other strategies which are helpful when taking notes are:

- Use colour to separate topics or issues.
- Use highlighter pens to emphasise key points.
- Devise shorthand to make it easier to note certain commonly repeated words, but keep it simple.
- Keep the material well spaced.
- Add examples, if possible.
- Use headings.
- Make lists.

Organisation of notes

It cannot be emphasised too strongly that organisation is the key to successful learning whatever activity is being undertaken. There is little point in learning to take successful notes if they cannot be easily accessed. There are several ways to store notes and each has advantages and disadvantages:

- looseleaf paper in files
- on computer
- in plastic boxes, on index cards
- in notebooks, one book per topic.

The choice of storage will depend on the space available and the preference of the user.

Poor note-taking skills can be at the root of learning difficulties, not only with the person who writes too few notes, but also with the student who tries to write down everything that is heard or read. It is a skill that needs practice but the dyslexic person is urged to concentrate on two questions:

- What is my learning style?
- What is the purpose of these notes?

If these questions are kept in mind the process of note-taking should become easier.

Lectures, talks and seminars

This section is closely linked to the section on note-taking. This form of teaching can be so difficult for dyslexic people who have auditory perception problems and a slow pace of processing. Why are lectures used? Why don't colleges, universities and training companies simply write the course and distribute copies to the students? A lecture should be an interactive experience and not a one-way absorption of information. Signs will be given about the importance of topics and issues by the body language of the lecturer, together with changes of pace and tone. Indications will be given about what is essential to know and what is not.

The main advantages of offering course information in lecture form are:

- It helps to summarise key issues and controversies.
- It explains difficult techniques and concepts.
- It includes the most up-to-date, unpublished information.
- It clarifies the scope of the course, identifying which aspects and components are most important.
- It engenders enthusiasm about the subject and raises interest, especially if the lecturer displays these qualities.

The student may wonder how it is possible to derive maximum benefit from a lecture, and the following advice may be helpful:

- Find out where the lecture fits into the sequence.
- Prepare for the lecture in advance: note the structure.
- If a reading list is on a handout or course booklet, ensure that it is open, ready to mark texts that are mentioned.
- Be proactive during the lecture. Think. Question.
- Request that the handout is produced with double spacing or wide margins so that notes can be merged with those of the lecturer.
- Review material as soon after the lecture as possible.
- Exchange notes with other students to find out if you have identified the same key points or missed any important facts.
- Do not try to write down too much.
- Signal to the lecturer if the pace is too quick: convey the impression of being hassled!

Essay writing

Essay writing is problematic for many adults with dyslexia. The main reason for the difficulty is that in writing an essay they have to demonstrate an expertise in a wide range of study skills: reading, note taking, organisation, and information gathering from all sources. In addition, they have to show that they can convert all their ideas into accurate, continuous prose.

   As with other aspects of study, organisation is a key feature of successful essay writing. The task becomes much easier if it is split into manageable sections and a time limit imposed for each stage. For example:

Stage 1   Collection of information (3 or 4 sessions of study time)
Stage 2   Planning (1 session of 2 hours)
Stage 3   Writing (3 or 4 sessions)
Stage 4   Proofreading (1 session of 2 hours).

The timings are only given as examples of how to plan, as individuals will know their own limitations. The point to remember is that it pays to plan in detail so that deadlines can be met and pressure of time is minimised. It is interesting to note that much more time is spent in collecting information, planning and proofreading than in the actual writing of the essay. The stages highlight the importance of these particular study skills for the adult with dyslexia, and are discussed in more detail below.

Stage 1: Collection of information

Libraries can be confusing places for adults with dyslexia. In order to find the materials they need they have to use a number of processing skills that they may find difficult: e.g. sequencing, reading, and note taking. As much time as possible should be allowed for this stage; being pressurised by time only makes the task more difficult. It is important to keep asking questions about the procedure: What exactly am I looking for? How much information do I need? Is this the most up-to-date account? Do I have evidence from both sides of the argument?

   If a vital text cannot be located it is essential not to give up. Rather, the library staff might be asked for help. Adults with dyslexia desperately want to be independent but sometimes they need to be able to know when to ask for help, especially when library staff are eager to provide it.

Another source of information is the internet. Search engines allow web users to find the information they require. Examples of popular search engines are:

Alta Vista   http://www.altavista.digital.com
Infoseek   http://www.infoseek.com
Yahoo!   http://www.yahoo.com/search.html

By entering key words, relevant information can be sourced. However, there are no editors or publishers evaluating the information that appears on the internet; therefore, the user must be alert and pay critical attention to the source of any information required.

Stage 2: Planning

The first step to planning an essay is to understand the question. There are three issues to address before making an outline plan:

1. Where in the course does this topic come?
2. What are the issues?
3. What precisely am I being asked to do?

The third of these questions involves understanding the processing words usually used or implied in essay questions: for example, 'describe', 'evaluate' or 'contrast'. Definitions of such words can be found in most books on study skills. A particularly clear table of common instruction words can be found on page 57 of *The Student Skills Guide* (Drew and Bingham, 1997).

A plan should be made, in diagrammatic form (see Figure 5.1), to break down the task into smaller, manageable chunks. A 4,000-word essay can seem an awesome task, but when it is broken down into sections of 500 words it can appear much more manageable.

Example question

Discuss the advantages and disadvantages of the social and individual models of dyslexia. How do these models relate to employment and education? (4,000 words)

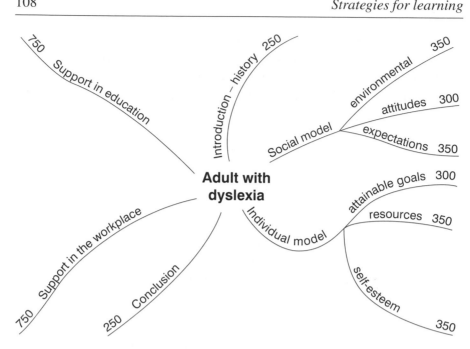

Figure 5.1 Breaking the example question into manageable chunks, with indications of wordage

There are three software programmes that help with the organisation of pieces of continuous writing:

- **Inspirations** is a flexible planning programme. It allows the user to plan in diagrammatic form then convert it, by pressing one computer key, to a linear plan. Equally useful to some dyslexic people who do not have good spacial perception, is the alternative approach, where text can be easily turned into a mind map.
- **Thinksheet** offers a mind map where text can be entered in each box. The text is not visible when the whole mind map is viewed. This facility enables the writer to be constantly reminded of the whole plan.
- **Brainbox** has basic mind-mapping facilities

Stage 3: Writing

A danger that adults with dyslexia must strive to avoid is a lack of sequencing in their writing. Often they have excellent, creative, informed ideas but do not order them in a comprehensive and logical manner. When a good plan has been made it must be adhered to. It is usually a good idea to place the plan so that it is visible during the writing of the essay to encourage the student to keep to the agreed order and not go off at a tangent.

A concise introduction will also help to give pointers to the reader about the direction of the discourse. An effective introduction will raise the key issues and identify the approach to be taken by the writer. The main body of the essay should present ideas from each section, one at a time. It is important that the line of argument is backed up by evidence of reading and research, which is correctly referenced. To avoid confusion, the draft of each section could be written in a different colour or a different typeface could be used. The conclusion will highlight the main points made in the essay. Adults with dyslexia find it difficult to be brief but they should attempt to summarise what they have said 'in a nutshell'!

Stage 4: Proofreading

Proofreading is problematic for dyslexic people. As they cannot identify errors in their writing, it may help to read the essay aloud. In this manner, it is sometimes possible to detect where a sentence should end or where a subject does not agree with the verb. Microsoft Word can assist with proofreading. The spell and grammar check can identify errors, but only writers know the exact meaning they wish to express. Other technological aids can help in proofreading: textHELP, scanner with text-reading software and Write: Outloud.

The adult with dyslexia might barter with friends in their group. In exchange for an oral discussion of the essay topic (an area where dyslexic people usually have great strengths), the friend could be encouraged to proof read the essay.

A simple checklist is the final procedure for the essay writer. Students should be encouraged to make up their own list because they will be aware of their own strengths and weaknesses. Some suggested questions for inclusion are:

- Have I kept to the essay question?
- Does the introduction signal what I have done in the essay?
- Have I demonstrated that I have read and understood the prescribed texts?
- Have I been analytical, critical and questioning?
- Does the essay flow logically?

- Have I linked the paragraphs?
- Does the conclusion show how I have developed the points?
- Have I kept to the recommended number of words?
- Have I included a reference section and bibliography?
- Have I adhered to the instructions for the production of the essay?
- Have I included the title?
- Have I given my own name or some other means of identifying the writer?

When the essay has been assessed and returned to the adult with dyslexia it is often important that verbal feedback be included so that the adult can ask questions that will lead to improved grades in subsequent assignments.

Report writing

Report writing includes many of the skills necessary for successful essay writing but has a more formal structure. It is a document that communicates important pieces of information in as precise a manner as possible. The clear structure of a report is helpful to the adult with dyslexia but the precise nature of the language can be problematic.

Presentations

Adults with dyslexia usually have good oral skills and communicate with people extremely well. Oral presentations, therefore, provide an opportunity for them to demonstrate their abilities to the full. However, there are three areas that must be considered:

- Preparation
- Anxiety
- Visual aids.

The most important thing to consider when preparing a presentation is to think about the audience. Who will they be? How much of the topic will they know already? Will they all have the same level of knowledge?

The structure of the talk could follow the plan for essay writing, as described in the last section. It will cover the following:

- introduction, where an overview is given;
- the main body, where issues are raised and discussed;
- the conclusion or summing up, where key issues are reinforced.

Since nervousness in a presenter is very uncomfortable for the audience, self-confidence is an important factor in successful presentations. To feel confident the presenter must be so well prepared that interesting and appropriate material is offered.

During the talk it is important to establish eye contact with members of the audience. Positive feedback increases confidence and relaxes the speaker. It is useful to anticipate potential problems such as awkward questions or how to respond if the thread of the talk is completely lost. It is important to ensure that any visual aids are entirely visible and are not obscured by the presenter.

Most presentations are accompanied by overhead projector slides. When preparing slides the following suggestions might prove useful:

- Make sure they can be read by the whole audience: use large lettering.
- Include only key words or phrases.
- Avoid too much technical detail.
- Select colour appropriately.
- Pie charts and graphs are easier to read than tables.

Revision strategies and examination techniques

Although other forms of assessment are being introduced to colleges and universities, written examinations are still the most common form of post-school assessment. To be successful in the examination situation adults with dyslexia need to acquire strategies to cope with processing difficulties associated with their specific learning difficulties: memory problems; working under strict time constraints; spelling and syntax inaccuracies; and, finally, what might be termed 'structure' challenges.

Revision strategies

Memory problems can be overcome by systematic, planned revision. The object of this revision is not to memorise the complete course but rather to enhance understanding of the issues and be able to develop important points in the examinations.

As with the other study strategies discussed in this chapter, the key to success for the adult with dyslexia is organisation. A study plan should be made in detail, including day-to-day living tasks (see the section on organisation above), and displayed on the wall. A duplicate could be made for family/flatmates so that interruptions will be minimised. Provision should be made for spare time in the plan in case extra work is required on one topic.

For each topic a programme of multi-sensory revision should be undertaken. It is possible to identify a number of helpful steps:

Step 1   Compile notes for the topic. Check that lecture notes are complete. Are comments on prescribed reading included?
Step 2   Dictate key points and issues onto tape, using a voice-activated tape recorder.
Step 3   Listen to information gathered on the tape.
Step 4   Listen a second time but on this occasion enter the information on a prepared mindmap or diagram.
Step 5   Write linear notes from the diagram.
Step 6   Put key words for each section on index cards.
Step 7   Place title of topic and three or four headings on a postcard.

Adopting a strategy of this kind will ensure that notes will become more and more sharply focused. The strategy allows the adult with dyslexia to use a number of different methods that will assist memorisation: reading, listening, drawing, and writing. In addition, categorisation of topics by colour in the notes will be a further aid to remembering and understanding. Revision, it must be remembered, is an active process, not simply a reading exercise.

After the whole course has been covered using the method described, a number of past papers should be tackled. This 'mock' test will give an indication of how effective the revision has been and engender confidence in the student.

Examination techniques

There are two stages to be considered in exam techniques: before the exam and during the exam. It is absolutely essential to know what the format of the exam will be. Familiarity with the layout of the paper will eliminate some of the anxieties on the day of the exam. A careful note should be taken of the precise time and location of the exam. By avoiding a last-minute rush, the candidate should be able to remain relatively calm and ready to tackle the final hurdle.

There are three areas where people with dyslexia can encounter difficulties in the exam itself: lack of preparation; time-management problems; and failure to answer the question. The first two points have been dealt with in some detail earlier in this chapter; the third point needs elaboration here. The most common error made by dyslexic students is to misread the question. An essay that is irrelevant, however well written, will almost certainly be penalised. Time should therefore be spent understanding what is being asked before an attempt is made to write the answer. A number of things can be asked about the exam question:

- From which part of the course does the question come?
- What issues are involved?
- What am I being asked to do with the topic?
- What is the processing word?

Only when a full grasp of the question has been established should the student begin to plan the exam essay. The processing word – for example, 'discuss', 'analyse' – should be placed at the top of the plan so that students will be reminded what they have been asked to do as they plan the answer. Students should be encouraged to make the plan on a separate sheet of paper so that they can keep it beside them as they write.

Importance of learning strategies

Learning strategies are extremely important for adults with dyslexia and high priority should be given to the development of these skills. The main study skills which have been discussed here are: organisation, reading strategies, note taking, information gathering, essay writing, presentation skills, and exam techniques. These are all crucially important. Although adults with dyslexia can be helped to acquire these skills they must take responsibility for developing them and using them in context, appropriately. Without doubt the most important of these skills is organisation. All learners, of course, need to be organised and systematic in their study habits. Given the particular difficulties experienced by learners with dyslexia, the need for well-practised organisational skills and routines is especially important. The adoption of careful routines may not entirely eliminate the difficulties experienced by learners with dyslexia, but there is no doubt that these will substantially improve their capacity to access information and ideas as well as to express themselves intelligibly.

Chapter 6

Disaffection, defiance and depression

Much of this book is about the positive aspects of dyslexia and the creative abilities of dyslexic people. The authors advocate that employers, and indeed all who work with dyslexic adults, should consider their needs particularly in the workplace. In some cases, however, the needs of dyslexic people are not met and too often they become disaffected – this unfortunately is the reality for some, perhaps many. Too often after speaking to audiences when we have been highlighting the positive aspects of dyslexia someone has approached us afterwards and retold a story of distress and dejection. Some it seems have considerable barriers to overcome. This chapter will therefore examine the area of disaffection and show how, in many cases, that disaffection becomes defiance. It appears to us, that it is too easy for the initial dissatisfaction to become disaffection, which, if left to develop, can so easily lead to anti-social behaviour or some form of inward negativity, which can result in depression.

While there are many and varied causes and symptoms of depression, the seemingly impossible hurdle and the succession of failures sometimes experienced by the dyslexic person may ultimately lead to depression. Once engulfed in that cycle of despair, considerable support and understanding is needed to fully appreciate and address the difficulties. Sometimes the demands of a busy workplace, coupled with the priorities of a society which holds literacy in high esteem, can prove extremely challenging for adults with dyslexia. This chapter will provide some explanation, examples and suggestions in relation to the cycle of disaffection, defiance and depression.

Disaffection

Disaffection implies that in some way the person is not obtaining satisfaction from the current situation. For many people with dyslexia this can begin early in the school years when their specific needs may not be understood or even acknowledged. We have noted many times how some dyslexic people who are seemingly successful in their particular area of work often minimise their achievements. This can be due to the long-standing feeling of inadequacy in an education environment which favours skills in literacy over unconventional processing avenues and creative, visual/spatial skills. The result is that the person can and often does experience feelings of failure which lead to a low academic and personal self-concept (Burns, 1986).

So what are the sources of disaffection which have such a powerful influence on the educational and social development of the dyslexic person? This will be discussed under the headings of identification, support and misunderstanding, which are the influential factors relating to disaffection.

Identification

Clearly identification, and early identification in particular, are important and recently many advances have taken place in that area. For example, a computer screening programme – Cognitive Profiling System (Singleton et al., 1997) – attempts to identify children who are at high risk of displaying dyslexic difficulties. This information is obtained from the responses to a cognitive computer assessment which can be administered to pre-school children. Additionally, Fawcett and Nicolson (1997) have developed a Dyslexia Early Screening Test which can also identify high-risk children before the onset of literacy and for many dyslexic children before the cycle of failure is established. Weedon et al. (1999, 2000) recognising that many of the difficulties with identification lie in the administration time required by tests and the conflict this places on a teaching profession with ever-increasing demands, have developed a Listening and Literacy Index, a group test, which can be administered to a whole class at the same time. The Index can identify potential specific learning difficulties and particular discrepancies within the developing literacy skills of the young child.

Muter et al. (1997) have produced a Phonological Abilities Test which is directed to the phonological development of children at a young age and can also highlight the early signs of dyslexia. This is clearly important since it is widely recognised that phonological development is an important factor in literacy development and is associated with dyslexia.

It can be noted that the tests mentioned above have all been developed in the last few years; therefore, for many dyslexic adults appropriate mechanism for identification was not widely available when they were at school. Identification may have been reserved for the most extreme cases or perhaps not at all. It is encouraging that now, coupled with the advances in early identification, many education authorities have policies in dyslexia which focus on early literacy development and early identification. Additionally a Dyslexia Friendly Schools pack has been compiled and circulated to all schools in England and Wales (BDA, 1999). This emphasises how crucial it is for teachers to have awareness in dyslexia and for dyslexic children to be identified early. It is not surprising to suggest that failure to identify dyslexic difficulties can lead to failure to develop literacy and can result in a cycle of failure which can highlight disaffection and the implications of that for the person's self-concept and academic self-esteem.

Support

There is little doubt that the availability of support when it is most required is crucial. Support clearly needs to be available from an early age to help the dyslexic child to cope with literacy and other demands of the curriculum. Intensive input at this vital early stage usually pays dividends. What we find, however, is that support is only part of the picture. Two aspects come to mind. Firstly, support should be provided in a way that will ultimately help the dyslexic person to achieve autonomy in learning. Support should therefore not be in the form of a crutch which, when removed, leaves the person at a loss and incapable of functioning without the support. Secondly, opportunities for support should be available when the dyslexic person requires it. We find that there are crisis points in people's lives – for example, when changing school, or due to family changes, peer difficulties, employment problems, personal problems, locational changes or significant changes in lifestyle. These situations may not necessarily be accompanied by crisis but the vulnerability of the situation can promote a crisis situation. At these times people with dyslexia can be at their most vulnerable and this is when support may be necessary, often stemming from a lack of self-confidence. The British Dyslexia Association and the Adult Dyslexia Organisation in the UK operate a helpline for dyslexic people. This type of service is invaluable yet is operated by volunteers, often overwhelmed by demand. Given the value of support at various points of a dyslexic person's life and the need for that support to be available as the need arises, there should be a strong case for this helpline type of facility to be offered as part of the government services to dyslexic people, indeed to all those who fall under the categories of the Disability Discrimination Act and similar legislation in the USA.

Misunderstanding

Dyslexia is perhaps the best known but least understood of the disabilities affecting children and adults. The media term 'word blindness', used to describe dyslexia does little to promote a real understanding of dyslexia. This is probably the most inappropriate of the terms used to describe dyslexia. The educational description of dyslexia based on recent research, as described in Chapter 1 of this book, should testify to the inappropriateness of the term 'word blindness'. Additionally we hear of almost daily 'cures' for dyslexia, a magic pill, some substance or an expensive training programme. This does little to promote a real understanding of dyslexia and, if anything, can lead to a misunderstanding among the general public and employers. It needs to be appreciated by all that dyslexia is neurologically based and developmental. This means that a dyslexic person will always be dyslexic but with support, training and appropriate education can compensate to a great extent for the dyslexic difficulties. It should also be noted that dyslexia can have many positive attributes. The success of famous dyslexic people such as Richard Branson, Anthea Turner and Duncan Goodhew is well known, but there are many dyslexic people who are successful in so-called 'ordinary' jobs, contributing to team meetings in the workplace, showing inspiration with new ideas, or initiating a new method of managing a business, an office or even a filing cabinet! Although awareness of dyslexia has increased in recent years, as has the body of research knowledge, publications, web pages and media coverage, there is still much ignorance regarding dyslexia among employers and indeed the general public. As long as misconceptions exist, dyslexic people will continue to hesitate about revealing their dyslexia on a job application form or course application. While we always encourage dyslexic people to declare their dyslexia on an application form, we are aware that the lack of knowledge and some of the misunderstandings which prevail may mediate against them in what is usually a competitive situation. One, perhaps extreme, example, which highlights a lack of knowledge and understanding was when an employer, on being informed that a interview with a dyslexic person had been arranged, asked if a ramp would be necessary! Perhaps this serves to highlight the confusion that can arise with the current amalgam of 'dys' labels which can confuse as well as clarify.

Defiance

It is not too controversial to suggest that if people fail and continue to fail they may display anti-social or anti-establishment behaviour. Much of this is due to a low self-concept as well as the inability to fit into a particular family, educational or social situation. Peer pressures, family pressures and the education system can lead a dyslexic person to a trail of defiance and perhaps even deviance.

Crime and prison

Studies which have been conducted on the prison population have revealed that between 30 and 50% of the prison population may be dyslexic (Kirk and Reid, 1999).

Alm (1997) described a study carried out in three penal institutions in Uppsala County in Sweden. The study covered a total of 80 inmates aged between 18 and 67. The results showed significant differences between decoding and comprehension in 31% of the sample.

Over 30 years ago the following comment was made: 'the ease with which dyslexic teenagers slip into crime demands serious attention' (Critchley, 1966). Although over a third of a century has passed since Critchley highlighted this issue, it is only very recently that some attempts have been made to identify the real extent of the problem. Today the relationship between dyslexia and anti-social or criminal behaviour is arguably one of the most controversial in the field of dyslexia. Some studies, which have attracted significant media attention, have claimed to detect a significantly higher incidence of dyslexia among those in custody compared to the general population. If it is valid, that finding is remarkable and worrying for it might be inter-preted to suggest that there is a causal connection between dyslexia and social deviance. Since it is now acknowledged that dyslexia is at least in part influenced by heredity – it has been described as an innate neuro-logical dysfunction – it would be extremely serious if this disabling condition predisposed people to criminal or anti-social behaviour.

At first glance dyslexia may induce anti-social behaviour. The able school pupil, whose dyslexic condition is not diagnosed or, having been diagnosed, receives insufficient or inappropriate support, might very well begin to feel devalued at school and to turn to forms of deviant behaviour as a way of responding to the sense of low-esteem induced by school and as a way of achieving recognition by peers. A pattern of anti-social or maladjusted behaviour at school might very well lead to more serious forms of deviant behaviour that end ultimately in imprisonment. If that pattern of behaviour was established it would not prove that dyslexia **caused** people to become delinquent: it would suggest that, if dyslexia is not carefully diagnosed and proper support provided, social disaffection might result. That is, dyslexia might be shown to be indirectly rather than directly related to offending behaviour. Once that relationship is estab-lished it will then be necessary to consider the implications for the training of those who carry responsibility for young offenders.

However, speculation of that kind is inappropriate until evidence is established of the relationship between dyslexia and anti-social behaviour. Of course, the findings of such studies will not by them-selves demonstrate that a relationship exists, but the results will lend support to one side of the argument or the other in what has become an extremely controversial topic.

Research studies on dyslexia and young offenders

STOP project

Shropshire Probation Service in partnership with Shropshire Chamber of Commerce, Training and Enterprise developed the initiative,

Specific Training for Offenders on Probation. The aim of this project was: to investigate the levels of basic skills; to find the incidence of dyslexia among young offenders; and to make recommendations about support for them. The time-scale of the project was from October 1995 until December 1997. It also involved Dublin City vocational education Committee and CelS of Belluno in Italy.

Three main issues were addressed: screening, assessment and training.

Screening

Firstly, a screening tool had to be established. The researchers had concerns that no one test was available to them, therefore a screening package was devised containing the following elements:

1. A sample of the offender's writing via a completed proforma.
2. Checklist 1 recorded basic skills difficulties and some indicators of dyslexia as found in the writing task.
3. Checklist 2 recorded various behavioural and other indicators.
4. The Adult Dyslexia Questionnaire which was researched and validated by Dr Michael Vinegrad, and subsequently adopted by the Adult Dyslexia Organisation.
5. Four tests of reading made up of performance-based tasks of real-life situations were given:
   - A poster advertising a pop concert provided the material to be interpreted by the young offenders
   - Offenders answered questions relating to a simple road map
   - An advertisement for a job was the focus for questions
   - Offenders were asked to extract information from a block graph.

The screening took between 20 and 30 minutes to complete. The Probation Officers found that the information obtained was very useful, of good quality and the fact that it was linked to National Standards gave it added respectability.

The screening process identified young offenders who required fuller assessment. These criteria included one or more of the following:

- Below Entry or Entry Level reading
- Below Entry or Entry Level writing
- Eight or more positive indicators on the Adult Dyslexia Questionnaire.

Assessment

Secondly, in addition to devising an appropriate screening test the research project had now to devise an assessment instrument that could be delivered by Probation Officers who had undergone training. This assessment tool comprised six tests in two stages:

Stage 1   The Schonell single word reading test
           The Schonell single word spelling test
           Raven's Progressive Matrices
           The Bangor Dyslexia Test
Stage 2   A basic skills checklist
           An action plan for support.

The whole assessment process was fairly lengthy – over 4 hours to complete. However, the Probation Officers found the process useful, often giving them the opportunity to spot discrepancies in the learning profiles of the young offenders and enabling them to identify potential dyslexics. The young offenders also found the experience useful and enjoyed discussing their learning difficulties, perhaps for the first time in their lives. The key findings of this stage of the project were:

- 12% of offenders were virtual non-readers;
- a further 29% had reading skills so poor they would seriously affect their employment opportunities;
- 24% could not write their name, address and personal details on a simple form;
- a further 46% could not write simple text at a level acceptable to employers;
- 31% had positive indicators of dyslexia.

Training

The third, and final, task the researchers had to address in this project was the training needs of the Probation Officers and others involved in dealing with the learning difficulties of young offenders. The training needs of a number of different groups had to be considered:

- Probation Officers
- Senior Probation Officers

- Magistrates
- Police Custody Sergeants
- Volunteer Mentors
- Employers
- Education staff from Dublin Prisons
- Psychology/training staff from CelS, Italy.

Four different courses were devised to offer training in the identification and supporting of dyslexic offenders. The project team acknowledges that many other factors contribute to offending behaviour but that literacy is a significant factor that contributes to re-offending. Through the training courses the difficulties can, and should, be addressed.

The Dyspel project

The Dyspel project was an 18-month pilot project which ran between September 1995 and March 1997. The aims of the project were three-fold and similar to the STOP project:

1. To increase probation officers' awareness of dyslexia and its relationship to offending.
2. To develop an initial screening tool to identify offenders with strong indications of dyslexic difficulties.
3. To increase education and training opportunities for offenders through diagnosis, counselling, appropriate specialist teaching and building links with education and training institutions, in order to reduce offending.

The first aim was met by providing a one-day and two half-day training courses for Probation Officers. The content included:

- Definitions and features of dyslexia
- Language processing difficulties
- The dyslexic learning/thinking style
- The experience of dyslexia
- Implications for offending
- Indicators for identifying dyslexia
- Screening: questionnaire and tasks

- Language and cultural issues
- Implications of dyslexia for the probation officer
- Counselling issues
- Dyslexia and the criminal justice system.

The second course, targeted at Tutors, was for 30 taught hours plus practical assignments, and had university accreditation.

A joint follow-up session was held to address questions and difficulties thrown up on the training course. From this meeting new developments such as written guidelines for the screening questionnaire were devised.

The second aim, that of devising a screening tool for dyslexia, was then addressed by designing a questionnaire, and, additionally, the Bangor Dyslexia Screening Test was included. The resulting questionnaire was made up of six sections:

1. Reading and writing
2. Memory and learning style
3. Education history
4. The individual's personal likes and dislikes
5. The Bangor Dyslexia Screening Test
6. A short reading and writing task.

The whole test took around 40 minutes to administer. Positive responses on a range of indicators, including difficulties in five or more of the Bangor Test tasks, meant that a referral should be made. In addition, Probation Officers were encouraged to refer if they had any doubt about the pace of processing, or other difficulties related to processing language.

A research study by Wally Morgan, using the Dyspel screening test, was carried out in Camberwell Centre EWE in May 1996. The results of this showed that 52% of those screened had strong indicators of dyslexia. This figure, although greater than that given by the STOP project, was in line with those found in projects in Sweden and Louisiana in the USA.

Of the 50 offenders diagnosed, 45 were positively identified as dyslexic; 33 then attended tutorials given by tutors who had taken part in the training scheme. Some of those proceeded almost immediately to college, others required a longer period of one-to-one tuition.

Comments about the project from different perspectives indicates its success.

- From a probation officer:

    Throws a whole new perspective on recognising clients' behaviour, abilities and propensity for certain conduct.

- From a tutor:

    It greatly enhanced my teaching in general.

- From a student:

    Alleluia! At last I know why I have struggled for 39 years. I can say I am dyslexic now – people used to say I was lazy and stupid. I feel so relieved.

Issues and critique

Many of the issues raised by the projects described above were subject to scrutiny from further studies, principally one at the University of Cambridge Institute of Criminology (Rice, 1998) where it was found that reading abilities of prisoners either match or exceed those in the general population. In relation to their reading skills they were overdependent on contextualised clues, and the likely causes were the low levels of reading experience, inadequate instruction, emotional disturbance, low motivation and low attitude. The research team concluded that:

We found no support for the belief that developmental dyslexia is more prevalent in the prison population than in the general population. We accordingly found no support for the claim that dyslexia entails a significantly enhanced risk of criminality.

Further, Rice (1998) suggested that the Dyspel project was fundamentally flawed on grounds of sample selection, measures used and the criteria used to indicate the presence of dyslexia. In a cross-sectional study of 323 prisoners in England and Wales, Rice (1998) asserted that there is no support for the claim that dyslexia is more prevalent among prisoners than among the general population.

While there remains questions about the generalisability from smaller scale studies, the findings of the studies criticised by Rice cannot be discounted. It can be argued that Rice's study followed a narrow definition of dyslexia using only reading performance as a measure of dyslexia ignoring the other manifestations of dyslexia (Nicolson, 1996)

Young offenders study

Kirk and Reid (1999) carried out a study involving 50 youngsters from a young offenders institution in Scotland. The study and its conclusions were the subject of a documentary screened by Channel 4 in the UK in July 1999, which resulted in considerable interest from viewers (Bruce, 1999 – personal communication).

The instrument used for the study was QuickScan, a computerised screening test for dyslexia (Zdzienski, 1997). This test had been piloted involving 2,000 students across many subject areas from the Universities of Kingston and Surrey. However, some of the vocabulary used to screen students in the south of England was judged to be inappropriate for young offenders in central Scotland. In preparation for the work to be carried out in the young offenders' institution, and in consultation with the author, the vocabulary in the questions was amended. Changes were made and carefully checked to make sure that the sense of the question remained the same. An example of the linguistic difference is: the word *task* has different connotations in England and was replaced by the more familiar *job*. All the changes were approved by the author: she was happy that the results of the screening would be as valid as with the original questions. An additional reason for selecting a computerised test was that the offenders might respond more positively to this method of testing than to paper and pencil tests with which they may have had negative experiences at school.

Choice of sample

The choice of the size of the sample group was determined by the prison management. They stipulated the amount of time they felt was enough to allow the screening to take place but not to completely disrupt the training and discipline within the institution. Given this time restraint it was decided that it would be possible to have nine sessions of 30 minutes. Half an hour allowed time for discussion with the small group about matters connected with anonymity. They had exclusive entitlement to the results and a right to stop participating at any time during the screening. A brief description of the test was offered, and details of what it would measure. At this point the young offenders were given the choice of whether or not to proceed, but none of them refused to continue. Again the numbers taking the test were limited by the prison procedures: only six young people were allowed to take the test at any one time. This stipulation determined that our sample would be 50.

In order to provide a further test of the validity of the measure it was decided that every offender who exhibited dyslexic indicators would be offered a full psychometric assessment by a Chartered Educational Psychologist using standard tests, for example, WAIS and WRAT. However, as the number of those who displayed indicators was far greater than we had expected, and as the time restrictions remained the same, it was possible to give the full assessment to only a sample. This sample was chosen at random by the prison officers from a list of those who, from the screening test, had displayed dyslexic indicators.

Before the screening began the Educational Psychologist and the Dyslexia Adviser visited a workshop where the Young Offenders were engaged in making bird tables for a commercial retail outlet. There was an opportunity at their tea break to introduce themselves and talk about their reasons for the visit to the institution. They were then able to observe the Young Offenders at work. An informal attempt was made to identify indicators of dyslexia at this stage. They looked for evidence of cross-laterality, of ability to carry out instructions in sequence, of awkwardness in handling tools and of ability to concentrate on the task. An officer took a note of those identified.

Results

The QuickScan screening test reports on 24 different items. Of the 50 Young Offenders who were screened, 25 were found to have indicators of dyslexia. The continuum of dyslexia was as follows:

3 displayed most indicators
3 displayed many indicators
17 displayed some indicators
2 displayed borderline indicators.

Three of the 50 had been tested previously and found to be dyslexic. In each of these cases QuickScan showed strong indicators of dyslexia.

Self-esteem was significantly very low in all Young Offenders who were found to have indicators of dyslexia. Of the 25 positive Young Offenders, 19 admitted family awareness of dyslexia, while only 6 of the non-dyslexic 25 admitted family awareness. The scores for sequencing and memory difficulties were much higher in those who were found to be dyslexic.

Owing to time constraints it was not possible to give a full psychometric assessment to all those who had positive indicators of dyslexia, and six of the young men were chosen at random, each of whom displayed a cognitive profile associated with dyslexia. The findings of both the screening test and the psychometric assessment, however small the sample, concur with the findings of the STOP project and the Dyspel project that is, the incidence of dyslexia within the institutions was substantial. Moreover, that result is based on a valid measure of dyslexia. Each Young Offender who participated was sent a letter which not only thanked him for participating, but specified his individual learning style with suggestions on how to utilise that style in future learning situations.

Implications of this study

At present there are no arrangements in place to support dyslexic people in this institution. The time when these young people are serving a custodial sentence offers an ideal opportunity to address their specific learning difficulties. They could be made aware of their particular learning style and work on study skill strategies to overcome their processing difficulties. A programme of this type would not only raise their self-esteem but also prepare them for further education or employment when their period in custody is at an end.

Study support is only one issue to be addressed. Identification is another, both for screening and for full assessment. What tools are to be used and who can be trained to use them? These questions can only be answered by highly trained individuals, but they must first be asked and resources provided to allow them to find the answers.

One solution offered, and agreed with the governor of the institution, was that a staff development seminar would take place. This seminar was given to all members of staff to raise their awareness of dyslexia and the ways in which it can manifest itself. However, this measure is not sufficient. A programme of training along the lines of that which was devised by the STOP project team would transfer very well to the situation in this institution.

Four different training courses were devised.

1. Training in **screening** – a two-day course covering:

   - Basic skills awareness
   - Readability
   - Dyslexia awareness
   - Identification of difficulties
   - Delivery of the screening instruments
   - Recording of results
   - Referral.

   This course could be adapted to be offered to all staff at this young offenders' institution.

2. Training in **assessment** – a four-day course covering:

   - Learning styles
   - Assessment techniques
   - Assessment tests
   - Delivering and scoring tests
   - Recording, interpreting and documenting scores
   - Action planning
   - Feedback to offenders.

   This course could be adapted to be offered to all education and training staff.

3. Awareness training for Magistrates and Police Officers – a one-day course covering:

- Definitions of basic skills and dyslexia
- The range and scale of basic skills difficulties
- The effect on the individual
- The effects on society
- Issues of access to the service, including readability.

This course could remain unaltered.

4. Mentor training. The basis of this course was The City and Guilds Initial Certificate in Teaching Basic Literacy Skills, a taught course of 8 × 2 hour sessions. Added to this were four sessions to cover issues specific to the target group of offenders making the whole course 12 × 2 hours long. A similar course could be offered by the RSA or SQA.

Whichever training scheme is adopted, set procedures must be put in place so that, when dyslexia is suspected, identification, assessment and support can easily be carried out. There also should be procedures to ensure liaison with agencies outside the prison so that support can be continued when the offender is released. In the USA many studies have replicated this type of finding.

Saunders (1990) from the US perspective provides a range of arguments for linking dyslexia and delinquency. He suggests that 'dyslexia won't kill you but it can mess up your life' (Saunders, 1990: 232). Saunders further suggests that some theories relating to anti-social behaviour – such as the 'strain theory' (Binder, 1988) which suggests that school is a source of frustration for some young people and this frustration leads them into delinquent activities – are relevant. Rebellion can be an alternative form of achievement for many youngsters. Saunders rightly suggests that dyslexia is not a cause of delinquency but can be a contributory factor. Saunders advocates the practice of community projects such as the one conducted in Maryland in 1990 – Maryland Associates for Dyslexic Adults and Youths (MAYDAY) – which he suggests can promotes a 'healthy therapeutic alliance … which results in a more wholesome self-concept … and leads to a more productive adult life'. Giorcelli, in an inspiring memorial lecture in honour of Des English to the Australian Association of Special

Education (Giorcelli, 1995), argues that the multi-faceted challenges of students with special needs are not the sole responsibility of schools but that of the community and society. The curriculum should be nourished by a strong foundation of equity and social justice principles nourished by a flexible and inclusive curriculum. She also has reservations about the Australian Disability Discrimination Act 1992, because the evidence shows that discrimination legislation does not necessarily mean an end to discrimination in the education system in either 'the pedagogical or social justice sense'.

Self-concept

Without doubt self-concept and self-esteem are important factors in the development of a positive attitude to learning and to one's dyslexic difficulties. The research on 'self' as a psychological concept was first brought to prominence by James (1892) who highlighted the 'self' as the 'I' now referred to as the 'categorical self' (Lewis, 1990). This view looks at the awareness of one's own life events, the uniqueness of one's own experience, one's identity and the awareness of one's own awareness of self. This internal view of self has been accompanied by the sociological perspective (Cooley, 1902; Dunn, 1988). Cooley believed that the notion of self is built through the reaction of others to us and how we believe they view us.

This 'looking glass' self is well established as an important determinant of self-concept. This view is further reinforced by Mead (1934) who saw the self and the social world as interwoven – emphasising the importance of language and interaction. This is important when one considers the relationship between self-concept and academic performance. Wood and Burns (1983) suggest that the body of research evidence indicates that children have a specific self-concept for reading ability and this can influence reading attainment. Since some studies actually suggest that poor achievement causes low self-concept we must view the relationship as reciprocal. Vail (1992) suggests that a child who has experienced school failure often enough will anticipate failure. This highlights the view of 'learned helplessness' which Abramson et al. (1978) suggest emerges when individuals feel they have no control over a specific academic outcome. This cycle of failure is, of course, reciprocal and reinforcing. Therefore anticipating failure will result in failure, which will further reduce motivation, expectations of success and self-concept. It is not surprising, therefore, that the study by Fairhurst and Pumfrey (1992) into the self-concept of third-year secondary students in three schools showed that pupils with reading difficulties in all three schools had lower self-concepts as learners than the independent readers.

The points discussed above underline the importance of self-concept not only in a social sense but also in an educational sense. The view is that the emotional needs of individual people are often overlooked at the expense of education and social conventions (Vail, 1992; Healy, 1991). Lawrence's studies (1985, 1996) show the importance of integrating self-esteem considerations with attainment factors. In his studies the group of poor readers who were given a dual-purpose programme, consisting of a reading programme and a programme designed to enhance self-esteem, fared significantly better than students who did not get the self-esteem programme. Peer (1998) maintains that the area of self-esteem is one of great concern in relation to dyslexia. She suggests that dyslexia is almost like a 'hidden disability'. Some disabilities are easily identified but dyslexic students may look the same as any others and she claims that this may lead to their specific needs being overlooked. Hales (1994) argues that we must not separate the individuals' dyslexia from other aspects of their existence as people. He further argues that social and emotional needs should be incorporated into assessment and support.

Dyslexia can have a significant effect on a person's self-concept and potential for academic success and personal fulfilment. It is not surprising then that dyslexic children and adults can experience increasing anxiety in some situations.

Anxiety and stress

As indicated above, it is not surprising that dyslexic people can have feelings of anxiety in many situations. This can be particularly acute, for example, when working under timed pressures or carrying out a task which requires considerable precision. Some anxieties, however, may only be situational which means that people are only anxious while they are carrying out one particular task. If such tasks become a major part of the person's work and life then the anxiety can be converted to work stress, which can have health implications and has the potential to become a chronic condition.

Work stress

Like dyslexia, the term 'work stress' is also an overused but little understood term. It is now used openly and freely in a range of work environments to describe the harmful effects of the interaction between employee and employment. Proctor (1993) suggests that the popularity of the term unfortunately leaves it open to misuse and misinterpretation.

One of the most thoroughly researched models of work stress is the transactional model – The Theoretical Model of Processes Involved in Psychological Stress, Causation, Continuation and Change (Psystress), (Hinton and Burton, 1992). This model looks at the imbalance between perceived demands and perceived capabilities – a process which occurs through cognitive appraisal. The important aspect about this model for dyslexia is the word 'perceived'. This is not the actual demands or capabilities but how the person perceives those demands and his or her own capabilities. An anxious dyslexic person with a long history of academic failure may have a different perception of perceived demands and capabilities than, for example, an employer.

Organisational climate

Reid and Hinton (1999) discuss the view that organisational climate is a key aspect of work stress and a positive climate within an organisation or the workplace can do much to prevent work stress among employees. In their study, management concern for employee involvement, and social support, ranked high in the organisational climate dimensions in relation to the Psystress model of perceived stress. This means that employers can help to prevent stress by promoting a positive climate within the workplace. This is important to those who may be vulnerable to perceived work stress, such as dyslexic people.

In the education context, Dunham (1992) suggests that perceived demands and interpersonal communication within institutions are important and any stress reduction programme should be generated by the workforce themselves. This implies that different individuals will react in a different way to similar work demands and be more sensitive to different organisational and work climates.

Depression

The previous section indicated how the term 'stress' has become overused to the extent that it has lost much of its actual meaning and impact. The same also applies to the term 'depression'. It is therefore with some caution that we use this term in this chapter but for some adults with dyslexia the deep-rooted and long-standing difficulties they have encountered have impacted on their lives to such an extent that depression can become a reality. Today the actual term 'depression' is used too loosely to be really meaningful. It is used often to describe a fluctuating state of feeling low or down rather than a clinical diagnosis of an actual medical condition.

Despite this, the state of depression and its associated symptoms – such as lack of interest, low motivation and low self-esteem – can be outward signs of very real inner trauma. Other factors which are associated with depression include obvious personality change, loss of sociability, anxiety and irritability, sleep problems, fatigue, despair and helplessness, lack of concentration, memory impairment, feelings of guilt, mental confusion and physiological factors affecting health such as digestive problems, imaginary aches and pains and headaches (MacLaren, 1996).

Triggers

There are many factors which can trigger depression and some of these are beyond the control of the individual. Control appears to be a significant factor in stress-related conditions (Hinton and Burton, 1992). There are a considerable number of life events over which individuals have little control. Again there are a number of reasons why certain events can have a prolonged and devastating effect on one but not on another.

Influential factors include personality, range of support and level of preparedness to cope with difficult situations. That preparedness can take different forms and, indeed, being able to access the right kind of support at the right time can make a considerable difference to an individual who may be vulnerable to becoming depressed following, or due to, a series of difficult life events. It is inappropriate to suggest, therefore, that certain situations can result in depression as there are many intervening variables. We are not suggesting that dyslexia can cause depression, but for some individuals a life struggle and conflict resulting from their dyslexic difficulties can be very influential in how prepared they are to cope with potentially traumatic situations.

Dyslexia and depression

No large-scale controlled study has been carried out to examine the relationship between dyslexia and depression, but it is clear that life events, and particularly those which occur during the early years, can have an enormous effect on the coping capacities of the individual for dealing with potential trauma. Failure during this period can generate a feeling of lack of self-worth and inability to please significant others, whether it be teacher or partners. A feeling of 'learned helplessness' can dominate and this can result in a lack of will and essentially an 'opting out' to avoid a confrontation with situations that can make the individual feel vulnerable. Quite a number of the dyslexic adults we have interviewed report a feeling of learned helplessness, often stemming from a lack of understanding and support during critical periods, at school, at work and indeed at home.

Support and understanding can make dyslexia a positive condition rather than a negative one. An excellent example of this is seen in the video 'Dyslexia: An Unwrapped Gift' (Hertfordshire Dyslexia Arts Group, 1999). The video highlights the positive aspects of dyslexia by viewing the problem as a gift. The caption at the start of the commentary states that one in twenty-five people are dyslexic. At the end of the video, following an explanation of how reading and writing may be 'merely an eye-blink of mankind' and how people with dyslexia may be at an advantage in the advanced visual communication systems of the future, the caption proudly states that twenty-four out of twenty-five people miss out on the opportunity to be dyslexic! This type of message can do much to prevent stress, anxiety and depression from affecting the life and life-style of the adult with dyslexia.

Support leading to self-help is an important factor in the sometimes-necessary attitude which needs to occur before the person with dyslexia can convert his or her dyslexic learning profile into a positive one. For those who feel that the obstacles they need to overcome are too formidable for them to deal with, professional help should be obtained and specific therapies can be recommended. These therapies can be palliative or direct action. Palliative therapies are those that seek to allow access to a state of relaxation which, in turn, helps the individual to deal more effectively with obstacles and potential trauma. These include yoga, gestalt therapy, art therapy, Tai Chi and breathing exercises. Direct action can stem from counselling, person centred or behavioural, but the implication is that the answer or response to the situation lies with the individual and the key is to prepare the individual so that self-help is possible.

Certainly, individuals with dyslexia have more to overcome than dyslexia; they have also to deal with attitudes and obstacles in education and employment, much of which can be weighted against them. There have, however, been vigorous and successful campaigns from pressure groups, and, spurred on by disability legislation, the tide can now be turning to provide more equitable opportunities for people with dyslexia in both education and employment to fulfil their potential and equip them to deal with life events and avoid the cycle of turmoil characterised by situations of disaffection, defiance, deviance and depression.

Disaffection, defiance and depression: support and training

Given the importance of fostering a positive self-concept and attempting to prevent anti-social behaviour or depression, it is important that the significant professionals in particular are aware of the potential difficulties and trained in some way to deal with these difficulties at college level or in the workplace.

There are many different programmes and strategies that can be used. For example, at school level the circle time programmes (Moseley, 1996) have done much to facilitate emotionally healthy classrooms with a programme of daily activities called 'circle time' which can actually influence the dynamics within an educational or work-setting ethos in a positive way by encouraging people to be aware of the needs of others and promoting a feel-good factor within the school.

Similarly, social skills programmes such as those developed by Hopson and Scully (1982) have a detailed list of activities which can be carried out by teachers to promote effective social skills and self-concept.

Reid and Hinton (1996) developed a programme of support for staff consisting of key elements within the organisation which can contribute to work stress. This programme, although aimed initially at schools, can be equally applicable to a variety of work settings. The four sessions of the programme were:

- Personal organisation
  - time management
  - planning and preparation
  - diary and record keeping
  - general awareness
- The organisation
  - organisational components
  - organisational models
  - vulnerable aspects of the organisation
  - staff interaction
- Interpersonal support within the organisation
  - features of a supportive organisation
  - examples of interpersonal support
- Organisational climate
  - role of management
  - organisational climate dimensions
  - assessing climate.

This model and training programme highlights the reciprocal nature of work-related stress. The elements which can potentially generate stress should be addressed. Therefore the organisation, the task and individual factors all need to be considered. In this way the people with dyslexia will clearly benefit, but also they will not necessarily be singled out for separate 'treatment'. This implies that dealing with stress in the workplace is whole-workforce responsibility, both management and staff.

Although this chapter has addressed some negative consequences of dyslexia the situation for dyslexic people is far from doom and gloom. Indeed, the next chapter highlights this by focusing on the positive aspects of dyslexia. Essentially it is important for dyslexic people to try to obtain the support they need, but moreover attempt to take control of their dyslexia and realise that the solution is in their hands and work towards their goal in a proactive manner. Make plans, have goals, recognise and celebrate your achievements.

Chapter 7

'The whole of the moon'

'I saw the crescent, but you saw the whole of the moon.' These are the words of the popular hit song by the Waterboys. The song is not referring specifically to dyslexic people, but the words, and particularly the implication that the person to whom the song refers can see the whole picture, may well refer to the processing style of adults with dyslexia – they can see the whole of the moon!

The previous chapter looked at the negative consequences of dyslexia. By contrast this chapter will focus on the positive aspects of dyslexia, the skills and aptitude some dyslexic people have in visualisation, in problem solving, in literature, poetry and in dealing with everyday work situations utilising individual and often well-developed learning and coping strategies.

Dyslexia and visualisation

West (1997a, 1999), an author and dyslexic from Washington, DC, refers to the dyslexic person as one who can see the unseen, understand patterns of incomplete information, and comprehend the complex whole. It is not surprising then that many people who work in the film industry or the art world are dyslexic. In fact if one is entering those professions it may even be an advantage to be dyslexic, to comprehend the complex whole and to get the best angle in a shot.

Furthermore, West suggests that the rapid advances in computer technology have paved the way for the visual thinker, using scientific and graphic visualisation, to have the skills of the future. West argues that the 'eye–brain' system with its great pattern recognition capabilities is finding its way into business, trade and finance. Specialists in many fields are recognising the power of visual approaches. West (1999) has consulted with the Confederation of British Industry and many other organisations throughout the world, including business leaders and media innovators at the Aspen Institute in Colorado. His ideas have been recognised by the Japanese business community and a Japanese edition of his book has been published with the title *Geniuses who Hated School*.

Yet West asserts that these skills are often highly developed at the expense of weaknesses in other areas of information processing – usually the verbal/linguistic area. The message of this observation is simple: dyslexia should be viewed as a difference not a deficit and the strengths often seen in dyslexic people in visualisation should be utilised in learning and job training. West suggests that educators will need to adapt to the new realities and free themselves from the 'almost universal preoccupation with written symbols, the instruments of old technology'. It is important that his message has some impact on trainers, employers and dyslexic people.

Art and artists

Through its publications and exhibitions, the Arts Dyslexia Trust in the UK has done much to promote the talents of dyslexic artists. In some art colleges almost a third of the student population are dyslexic and this has considerable implications for support and assessment. In every higher degree in art there is likely to be an element on history of art and theoretical and contextual considerations of the period. The quantity of reading, and writing a critical comment on the content, can prove difficult for the dyslexic art student. It is vital that support and under-standing are available to allow the dyslexic person to develop his or her creative talents (Everatt et al., 1999).

This does not appear to have happened in the case of Vanessa, a dyslexic artist, who provides an account of her experiences in Chapter 8. She successfully completed a degree in fine art and subsequently exhibited her work in several galleries despite the barriers and diffi-culties stemming from lack of understanding and support.

Fabian Hercules, a leading figure in the Arts Dyslexia Trust in the UK, who co-developed 'Pencil' – Teachers Pack, suggests that it is vital that dyslexic artists exhibit their work as this provides the opportunities to develop their skills and, very importantly, their confidence. The Arts

Dyslexia Trust (1996) suggests that dyslexia is not so much a 'learning difficulty associated with written language development but rather a learning characteristic or style associated with visual spatial ability'.

Graves (1999) suggests that the education system and the employment system waste valuable time concentrating on the weaknesses of dyslexic people rather than their strengths. She suggests that dyslexic people see the overall pattern and grasp sophisticated ideas more easily than simple ones. Additionally, because of their short-term memory difficulty, they have often to get their ideas down quickly, and being intuitive thinkers may not be able to explain their thinking process easily to themselves or to others. She also suggests what must be the ultimate coping strategy – 'they are brilliant at converting mistakes into assets'. Her work as a specialist dyslexia tutor at a College of Art and Design has convinced her of the close relationship between dyslexia, visual–spatial ability and creativity.

Tanja Lannen, a PhD student in computer design specialising in children and adults with special needs, suggests that virtual reality programmes can offer an avenue for social, cognitive and educational development for dyslexic individuals. The area of virtual reality is largely confined to games but Lannen's hypothesis is that it can provide considerable opportunities for creativity and the transfer of skills to other areas by developing cognitive skills such as memory, decision making, discrimination and problem solving. This strategy may be particularly appropriate for dyslexic people because it is interactive, visual and kinaesthetic.

Creativity

It has been suggested that dyslexic people can have particularly creative skills and abilities and this can be noted in people who have succeeded in business, the arts and the sciences (West, 1997b; Bruce, 1999). Interestingly, Treffinger and Selby (1993) have shown links between creativity and learning styles. Treffinger (1991) suggests a model of creativity with four basic components;

- *Characteristics*, i.e. the cognitive abilities.
- *Operations*, i.e. the strategies used, the clear management of thinking.
- *Context*, i.e. the environmental resources and restraints.
- *Outcomes*, i.e. the success of the process, the result.

Treffinger's model reveals areas where people with dyslexia who may have the cognitive potential to be creative might be thwarted in their efforts to reveal their real abilities. They may choose inappropriate strategies and may not be able to manage their thinking without someone creating a structure or some kind of organisational framework. Additionally, the context must be conducive to the dyslexic people otherwise their skills may not be obvious. A context which places time demands, or one where many facts have to be dealt with in quick succession, can be stressful and the creative abilities may not be revealed in this type of environmental situation.

The final component of Treffinger's model relates to the outcomes, i.e. the success of the operation, yet many people with dyslexia may have successfully completed a task but not feel successful. During our interviews with dyslexic adults we have noted on many occasions how successful dyslexic people appear to disregard their successes with some flippancy and actually highlight the areas in which they have difficulty. This may be because of a long-standing low self-concept or because they have simply experienced repetitive failure to such an extent that they cannot recognise success. It is important, therefore, that the success of a venture or activity is fed back to them so that they are in no doubt that they have been successful. In relation to learning style and creativity, Treffinger and Selby build on their four basic components through practical applications to the learning situation.

- *Characteristics*: How am I creative? How can I create a learning or working environment that will bring out my best?
- *Operations*: How can I use my preferences best? Why do some strategies seem to work better than others? What conditions make it more difficult for me to learn and use strategies?
- *Context*: What environmental conditions seem to enhance or inhibit my performance? What conditions distract me? How can I contribute best to a group?
- *Outcomes*: Where will I most likely need the support and help of others? How will I know when I have reached my goal? How can I build on my natural style to achieve my goal?

Although Treffinger and Selby were not specifically focusing on dyslexic people, many of their suggestions apply because dyslexic adults can be creative and generally have a right hemisphere processing style. Maston (1989: 752) suggests that there is 'a positive relationship between creativity in general and having a right hemisphere learning style'.

Many biographers have reported that creative geniuses have performed very poorly at school (Simonton, 1988). As Runco and Sakamoto (1993) point out, traditional education seems to offer students few opportunities to work and express themselves in some domains other than Gardner's (1983) logical–mathematical and verbal–symbolic domains. Yet creative learners may only flourish when given the opportunity to work in domains that are interpersonal and kinaesthetic.

In the USA, Gadwa and Griggs (1985) reported on the learning styles of students involved in a Washington High School alternative programme who were at risk. It was noted that the students showed many right hemisphere, global characteristics and preferred learning with music, low light, an informal design, short assignments with break time between and high peer motivation (Dunn et al., 1990). Additionally, the study showed that this group were not morning alert learners and required a variety of teaching methods rather than traditional and routine methods. This confirms the findings of Dunn and Griggs (1988) who suggested that the following seven learning style traits (adapted from Milgram et al., 1993) characterise high-risk students from others:

- Need for mobility while learning.
- Require a variety of teaching and learning approaches and peer learning.
- Most productive learning time is late morning, afternoon or evening, but not early morning.
- An informal seating design for learning, not traditional desks and chairs.
- Low illumination.
- Tactual and kinaesthetic learning, certainly when first learning a new topic or skill.
- Multi-sensory teaching packages.

In a Canadian study, Broadhead and Price (1993) found similar results while studying the learning styles of creative students. Like the US students, the Canadian students also preferred working in groups, preferred music, afternoon or evening learning, and tactile and kinaesthetic learning. Indeed in a cross-cultural study of high-risk, creative students from seven countries (Brazil, Canada, Guatemala, Israel, Korea, The Philippines and the USA), Price and Milgram (1993) found many similarities such as the need to learn kinaesthetically and self-motivation. There were differences such as the scope for creative activity and the researchers suggested that cultural factors influence the individual's creative activities. In general, however, the study did support the notion that creative students, particularly in relation to a specific domain, such as art, drama, literature, music and dance, do have significantly similar learning styles to each other but significantly different from other groups of students with different abilities.

This is particularly relevant because dyslexic adults have been described as creative and can be at risk of academic failure. Training programmes for employees who are dyslexic should take learning styles into consideration. This has the potential of enhancing learning and making the learning experience efficient, pleasurable and cost effective.

Words making sense

Many dyslexic people study and become successful artists, engineers and architects; however, many enter courses or professions which appear to be unsuitable for them. Many opt to study History or English Literature, subjects with a considerable amount of reading, but they would probably have been advised against selecting these subjects if they had sought advice prior to selecting their courses. However well meaning the advice, it is wrong to deter a dyslexic person from selecting a subject about which he or she is enthusiastic. Every subject and every career has scope for some form of creativity. Usually the more potential for creativity the more likely the dyslexic person will be to chose that profession. Our advice to counsellors, tutors and employers is to listen – listen to dyslexic people, they may have the idea that you need for your company or they may help to run a happy and successful workplace. Listen to their words, they may make a lot of sense. Tom West, author of *In the Mind's Eye* (1991), summed this up well when he said:

We ought to begin to pay less attention to getting everyone over the same hill using the same path. We may wish to encourage some to take different routes to the same end. Then we might see good reasons for paying careful attention to their descriptions of what they have found. We may wish to follow them some day.

An interesting account of how one dyslexic adult we came across used his abilities to write poetry and short stories is described in the following chapter. Bill was 50 when he was first diagnosed as dyslexic and this seems to have opened a number of doors for him. He has had a number of short stories and poetry published, as indeed have a number of dyslexic people we have met. This reinforces the view that no avenues, courses or careers are beyond the reach of dyslexic people.

Some of the more noted strengths and abilities of dyslexic people are shown below:

Strengths and abilities

- Good visual and spatial skills in creative areas such as mathematics, engineering and the physical sciences.
- Abilities to recognise patterns in information and to represent three-dimensional images in work with computers.
- A special facility for mentally rearranging designs and information would have a contribution to creative and novel design, as for example, demonstrated by Leonardo da Vinci, Auguste Rodin and Albert Einstein.
- A more holistic way of viewing the world, which aids the discovery of problem solutions.
- Rich colour memory and ability to use fast multi-sensorial combinations.
- Willing to meet expectations and have high regard in work.
- Can have good social skills.
- Ambitious – a need to achieve.
- Enthusiasm.
- Creativity.
- May have good kinaesthetic skills.
- Critical thinking skills.
- Better verbal skills than writing skills.

There are many other skills and abilities which can be found in dyslexic people, and these abilities need not be thought of as exceptional. Dyslexic people need not be famous to be successful. Success is a very personal attribute but it is important that if they have succeeded with any type of task, however small it might seem, they should be able to acknowledge that and give themselves some credit for the achievement (Reid, 1999a).

Attention Deficit Hyperactivity Disorder

It is appropriate to briefly discuss Attention Deficit Hyperactivity Disorder (ADHD) in this book because many dyslexic people who process information globally can be misdiagnosed as having ADHD when in fact they are merely utilising their preferred and natural processing style. ADHD usually occurs when an individual has difficulty in focusing on one stimulus for a period of time and this should not be confused with the simultaneous processing sometimes experienced by dyslexic people.

Attention Deficit Disorder (ADD), or Attention Deficit Hyperactivity Disorder (ADHD), has received considerable attention in recent years and there is a growing body of knowledge on the characteristics, identification and intervention strategies to deal with the difficulties associated with the disorder (Lloyd and Norris, 1999). Lloyd and Norris, however, point out that much of the academic literature on ADHD has been written by enthusiastic proponents and within a strong psychological and medical perspective. They suggest that, in general, the literature is unquestioning in relation to the concept and incidence rates of ADHD and considerable public attention has resulted from press coverage.

While it may be accepted that there is a neurological and cognitive basis for ADHD, many who are diagnosed as having ADHD may have a random processing style and a preference for learning globally. Some of the symptoms commonly associated with ADHD are inattentiveness, impulsivity and hyperactivity. Lloyd and Norris (1999), however, suggest that sociological and environmental criteria can be influential factors in ADHD and that dealing with the presenting behaviours and the sociological causes can be more effective than, for example, medication. This view is supported by the developmental, contextual perspective (Pellegrini and Horvatt, 1995) who acknowledge the inter-action between biology and environment.

A programme on ADHD developed in 1995 by the New South Wales Department of Education in Australia (*Talk, Time,Teamwork*) illus-trates the multi-faceted dimensions of ADHD by indicating that no single intervention method is sufficient to produce either short- or long-term behavioural change and interventions for ADHD should include individualised instruction, social skills training, behaviour management programmes, family programmes and medication (if appropriate). This is consistent with the views expressed by Grainger (1999), who suggests that it is important to build as many connections as possible addressing writing, spelling and linguistic aspects of print and speech sounds. Therefore, a multi-sensory and multi-connectionist approach should be employed.

Giorcelli (1999), who has pioneered inclusive approaches to managing ADHD by considering both within-person factors and systems approaches agrees that a multi-faceted approach is necessary to fully comprehend and advise on the difficulties associated with ADHD.

While it is not appropriate to discuss the complex and contro-versial ADHD debate in this book, the sociological perspectives discussed by Lloyd and Norris are relevant to adults because they indicate that environmental influences are as important as the need to attribute the difficulties experienced to factors within one's control. This does not in any way invalidate the concept of ADHD and for many a medical palliative is a necessary expediency. The two key points being made are:

- There are a number of causal and behavioural factors associated with ADHD (e.g. neurological organisation, biochemical, genetic, cognitive and sociological).
- The criteria for identification is not well defined and many dyslexic individuals with a fairly typical dyslexic random processing style can be misdiagnosed as having ADHD.

It is important to make these points because the processing style used by some dyslexic adults is not one that should be characterised by deficits but by differences. This implies that one has to appreciate the particular thinking style of dyslexic people and, if necessary, make workplace accommodations to maximise their skills. At the same time it is important that adults with dyslexia have self-knowledge as this will help them to accept themselves, which is necessary for taking responsibility for and control of life events.

There can be some overlap and confusion between the difficulties associated with dyslexia and the difficulties each of us experiences in the course of life events. It is important that dyslexic individuals are able to see this clearly and although dyslexic difficulties can exacerbate some aspects of life and work they should not be used as an excuse for opting out or perceived failure. The very point of this chapter is to highlight the positive aspects of dyslexia and to avoid confusing 'differences' with 'deficits'.

Hemispheric specialisation

There is now growing evidence that the dichotomy between left and right hemispheres may not be as clear and as distinct as believed some years ago and there is still some value in examining the skills principally associated with each hemisphere.

The importance of Figure 7.1 is that it highlights some of the possible strengths of dyslexic people and provides some guidance on how they may learn more effectively. One factor which is usually associated with

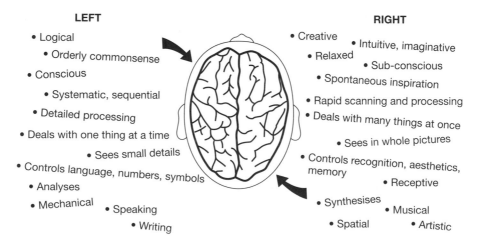

Figure 7.1   Functions of the two sides of the brain (reproduced with permission of the publishers, Red Rose Publications 1998)

the right hemisphere is visualisation. This can be important to dyslexic people in learning and remembering information. This was briefly discussed earlier in this chapter and is referred to more specifically below in relation to specific strategies.

Visualisation and strategies

Visualisation can be a useful skill to help to remember and process information. Dyslexic people may have some advantage in visual processing, but it is still important that they receive some training in using their visual skills to advantage. Visualisation can be used not only to remember, but to help one to relax. Ward and Daley (1993) suggest that visualisation and relaxation go hand in hand and a relaxed state can help to induce further visualisation techniques.

Visualisation techniques can help to develop positive images through visualising a positive situation when you are doing a task which you may find difficult. As some people have difficulty visualising this type of situation and visualising themselves achieving success, this is therefore an area that can be addressed and practised. The benefits of being able to acquire positive visualisation techniques are considerable and this skill needs to be practised until it becomes an automatic part of one's lifestyle.

Kinesiology

Kinesiology can be used to induce a relaxed state and help people to reach their maximum potential. Administered by a trained kinesiologist, a series of exercises can help to balance and harmonise the body and brain. This system has been applied successfully to education through the programme known as Edu-K or Brain Gym (Dennison and Dennison, 1989), which involves a series of physical exercises and personal affirmations that can help to integrate the two hemispheres. Essentially it involves across body movements that help to integrate the two hemispheres: lengthening movements that help to relax the body and release tension, and energising movements that help the individual to focus and control emotions and thinking. People who use kinesiology seem to report a greater feeling of calmness, confidence and achievement in their everyday lives. It is a lifestyle approach and not a quick fix as it involves diet and lifestyle and links with yoga, accupressure, optometry and alternative medicine.

Mind mapping

Mind mapping has already been discussed elsewhere in this book since it is a strategy which can help with organisation and study. It can, however, have a considerable visual element and those who have skills in this area can develop mind mapping very effectively. Essentially mind mapping involves viewing a topic in a holistic and lateral manner rather than sequentially and linearly. This can give a breadth to processing and organisation and the use of visual symbols can aid remembering. Though a considerable amount of information can be learnt in this manner, it is best when one begins to use this strategy to start with something less ambitious such as one's plans for the day or week. The works of Buzan (1993) and Margulies (1991) have been very influential in this area and both have produced useful literature which is readily accessible.

Visualising and verbalising

Bell (1991) has produced successful and substantial materials used to teach dyslexic children and young adults skills in visualisation and then relating this to language development. One of the aspects on which the programme called Visualising and Verbalising for Language Development and Thinking is based is that many conventional teaching approaches focus on left-hemisphere skills and of course this is the area in which dyslexic people are usually weak. Bell argues that by focusing on this area one is neglecting the right hemisphere, and therefore the visualisation area, and indeed comprehension. She suggests that more visualisation techniques can develop not only visual skills but also comprehension. One is encouraged, therefore, to actively visualise an object and describe some of its features. The individual can then provide detail around the key words.

Multiple intelligences

The work of Gardner (1985) and others has emphasised the benefits of focusing on different abilities apart from verbal and linguistic ones. Gardner's model suggests there are at least seven intelligences that can be influential for education, learning and individual success. These are verbal–linguistic, visual–spatial, interpersonal, intrapersonal, logical–mathematical, bodily–kinaesthetic and musical–rhythmic.

It is suggested that the education system and, consequently, one's opportunities for academic success rest to a great extent on the verbal–linguistic area which is usually the weaker area for many dyslexic individuals. Lazear (1994) suggests that the curriculum should be more focused on the other intelligences and each of these can in fact be integrated into assessment and teaching approaches. Different types of questioning can relate to the different intelligences. Lazear suggests that verbal–linguistic questioning would ask about key words; logical–mathematical about patterns and sequences; visual–spatial about scenes; bodily–kinaesthetic about actions; musical–rhythmic about sounds; interpersonal about observations on different characters; and intrapersonal about emotions and feelings. Games and other curricular activities can be developed around these aspects to make the student an active learner, and assessment should be developed to enhance student learning, not only to test it. Lazear advocates assessment through 'metacognitive process-folios'. This appears to be extremely exciting and far reaching. Lazear's model involves six different types of processing–objective, affective, cognitive, process, metacognitive level, and applications. This model relates to knowledge, how that knowledge was obtained, understanding and transfer of learning to other aspects and understanding of one's own thinking process. There are benefits of this assessment paradigm for dyslexic people.

Emotional needs/support groups

It is important to appreciate the emotional needs of dyslexic people. For that reason an assessment and follow-up support should be administered by a qualified and experienced professional. Support groups can also be helpful for some people and these are found in many areas. Usually they have helplines which can often provide the advice needed on the spot without any lengthy wait for appointments which can be quite offputting for some dyslexic people. Jameson (1999) suggests that support groups should have a programme, of which there are four choices: a discussion group for adult dyslexic people only; an open discussion group that welcomes partners and friends; a programme of invited speakers; or a mixture of the above. She also suggests that a support group should have a development plan – which could encapsulate a mission statement, keep a record of activities and obtain charitable status.

A study by Riddock et al. (1999) suggests that dyslexic adults have relatively low self-esteem, and significantly that this low self-esteem is not confined to academic self-esteem. The researchers therefore concluded that there may be a number of risk factors in the lives of dyslexic adults which can contribute to low self-esteem. The study suggests, as the researchers point out, that there are more factors to consider in supporting dyslexic adults than literacy attainment. That is only one aspect of a much bigger picture and, clearly, low self-esteem – possibly accompanied by high anxiety (Riddock et al., 1999) – need to be considered as these factors can affect every aspect of the lives of dyslexic adults. Emotional needs and support from qualified and empathetic people are important for the well-being and social, educational and employment needs of dyslexic people.

Conclusion

This chapter has drawn together a number of different factors relating to the potential and positive aspects of dyslexia in adults. It is important to value the dyslexic person as an individual first and foremost to ensure that all his or her individual needs are met. It should also be remembered that the presence of dyslexia can accentuate some of the difficulties and barriers which often prevent individuals from reaching their desired goals. Though dyslexic people can have considerable skills in some areas, it is important that a holistic view is adopted in relation to support so that their emotional and social needs can also be considered alongside the strengths they can bring to the workplace and the workforce.

Chapter 8

Speak for yourself

Self-advocacy is important when attempting to establish 'rights' which may not be easy to achieve without some form of struggle, lobbying or persuasion. In many cases dyslexic adults have to be assertive about their entitlement for support. For some adults this is difficult to achieve.

There are support groups in existence which can help with this but often in the day-to-day situations faced by adults with dyslexia support groups are not available. They have to be their own advocate and determine their own rights in whatever situation they face in their daily work and life. Support groups offer valuable assistance and have set many adults on the road to success. Such groups can offer valuable guidance and can boost the confidence of the dyslexic person.

A shift towards greater personal responsibility, self-direction and self-advocacy is crucial to the attainment of employment success (Klein, 1993; McLoughlin et al., 1994; Brown, 1997; NJCLD, 1987). Employment success may be dependent upon whether a disabled individual knows the dimensions of his or her disability well and to know how, and when, to compensate for them within the job contexts.

Perhaps one of the reasons that self-advocacy is difficult to achieve is because there are few opportunities to practise these skills at school. Even in further and higher education self-advocacy is not seen as a priority. This point has been recognised by a group of special educators in Rochester, New York (Weimer et al., 1994) who developed a working proposal on self-advocacy for adolescents with special needs. Their proposal suggests that self-advocacy should begin at least by the middle school because that is when students are given more curriculum choice and encouraged to think independently. Weimer and colleagues recognised that even in high school and post-high school, many students still lacked skills to evaluate their strengths and weaknesses. Three of the goals in their self-advocacy programme include:

- developing an understanding of self-advocacy and how it can apply to the student;
- the importance of the knowledge gained on self-advocacy and self-awareness and how that can be transformed into life skills and techniques;
- allowing the student to understand that success in life can depend greatly on one's ability to self-advocate.

Weimer and colleagues suggest that if this type of structured programme is introduced early in the school years, it can help students with all types of special needs to overcome the barriers they will very likely meet in education, employment and sometimes in interpersonal skills.

Experiences of adults with dyslexia

This chapter describes the different situations faced by many dyslexic adults in a range of employment and other situations.

Melanie

Occupation: Speech and Language Therapist

> I was good at science at school and I sort of drifted into university, I suppose I was influenced by my parents a bit. I struggled at university and in the end I just wanted to pass and get a job. In my job as a speech therapist I sometimes have time management difficulties, planning my diary and writing up my case notes can be difficult. I get very involved with the client and spend a lot of time discussing different aspects but then when it comes to putting it into words – that is when it becomes very difficult. I usually need a lot of time to write reports and filling out forms at work can be a nightmare. Usually I miss out something in a form and often I am pulled up by my boss for such omissions.
>   Yet at meetings and in informal discussions with colleagues I always seem to be able to see things or think of things which other people miss. Some of my colleagues are quite rigid in the way they

process information. I feel I can see things as a whole and I can often add points at meetings. I feel the main thing is knowing your strengths and use these as far as possible.

Melanie makes some very relevant points in her statement. She came to us to be assessed as she was about to embark on a further course which would develop her career. She knew the pace would be fast and was now more confident than she was at university; she was also determined to assert her rights as a dyslexic student – which is something she was reluctant to do when she was first at university. She is now 28 years old. Her WAIS profile showed a significant discrepancy between her verbal and performance scores. Apart from Digit Span, her verbal scores were all well above average, yet her performance scores were all well below average. Her verbal expression was good but she had a significant difficulty with written expression. It is interesting that, despite having some difficulty with some aspects of her work, she does see herself, and quite rightly, as successful. This has given her the confidence not only to embark on further training but to ensure that her dyslexia is recognised.

Valerie

Occupation: Teacher of English as a foreign language

I was thirty-eight when I was diagnosed as dyslexic and that was because of a crisis point in my career. I had to pass this exam, two three hour papers, and already I had failed twice. My teaching reports were excellent, there was no doubt I could do the job – and do it well. In fact I usually supervised and helped other staff who had passed the exam but they still came to me for assistance. My problem was transferring my knowledge into a written assignment. Yet the strange thing was that I could tell others how to do just that, as in my teaching role I had to provide students with help in study skills and help them pass the exams – but I couldn't do it myself. I found this quite demoralising and really shattered my confidence. I really needed extra time in the exam but always felt reluctant to come for an assessment. My first degree was in fine arts yet I wouldn't say I am a brilliant artist, but it just seemed interesting and less threatening. Certainly there was less reading and writing for this than there would be in some other subjects.

Valerie was quite near the end of the road when she came to us for assessment. She felt fairly low in terms of her academic confidence yet had achieved much, having already received a fine arts degree and was working very competently as a teacher in a Further Education College. Interestingly her verbal WAIS profile was very high and she scored virtually full marks in vocabulary and comprehension, yet her short-term memory scores were well below average. Another interesting aspect was that although she opted for a fine arts degree her performance profile showed that she was just around the average mark for three visual sub-tests and well below average in the picture completion sub-test which focuses on visual perception. Although Valerie was well advanced educationally when she was assessed it was certainly useful and provided her with explanations and possible courses of intervention as well as course support in exams. This increased her chances of eventual success in the exam she had previously failed.

Rose (aged 43)

Occupation: Teacher of children with special needs

I really like my present job, but being dyslexic does create some difficulties for me. For example, I sometimes see a gap between what needs to be done and what I can actually do and this becomes quite frustrating. But the advantages of being dyslexic are that I know where the children are coming from and I can understand the children's difficulties and their frustrations because I went through those myself. Sometimes I can identify with the children better than with my colleagues. I can understand the children's agendas better than some teacher's agendas.

I always wanted to be a teacher from a very young age but was not sure if I could cope with, firstly, the training, then getting a job and coping with the daily work. At first I thought I would be an art teacher but when I observed what an art teacher does I thought that I would have difficulty with the organisational aspects of the job, supervising and handling all the equipment. Each art lesson seems to need so much planning and organisation and I thought perhaps I would be better teaching another subject. So I decided to teach Religious Education. I like stories and telling children stories and R.E. seemed to be a holistic subject in that it can involve many different types of skills and activities.

My training was a difficult time for me. I had difficulty with exams and particularly spelling. My tutor said that I should not become a teacher because I could not spell and I had difficulty in getting interviews for a teaching post.

I think I have developed good coping strategies in my work although often I have to wind myself up to do administration and there seems to be so much paper work now. But my dyslexia has made me determined to do well, to help others and to achieve – at the moment I am doing my Masters in Education part time!

It was interesting to listen to Rose as she recounted her experiences, particularly as at the time she undertook her teaching qualifications the same level of awareness was not available compared to the potential understanding of tutors and employers today. Rose very likely played down her difficulties during the interview because she now has good coping strategies which she has accumulated with experience and this is probably the reason why she now feels able to tackle a high-level qualification such as the Masters degree. The other interesting aspect to emerge from Rose's comments is that despite the lack of support she seems to have persevered and evaluated the work demands for herself and made her own decisions very likely against some people's advice to enter teaching. This helped to make her determined to succeed and also have the confidence, for example, to change from Religious Education to Special Needs.

John (aged 43)

Occupation: Mechanical designer

At junior school no one knew about dyslexia, I was good at art, but not English. I was always on report because my English was so poor. The Head told me I would go nowhere unless I improved drastically. Perhaps that is the reason why I forced myself to go as far as I could in my career.

Some teachers were able to pick up my difficulty, but it meant that I had separate classes and tuition, and when I went back to the main class I had missed a lot of work which made me feel that I was different and not as able as other people in the class. My happiest time at school was the last few years before I left because I had a choice of subjects and I could choose those I liked and was good at.

When I left school I had to do a course in basic skills before I could get into a technical training course because my school leaving qualifications were not good – except for technical and art all my other grades were very low. At college I struggled in the basic skills class, all my grades were around 30% whereas in my practicals I was scoring 100%.

I was not formally diagnosed as dyslexic until ten years ago. No one at work knows I am dyslexic and I try to spot my mistakes before they do. When I am learning a new skill or task at work I need a basic framework, that is usually quite difficult as it takes time but once I get that basic framework it is easier to learn and remember.

I like working with machines because it is a multi-perceptual activity, in other words I can feel, see and experience whatever I am working on. I think this is important to me in my occupation – to see products in different dimensions using different modalities.

My employer does believe I am very competent and I now also believe in myself, but it can be difficult. It does not take much to erode my self-confidence. Life events can be confusing and difficult for me and sometimes I have to write my thoughts and feelings down on paper. I have had some stress-related difficulties because I found it difficult to separate the normal stresses in life events from those associated with my dyslexia. There may be some overlap but I think it is important to separate the two aspects. This was difficult for me but fortunately the professional help which I sought was extremely beneficial and helped me identify the different strands in my life and helped to control my dyslexic difficulties. I am now an active member of a dyslexia support group.

Talking with John was very interesting and clearly the lack of an early diagnosis has affected his education, career and self-concept a great deal. We felt that the identifying of normal life stresses and dyslexic associated difficulties was a useful distinction, but perhaps a difficult one to make.

We also felt the multi-perceptual aspects and particularly the sensitivity of touch when John was working with a design or a metal creation in a machine was an important point and highlights that dyslexic people can have considerable strengths in other modalities, particularly visual and tactile – and of course can be very sensitive to whatever they are creating or to the learning environment.

Doris (aged 55)

Occupation: Youth worker

I have asked the question 'why' since I was four years old! Why can other people do this and I can't. I also think I had an enquiring mind but at school I was not able to get the support and opportunity I needed. I had very bad school experiences, I wanted so much to learn and I tried very hard but I was told I was 'thick' and I am still very bitter about the way I was treated. I had to stand up in class and read aloud, I always stuttered and eventually through sheer frustration lost control, scattered the objects on my desk and ran out of the room in tears. I spent a lot of time in the corridor!

I get on well with people, particularly young people. I can relate well to them. I am interested in young people and they accept me. Sometimes I can feel inferior to teachers and other adults and when someone says to me 'Are you sure?' I always doubt myself and this kind of question makes me hesitate and I always say 'No I am not sure', when in fact I probably was sure.

I have been a youth worker for 25 years, then three years ago I was told I had to obtain a formal qualification. I immediately panicked but was confident and sensible enough to tell my employers that I was dyslexic and would likely have difficulty obtaining the qualification. I consulted my trade union and my employer provided the cost of a dyslexia assessment from a psychologist.

I had to attend an access course to prepare me for the qualification. At first I panicked and 'took off' instead of attending the class. My first year was difficult but I still managed to get a credit in sociology and psychology but I needed quite a bit of support and coaxing to get through my first year.

I am now successfully through my second year. I get support from a scribe and reader and my employer pays for this support.

I find it therapeutic to write down my own dyslexic experiences. When I show what I have written to other people they are surprised and often ask who taught me to write like this. Did I go to lectures on writing? No, I reply. It is just good to get it all out!

Doris's story is very touching and she has obviously been disadvantaged by a school system which at that time did not recognise dyslexia. The strengths shown by many dyslexic people of being sensitive to other people and particularly young people with their own particular difficulties is clearly one of Doris's strengths and motivating interests.

Although returning to formal education has been difficult for Doris, she has been successful and perhaps it has provided her with the opportunity to convince herself that she does have considerable academic ability and potential.

Jean (aged 84)

Occupation: Retired

Jean is an alert and intelligent lady with considerable self-knowledge regarding her dyslexic difficulties and her processing strengths.

> I was not formally diagnosed until I was 73 years old. I know I was different at school but was determined not to let that bother me as I realised that there were many tasks that I could do better than others. I am very musical but have difficulty reading music. At school I developed a range of strategies for dealing with my difficulty which of course I did not realise was dyslexia. I ingrained a mark in my hand with ink to help me distinguish left from right and the mark is still there today.

Jean recalls:

> I felt fortunate at school as I benefited from considerable support and my (dyslexic) difficulties were accepted by my teachers as just being part of me. When I left school I became a saleswoman, which I enjoyed because the paper work was minimal and I met many different types of people. Recently I have been studying at university level and was successful with the course work but found the exams difficult!
> One of the difficulties during my younger years involved figure marching. This involved marching in lines of four columns and each column passing through the other in various figure formations. I enjoyed this activity except when it was my turn to lead.

Jean laughed and said: You can imagine the result of that – chaos. She continued:

> I found swimming difficult, particularly the breast stroke as it required more co-ordination than some other strokes and of course learning to drive was also a problem. But I didn't fuss about my dyslexic difficulties and felt quite confident knowing that perhaps I could not do that

task but I could do something else. But I always knew I was different but I did not realise it had a name. My memory is poor but I can remember plots and storylines very well. I feel I have accepted my dyslexia very well but I was fortunate in the support I had around me. But one thing I find quite peculiar – when I dream I always dream of being lost!

It was interesting talking with Jean who displays a good example of someone utilising her strengths and accepting her difficulties. Although dyslexia was not widely acknowledged when Jean was younger she clearly still benefited from a supportive learning environment. This is very important in allowing people the opportunity to accept their difficulties and experiment in using their strengths.

Alex (aged 35)

Occupation: Student (formerly, stone mason)

I had a sort of mixed school experience. To begin with I enjoyed school but later when I moved to a different town I felt I was not accepted by teachers and some other children. This made things quite difficult for me and at times I felt quite threatened. My dyslexic difficulties were not identified at school but I was taken out to a remedial class several times for extra tuition. It was my father who noticed that I was not reading accurately – he noted that, when he mistakenly turned two pages of my reader, I continued reading what I thought should be on the page. I was clearly reading for context and did not realise that two pages had been turned by mistake. Perhaps looking back I felt I was probably forgotten about at school – perhaps the problem was that I was not able to say what I wanted to say. I was often reluctant to be involved in discussion in case I made a fool of myself.

When I left school I was fortunate and managed to get an apprenticeship as a stone mason with a very small firm who did not ask me to attend any college course. My apprenticeship was all practical but of course it means that I do not have a formal qualification.

My health condition which affects my joints began to have some effect on my employment so I had to leave and eventually I decided to embark on a full-time course of study. I decided to study Anthropology and Social History and ideally I would like to do some type of community education work when I complete my degree.

I have just started my degree and I also have just been diagnosed as having dyslexia. I was finding it difficult in lectures taking notes and often have to re-read material several times. Sometimes I feel I have a mental block but I think that is likely to be due to anxiety about my studies. I probably over-prepare for tutorials and read too much, but I feel comfortable in tutorials as long as I have prepared for them. I think my experiences and maturity help me in tutorials and I feel I can give a balanced perspective on some issues.

On reflection I wish I had been motivated a bit more at school and that my dyslexic difficulties had been recognised. But at least now I have a second chance and also see myself as being more reliable and certainly more socially aware.

Alex's situation is not unusual among mature students as often they experienced being placed in remedial classes as their dyslexia went undiagnosed. Despite some unfortunate school experiences, Alex seems to have coped well. Unforeseen health circumstances were probably the motivating factors for his decision to embark on full-time education, and this will give Alex an opportunity to maximise his potential and perhaps achieve a career to which he is more suited.

Alex's account also highlights the difficulties that can be associated with a change of school. Alex mentioned this to us several times during the interview and the unfortunate memories of trying to fit into a new school in a new area seem to have remained with him. Children with dyslexic difficulties can be very vulnerable when undergoing change, but if the school is supportive and have an awareness of the potential difficulties the change need not have a negative effect on the person. Similarly, dyslexic adults who are changing jobs may also be vulnerable, particularly if their dyslexic difficulties are unrecognised and therefore not fully supported.

Harry (aged 41)

Occupation: Student (formerly, a swimming pool supervisor)

I can only describe my school experiences as suicidal! I changed school almost every year because of my father's occupation. I found academic subjects very difficult but I was good at Art. I found it difficult to express my emotions at school and bullying was rife throughout the schools I attended. This helped me to become more assertive and self-confident. When I left school I worked as a chef then retail management. I had many different jobs, but I was a swimming pool supervisor for seven years.

Sometimes I feel unfulfilled. I know I can be quite creative but I really need some outlet for this; perhaps I am looking for something more challenging and stimulating. Yes, I do often feel a sense of frustration and I feel I would like to help others when I complete my degree.

Harry, in common with Alex, experienced a difficult time at school but seems to have survived the experiences very well. It is interesting that both wish to work with young people because they feel they can be good role models and gain some personal satisfaction from this type of work. Harry's experiences seem to have helped him become more self-confident. This is not always the case as some may be very adversely affected by the type of intimidation Harry suffered at school. Harry certainly came across to us as a mature and intelligent person who, given adequate education experiences and support, will do well. Harry will probably require reassurance and positive feedback throughout his course that he is doing as well as the others, and we feel sure he will!

Katalin (nationality Hungarian)

Occupation: Economics and tourism student in Hungary

I am studying economics and tourism at a university in Hungary. I have lots of problems with reading and writing but learning Russian was the most horrific thing in my life. All the information I learnt during these long hours I forgot the next day. I built a house one day which fell down the next. I am lucky because I am good at Maths and History and am very creative.

I was nearly 14 years old when my mother, who is a teacher, realised I had dyslexia. Some people actually told me I was too old to improve. My father is also dyslexic. He has two engineering degrees but he still had a hard time because he is dyslexic.

I started learning German in the catering trade High School at the age of 17. After the first year I worked in Austria and I could speak very well but my grammar was terrible. After five summers in Austria I was able to correct my grammar. When we read newspapers and used other materials my performance significantly improved. When I was quite good at

German I began to learn English. This language was much easier than the first one. I knew my disadvantages but I could handle them. Between the courses I spent some months in Australia and I worked in the Caribbean. I was chosen employee of the month after 90 days by one of the largest companies in America. But the hardest part of my story came after this.

To get my degree I needed to pass two national language exams. I passed the spoken exams the first time but failed the written exams several times. Fortunately my friend who is also a language teacher helped me and eventually I was tested and both dyslexia and dysgraphia were diagnosed. But there are no written regulation regarding this at the university so I still have to fight my battle with the university authorities. My aim is to get them to accept my performance in spoken exams instead of written papers.

Gillian (aged 52)

Occupation: Retired teacher

My school experience has been totally blacked out from my mind. I was made to feel a failure because I could not achieve what others felt I should achieve. Initially I did a course in physiotherapy after I left school but I had to give that up because I had difficulty copying from the board. I then did training in social work which I completed but found the report writing a nightmare – luckily I had a sympathetic manager. I was not diagnosed as dyslexic until much later in life. After I had my children I undertook a teacher-training course and became a Maths teacher. I am still very much interested in Maths and particularly how dyslexic people cope with Maths. I have undertaken a professional course of training in Dyslexia but I still find the written work quite difficult and very time consuming – it took me two days to do the references for the essay.

Many people mistook my dyslexic difficulty for laziness – at school and at university people simply thought that I did not work hard enough. I know different!!

Gillian's experiences of not being identified at school, or even at university, have had a considerable effect on her professionally and personally. It is interesting that she has completely blacked out her school experiences from her mind, which clearly indicates the pain she probably feels when thinking back to the difficulties she experienced as a result of her dyslexia. Her dyslexic difficulties have obviously had an effect on her self-esteem and very likely resulted in her inability to complete her first training course, and also very likely contributed to anxieties she had as a social worker particularly in the area of report writing.

Andy (aged 29)

Occupation: Medical student (already has a PhD in Biochemistry)

I was 28 when I was first diagnosed but I have suspected for a long time that I had dyslexic difficulties. Although I seemed to pick up reading well at primary school, I had real difficulty with arithmetic and handwriting. For example I was never able to subtract by conventional means, putting a 1 down the side of a column confused me. At school I was also very disorganised and this certainly became a problem when I entered middle school and I had to move from class to class. I was always in the wrong class and this became a big issue for me and I felt confused because of this difficulty.

I also learnt to spell in a very strange manner and joined up writing became near impossible. I did develop an effective exam technique at grammar school. When I am reading a text I do not start at the beginning. I need to find a focus and a framework before I can understand the text, so I usually build around the main points, or at least my main points.

I have always been determined to achieve academically and I eventually intend going into medical research. Yet sometimes I still feel unfulfilled, I am interested in disabilities and would like to research some aspects of that area.

The course I am currently doing has not been without some difficulties – for example, much of the teaching is in small groups and each group take a small part of whatever topic is being discussed. This is not effective for me because I need to see the whole picture and not accumulate bits from other groups. I need to work things out for myself. I now, however, am able to type my exams. I believe this is the first time this has been permitted in the medical faculty at this university. I am extremely relieved at this because my handwriting was becoming a big issue with my tutors.

> In lectures I find it infuriating when the tutors cover up part of the overhead transparency and only show it bit by bit – I cannot understand it until I see it all because I only process in the whole and not bits!

Andy's account is particularly interesting because he is a medical student and a high achiever and, moreover, has developed his own methods of coping with his difficulties. He is still, in some circumstances, at the mercy of others, for example course tutors, regulations and conventions and has to show determination as well as ability to succeed. He does, however, have good metacognitive awareness – that is, he knows how to learn or at least he has acquired this knowledge and can apply it to new learning situations.

Susan (aged 43)

Occupation: Writer

I was not formally identified as dyslexic at school and failed my 11+ exam, but my Head knew I was bright and this helped me get through on appeal. Grammar school was potentially tough but I soon learnt to use coping strategies and got considerable support from my English teacher who gave me individual support at lunchtimes and I managed to wriggle through all my 'O' levels. I was good at drama at school and this was also encouraged by my English teacher.

I am left handed and was poorly co-ordinated yet through determination I ended up being captain of a tennis club team. The problem of course was that the captain was responsible for writing all the score sheets. This included writing each person's name on the score card and tallying up the scores. This was a real challenge for me and I developed the strategy of delegation! This became a bit of a joke as most people did not realise why I was delegating this task, some thought I was lazy and opting-out of my responsibilities as captain.

I have been fortunate in the support from my family and friends. Becoming a writer was a real challenge for me and my friends were helpful with proofreading, but now my word processor does so much of that for me; it has been a great help. I like a challenge, which is probably why I became a writer, and I am also creative. The plot for the novel I have written came to me in a dream. This started me off in my career as a writer. I am now also a freelance travel writer. Looking back I suppose I would have had an easier passage at school if I had received some of the allowances which dyslexic people now get, such as extra time in the exams. This would have been ideal for me because I usually have to read my work several times to pick out the errors.

I suppose determination, support and good coping strategies have seen me through.

We view Susan's story as inspirational, and I am sure some of her teachers would have advised her against becoming a writer. It emphasises the value of support at the right time from the right type of person. Susan throughout the interview was full of praise for her English teacher and attaches much of her success at school to that teacher.

It also underlines the need for dyslexic people to be determined and usually they are and, like Susan, often tackle an activity to prove to themselves that they can do it. Usually they become very good at some tasks – as was the case with Susan at tennis, despite seeing herself as clumsy and poorly co-ordinated. Susan's story also highlights the need for dyslexic people – irrespective of the support offered – to accept the challenge, devise their own strategies and use their strengths.

Rebecca (aged 33)

Occupation: Classroom assistant

I was diagnosed as dyslexic when I was 31 and this has made a considerable difference to me. At school I had problems with Maths and I was totally unaware of what was going on in the classroom. I actually thought I had been away, but I hadn't. This and my other difficulties – I now know they were due to my dyslexia – resulted in low self-confidence. I would be reluctant to speak to anyone in authority. When I left school I got a job cutting the ends off socks in a factory. I continued working in a factory until medical problems meant I could no longer lift anything. This virtually ruled out factory work and I had to rethink my future.

I started to work with infant school children and found I really enjoyed this type of work. It also motivated me to examine why I had not achieved in terms of qualifications. I was assessed and it was found I had considerable dyslexic difficulties. I also benefited from, at first, using a blue acetate sheet, and now I wear blue glasses. Before I used the acetate I thought I was able to read. I now realise that I was not reading. Before I was only processing one word at a time and had little comprehension, but with the coloured acetate I can read whole lines. It seems to relax my eyes and I can now read with comprehension.

This has given me a real boost and I have now passed many exams in counselling, learning support and child care. I will never stop learning – it is like a hunger and I want to go on. Ideally I would like to become a special needs teacher.

Rebecca's account highlights that different types of strategies can be effective for different people. For example, blue acetate will not benefit all dyslexic people but it certainly seems to have been a considerable help to Rebecca. It is important that professionals involved in assessment and support should consider all aspects, and it would seem that coloured acetates can be helpful. It is a fairly simple procedure to include in an assessment battery. It was interesting that Rebecca actually mentioned that her sequencing score in the assessment was particularly low, which may well have provided some clue that she had some visual difficulty.

It is also interesting to note that, once started on the ladder of success, Rebecca wants to continue climbing. This a positive effect of a diagnosis and the right type of support. It is also the effect of a more positive self-esteem which is essential if a dyslexic person is entering further education for the first time. The 'hunger' for learning Rebecca mentions is not unusual. Many dyslexic people, having missed earlier opportunities, have such a 'hunger'; and it is extremely heartening to hear about that 'hunger' being satisfied. Realistically, of course, sometimes the support to make that possible is simply not available, and we hope that the increased interest in and knowledge of dyslexia may make that possible in the future.

Vanessa (aged 25)

Occupation: Artist

I was actually 17 when I was identified as dyslexic and in many ways it was a case of too little too late. I had a really horrendous school experience: I was in the bottom groups for English and Maths and this meant I was with children who were not interested in school and probably not very able. I was serious about my work but it was impossible to perform well in the class I was put into. I was bullied quite a bit and also given work which I knew was well below my capabilities. On two occasions I just felt I could not, and should not, have to cope with this and actually ran out of school. No one at that school bothered to investigate why I had difficulties as I was very good verbally. Dyslexia was kind of loosely mentioned at primary school but the school did not take it any further.

At secondary school I failed in virtually all my subjects except Art and Science, but I was even advised against doing Art at college. Looking back I feel I was written off at school and this still has an effect on my self-esteem.

It was fortunate that at college one lecturer took an interest and suggested a dyslexia assessment. He noticed that I was good verbally but my written work was unexpectedly poor by comparison. Being diagnosed as dyslexic raised many questions in my mind; for example, I did not know what dyslexia was and received very little feedback after the assessment. I was told my reading age was 13 and my spelling was at the 10-year-old level. Imagine how that made me feel – I was told nothing at all about the strengths in my profile. At college I received a computer but little else. I was not even shown how to use it and the computer I received was not the most appropriate for my course. There was no follow-up help and support. I would have benefited from help with structuring and writing essays. Even to get an assessment and a computer I had to do all the running and organising, which wasted valuable study time. I did not actually receive the computer until the start of my second year. My degree was in Fine Art but there was a lot of written work.

I worked as a team teacher in a school for dyslexic children after completing my degree. I thoroughly enjoyed that and I was given some responsibility for the art curriculum and the children produced some excellent work.

At the moment I am doing some freelance work and have just finished working in a nursery school. I enjoyed that but found reading aloud to the children very difficult and very embarrassing! Although I now read and have a good language awareness I still have problems in some situations such as writing a cheque in a shop. I always make mistakes writing out numbers in full as you have to do in a cheque. Thank goodness for Switch cards!

Vanessa's account highlights very clearly the difficulties and the obstacles that have to be overcome by dyslexic people and the need for support at different stages from school through to employment. Vanessa experienced many unnecessary situations, but unfortunately these events are all too common: the late identification, inappropriate curriculum, bullying, lack of appropriate course and careers guidance, and lack of follow-up after an assessment. Considering these factors we feel that Vanessa has achieved much and like many dyslexic people has a determination to succeed to a high standard.

Michael (aged 22)

Occupation: Transition from university to work

I was diagnosed as dyslexic when I was 8 and after that I received one-to-one support at school. I still felt there was a discrepancy between people's expectations of me and what I was actually achieving. I felt I would be a road digger when I left school because I did not feel I could achieve academically. In actual fact I got a degree in Genetics. But I feel that was due to my determination. I have set down my own goals and I was determined to improve my GCE grades so I did an intensive course which others thought was impossible, but I succeeded. I still feel a bit bitter about being dyslexic; sometimes I feel that everyone has an advantage over me.

At university I had many difficulties to overcome associated with my dyslexia such as note taking, time management and essay writing. I found that I became so immersed in an essay that I forgot which part was relevant. Also doing several projects at the same time was difficult. I could only focus on one thing as I had to put all my energies into one project and forget about the rest of my work. This was, of course, not too wise as I had a lot to catch up with when I had finished the project I was doing.

Michael's account also illustrates the determination often displayed by dyslexic people. Sometimes they achieve against almost impossible odds. It is also interesting to note the sense of under-achievement sometimes experienced by dyslexic people even though in actual fact they have achieved much – as is the case with Michael. The difficulties Michael experienced at university are very typical of those many dyslexic students experience. Almost certainly support and advice with essay planning and time management are essential.

Bill Thomson

Occupation: Author

We would like to end these accounts with an extract from a Scottish Dyslexia Association publication (Thomson, 1999). The extract is about the author of a selection of short stories and poetry – Bill Thomson who was diagnosed dyslexic at 50 and has now gone on to record many achievements.

> I was born and brought up on a farm and at secondary school I had real problems with reading and writing. My first job after leaving school was as a gardener and although I have had many jobs since then to this day I have maintained an interest in gardening. I won the best vegetable garden prize five years in a row; I have also been a champion bait fisherman.
>
> Due to ill health I had to look for another hobby and this was the daddy of them all. My daughter asked me to spell a word and I was unable to do so and I thought it was about time I did something about this. I went to an adult basic education class and with the help of my teachers I gradually improved and was diagnosed as dyslexic. Soon I was able to understand words and sentences. To my astonishment I found I was able to write poetry and short stories. The first poem I wrote was 'A Humorous Look at the First Night' and it was published in the British Poetry review 1994. Shortly after this I wrote 'The Working Men', which is displayed beside a miner, gamekeeper and a gardener. In June 1998 I was Scottish winner and UK runner-up at the Adult Learner of the Year awards. In June 1999 I was invited to a reception at 10 Downing Street to celebrate the UN Year for Older Persons and I met the Prime Minister and his wife. I feel fortunate to have benefited from family and community support.

Self-advocacy

Latham and Latham (1997) make the very important point that advocating for your legal rights does not necessarily mean filing a law suit in court. Many dyslexic people are able to get the support from their employer without resorting to stressful and time-consuming legal wrangles. The case of Doris described above illustrates that employers can be sensitive to the needs of dyslexic people and that these needs may change with changing circumstances. Latham and Latham suggest that the basic advocacy steps can be: communication, negotiation, mediation, and arbitration.

We certainly view communication as being of great importance. In all the accounts of dyslexic people's difficulties and successes described in this chapter, communication seems to be the key issue. That can often mean informing a manager or employer for the first time that one has a dyslexic difficulty. This 'coming out' can be difficult for dyslexic people (Biggar and Barr, 1996) but it can also be therapeutic. Dyslexic people usually benefit from talking, or indeed writing, about their experiences but they need to communicate with their employers in the first place so that they can then talk openly about their difficulties. Indeed this openness should, of course, begin with the application for a job then the employer will not be able to back down on any provision necessary for the dyslexic person. Of course, the flip side of this is that if employers do not have sufficient awareness and understanding of dyslexia they may be reluctant to employ the dyslexic person in the first place. The situation experienced by Rose and described in this chapter illustrates how lack of understanding can prevent one from obtaining an interview let alone a job! The legislation – Americans with Disabilities Act 1990 and the Disability Discrimination Act 1995 in the UK – should protect dyslexic candidates from being discriminated against in terms of recruitment, advertising and job application procedures.

The heartening and sometimes touching accounts described in this chapter show the determination and resilience of people with dyslexia and in some cases the support and understanding offered by friends, professionals and support groups.

Self-advocacy may be the responsibility of self, but it is not achieved in isolation. It is important that the dyslexic person receives the support, the encouragement and the message – *speak for yourself.*

Chapter 9

Reaching out

It is important that people with dyslexia are able to locate resources and sources of help as easily as possible. Sometimes it is not easy to find out who can help and from where the help can be obtained. Too often we have been informed of quite horrific accounts of dyslexic people being passed from one organisation to another in order to acquire the help they need. This can take considerable time, energy and conviction from the dyslexic person. Yet in this book we are encouraging dyslexic people and their supporters to take control of their own lives, their studies, their employment and their difficulties. It is through accepting and recognising that dyslexic people themselves hold the answer to their difficulties that progress can be made. But that is not to say that others have no role to play in the process. Employers, family, organisations and education staff all have a supportive role to play. This chapter will provide information, resources and contacts which may be useful to all who have contact with dyslexic people and, of course, to all dyslexic people themselves.

Disability and dyslexia organisations

Independent organisations

An extensive list of organisations for dyslexic adults is provided in this section. Some of the organisations listed below provide services in employment, others give support, counselling assessment and general advice. The organisations are listed in alphabetical order.

Adult Dyslexia and Skills Development Centre

5 Tavistock Place, London WC1H 9SN. Tel.: 0207 388 8744. Fax: 0207 387 7968.

The Centre aims to provide customised support to help adult dyslexics to achieve their full potential, and younger dyslexic people to become successful adults. It offers psychological and diagnostic assessment and/or counselling, tuition and training, advocacy and awareness raising through telephone advice, lectures, talks and workshops, and publications in journals or books.

Adult Dyslexia Organisation (ADO)

336 Brixton Road, London SW9 7AA. Helpline: 0207 924 9559. Admin.: 0207 737 7646.
E-mail: dyslexia.hq@dial.pipex.com
Website: http://www.futurenet.co.uk/charity/ado/index.html

ADO is a national charitable organisation founded in 1991. It has a network of both local and international groups. It offers advice about psychological and teacher assessments, tuition, a helpline, a research group, setting up support groups, a Newsletter (called *Dyslexia 2000*) and various pamphlets and videos. At present, it is developing a mentoring service for dyslexic students.

AFASIC

347 Central Markets, Smithfield, London ED1A 9NH. Helpline: 0207 236 3632. Admin.: 0207 236 6487. Fax: 0207 236 8115.
E-mail: member@afasic.org.uk

AFASIC is a registered charity, founded by parents over 30 years ago. They deal with children and young people with speech and language difficulties and their families. It organises a national network of support groups and promotes events in support of children with communication difficulties. Moreover, it produces a range of publications and some factsheets about dyslexia and specific learning difficulties.

Association for Children and Adults with Learning Disabilities (ACLD)

Suffolk Chambers, 1 Suffolk Street, Dublin 2. Tel.: 01 679 0276. Fax: 01 679 0273.

ACLD is incorporated with the Dyslexia Association in Ireland in supporting both children and adults with disabilities, including specific learning difficulties. The Group has just finished a pilot survey concerning the attitudes of Irish employers to employing people with disabilities, including dyslexia. The survey is funded by the European Commission and is in partnership with members from England, Spain, Italy and France. A report has just been published and is now available. Recommendations were also provided in the report.

Association of Educational Psychologists (AEP)

26 The Avenue, Durham DH1 4ED.

This is a professional representation of a variety of educational psychologists. They publish a journal, *Educational Psychology in Practice*.

Basic Skills Agency

7th Floor, Commonwealth House, 1–19 New Oxford Street, London WC1A 1NU. Tel.: 0207 405 4017. Fax: 0207 404 5038.
E-mail.: enquiries@basic-skills.co.uk
Website: http://www.basic-skills.co.uk

The Basic Skills Agency is a national (England and Wales) development agency for basic skills with the patronage of HRH the Princess Royal. It provides national information and support in promoting literacy for all ages, e.g. in primary, secondary, FE and adult organisations. It publishes information and resources, funds innovative research in the field and runs a national free telephone referral service to help adults to join basic skills classes. It presents a quality mark award to good literacy programmes.

A number of research programmes have been carried out with support from the Agency, e.g. *Basic Skills at Work* (1995), *Basic Skills Training at Work* (1995), *Influences on Basic Skills* (Parsons and Brynner, 1998), *Basic Skills Development in Lincolnshire*

(Walker and Chamberlain, 1999), *Improving Literacy and Numeracy, A Fresh Start* (Moser, 1999), National Literacy Trust Database and Information Service.

The Agency designed new teaching packs specifically for the training organisations to provide a quality and effective training to their New Deal clients. These are designed according to the themes of the New Deal options (e.g. environment, employment and voluntary sector). Each pack contains a 12-week 'off-the-peg' basic skills course covering reading, writing, spelling, oral communication and numeracy skills.

Broxbourne Dyslexia Unit

The Priests' House, 90 High Road, Broxbourne, Herts EN10 7DZ. Tel.: 01992 442 002.

The Unit is a centre for the Royal Society of Arts (RSA) and Specific Learning Difficulties (SpLD) courses. It provides assessment, advice, books and resources. It also offers training courses and In-Service Training (INSET) to specialists and other professionals working in the field.

British Dyslexia Association (BDA)

98 London Road, Reading RG1 5AU. Helpline: 0118 966 8217. Admin.: 0118 966 2677. Fax: 0118 935 1927.
E-mail: helpline@bda-dyslexia.demon.co.uk   or
        admin@bda-dyslexia.demon.co.uk
Website: http://www.bda-dyslexia.org.uk

The BDA is a national charity organisation interested in specific learning difficulties. It was founded in 1972, and represents over 100 dyslexia associations, 28 support groups and 86 corporate members. The BDA handles over 40,000 enquiries per year. Its aims are: to present its policies to the government and local authorities on issues concerning people with dyslexia; to provide a support network throughout the UK via helpline, computer, advice service, publications, teacher training, conferences and exhibitions; to provide training for befrienders and other volunteers; to participate in research activities; and to support member organisations.

As in the support for the dyslexic adults, the BDA offers information to dyslexic adults wishing to study in FE/HE on employment and continuing education. Moreover, they emphasise both the needs and abilities of the dyslexic adult in the workplace and encourage employers to take part in their support.

Local dyslexia associations are mostly registered charities. They are affiliated to the BDA and have representatives on the management board, but they run their own affairs when offering support to dyslexic people and their families on the ground.

Corporate members are not affiliated to the BDA but many have representatives on the management board. They organise collaborative activities with the BDA based on common aims, providing educational or specialist dyslexia services. Categories include independent schools, mainstream schools or units, FE/HE, health, research institutions and commercial organisations.

A magazine, *Dyslexia Contact*, and an annual *Dyslexia Handbook* are also produced by the BDA. The BDA also collaborates with John Wiley and Sons (publishers) to publish the international research journal, *Dyslexia*.

British Institute for Learning Disabilities

Wolverhampton Road, Kidderminster, Worcs DY10 3PP. Tel.: 01562 850 251. Fax: 01562 851 970.

British Psychological Society (BPS)

St Andrews House, 48 Princess Road East, Leicester LE1 7DR. Tel.: 0116 254 9568. Fax: 0116 247 0787.
E-mail.: enquiry@bps.org.uk
Website: http://www.bps.org.uk

The BPS was founded in 1901, and became incorporated by Royal Charter in 1965. At present, BPS has 32,000 members. The BPS aims to promote events and network in the field of psychology, provide training, organise conferences and represent the members' views and opinions. There are 8 divisions and 11 sections of which the Occupational Psychology (OP) is the largest (more than 2,300 members). The OP section focuses on issues such as selection methods, training, work counselling and unemployment, occupational stress, job satisfaction, person–machine interface and the impact of new technology. In addition, it publishes a monthly bulletin, *The Psychologist*, and the *Journal of Educational Psychology*.

Career National Association

20–25 Glasshouse Yard, London EC1A 4JS. Tel.: 0207 490 8818.

Career Services

There are many career services offices and they are often seen to be linked with Training Enterprise Councils (TECs) and Local Enterprise Councils (LECs), but are separate from them and are often run by private companies contracted by the DfEE.

Dis-Forum

This is a network discussion group for people who would like to discuss issues relevant to disabilities.
E-mail: dis-forum@mailbase.ac.uk
Website: http://www.mailbase.ac.uk/lists/dis-forum

Disability Action

2 Annandale Avenue, Belfast BT7 3JH, Northern Ireland. Tel.: 01232 491 011.

Disability Scotland

Princes House, 5 Shandwick Place, Edinburgh EH2 4RG. Tel.: 0131 229 8632. Fax: 0131 229 5168.

Disability Wales/Anabledd Cymru

Llys Ifor, Crescent Road, Caerphilly CF83 1XL, Wales. Tel.: 01222 887 325. Fax: 01222 888 702.

Dyslexia Adult Support Group

Dyslexia Centre, 115a Market Street, Chorley, Lancashire. Tel.: 01380 850935/01257 232459 (drop-in centre, Tuesday and Friday a.m.).

The Centre offers a number of facilities for adults with dyslexia including a helpline, drop-in service, self-help group, and an advisory service. The Centre is also very active in research projects in the area of audio research and video close captions.

Dyslexia Advice and Resource Centre Ltd (DARC)

Unit 217, The Custard Factory, Digbeth, Birmingham B9 4AA. Tel.: 0121 694 9944 or 0121 248 2429.

DARC is a registered charity supported by the local council and TEC. It is committed to serving dyslexics by identifying methods of reducing their problems, and championing their abilities.

The Centre has produced a unique training programme, the RiBboN Programme, which aims to help dyslexic adults, and in particular to develop the awareness of coping strategies for life and social skills. Funding is available for the course through the Further Education Funding Council (FEFC).

Dyslexia Association of Ireland

31 Stillorgan Park, Black Rock, County Dublin.

Dyslexia Forum

This is a network discussion group for people who would like to discuss issues relevant to dyslexia.
E-mail.: dyslexia@mailbase.ac.uk
Website: http://www.mailbase.ac.uk/lists/dyslexia

Dyslexia Institute (DI)

133 Gresham Road, Staines, Middlesex TW18 2AJ. Tel.: 01784 463 851. Fax: 01784 460 747.
E-mail: dyslexia-inst@connect.bt.com
Website: http://www.dyslexia-inst.org.uk

The DI is a registered educational charity (non-profit making). It was founded in 1972 and has 25 local centres throughout the UK. DI offers psychological assessments (from ages 5 to 69), and tuition to those assessed by the Institute, and special needs teacher training. The Centre's core training programmes include the Dyslexia Institute Literacy Programme, Units of Sounds (LDA), Multimedia and the latest Dyslexia Institute Maths Programme.

Over 400 adults are currently enrolled in courses at the DI. Some of the DI centres are contracted by the Employment Service to provide basic skills to unemployed dyslexic adults. Courses are also offered to dyslexic adults in conjunction with other organisations such as the Probation Service and the Driving Standards Agency.

At present, it runs a one-year Postgraduate Diploma Course with York University at a number of centres, and short courses for specialist teachers and parents. Some of the courses are run in partnership with other organisations such as Tesco, Industry in Education, the Post Office and the JJ Charitable Trust.

It has its own professional body, the Dyslexia Guild, and it publishes a journal, *The Dyslexia Review*.

Dyslexia Institute (Scotland)

74 Victoria Crescent Road, Dowanhill, Glasgow G11 9JN. Tel.: 0141 334 4549. Fax: 0141 339 8879.

This is a regional office of the Dyslexia Institute in Glasgow. It provides psychological assessments and teaching to dyslexic children, training for professionals and specialists.

Dyslexia Teaching Centre

23 Kensington Square, London W8 5HN. Tel.: 0207 937 2408. Fax: 0207 938 4816.

The Centre is a registered charity which receives no funding from central or local government. It offers individually tailored courses, psychological assessments, counselling and one-to-one tuition for dyslexic children and adults. It organises adult support groups and conferences, and also runs programmes in conjunction with speech, motor or other therapy.

Dyslexia Unit (Bangor)

University College of North Wales, Bangor, Gwynedd LL57 2DG. Tel.: 01248 351 151. Fax: 01248 382 599.
Website: http://www.dyslexia.bangor.ac.uk

The Unit is self-financing within the University of Wales and is a corporate member of the BDA. It provides a wide range of services relevant to dyslexia, including consultation and advice, assessment, teaching, teacher training, support for students and research.

Dyspraxia Foundation

8 West Alley, Hitchin, Herts SG5 1EG. Tel.: 01462 454 986. Fax: 01462 455052.

European Dyslexia Association (EDA)

12 Goldington Avenue, Bedford MK40 3BY.
E-mail: eurodysass@kbnet.co.uk
Website: http://www2.soutron.com/eda

The EDA was funded by the European Commission, but is currently looking for independent funding. Its principal office is in Bedford. There is a plan that a new office will be set up in Brussels. It offers supports to dyslexic people, to promote links between groups, to publish news and information and to conduct studies and organise conferences.

Helen Arkell Dyslexia Centre (HADC)

Frensham, Farnham, Surrey GU10 3BW. Tel.: 0125 792 400. Fax: 01252 795 669.

HADC is a registered charity funded by grants from charitable trusts. It was founded in 1971 with the patronage of HRH the Duchess of Gloucester.

The Centre provides information, counselling, tuition and training. It works in partnership with teachers in schools in order to provide in-service programmes to teachers as well as to support dyslexic pupils – for example, the Centre's unique Schools Partnership Scheme. These programmes are also available to further and higher educational institutions. Moreover, it offers professional training courses to specialists; trains parent volunteers; and undertakes research activities. In the near future, the Centre plans to develop further the training with Local Education Authorities (LEAs), the training to training providers and employers, and information technology (IT).

Hornsby International Dyslexia Centre

Glenshee Lodge, 261 Trinity Road, London SW18 3SN. Tel.: 0208 874 1844. Fax: 0208 877 9737.
E-mail: dyslexia@hornsby.demon.co.uk
Website: http://www.hornsby.co.uk

The Centre is a registered charity dedicated to overcoming dyslexia. It offers advice, counselling and teaching including distance learning courses. The Centre also offers tuition and support to employed dyslexic adults who would like to improve their performance at work.

Hungarian Dyslexia Association

1114 Budapest, Villányl üt 11–13, Hungary. Tel.: ++165 8804. Fax: ++342 8019.

International Dyslexic Association (IDA)

8600 LaSalle Road, Chester Building, Suite 382, Baltimore, MD 21286–2044, USA. Tel.: (410) 296 0232. Fax: (410) 321 5069.
E-mail: info@interdys.org
Website: http://www.interdys.org

The IDA is an international, non-profit-making scientific and educational organisation dedicated to the study of learning disability and dyslexia. It was founded in 1949 in the USA (formerly called the Orton Dyslexia Society). It aims to monitor government legislation, offer information and support to teachers as well as to parents and dyslexic individuals, produce publications, undertake research and organise conferences.

IRLEN Institute

Irlen Centre, 123 High Street, Chard, Somerset TA20 1QT. Tel./Fax: 01460 655 55.

It deals with perceptual learning problems which affect some dyslexics and ono-dyslexics. Colour-tinted lenses and overlays may be prescribed from the Institute in helping to overcome the problem. Learning strategies are also recommended within the Institute.

Kelly's Business Directory

This gives information about companies based in the UK which may advertise particular types of work. As regards information about trade directories, the directory can be found in local libraries.

Lancashire Centre for Specific Learning Difficulties

22 St Georges Road, St Annes on Sea, Lancashire FY8 2AE. Tel./Fax: 01253 720570.
E-mail: Colin.Lannen@Btinternet.com

This Centre conducts psychological assessments on adults and children and provides advice on support and training. Counselling and training courses are also offered within the Centre's vision of a dedicated centre for supporting adults with dyslexia. The Centre is part of Dyslexia North West (registered charity), is a corporate member of the BDA and also runs the Red Rose School for dyslexic children.

Learning and Behaviour Charitable Trust New Zealand

Box 40, 161 Upper Hutt, Wellington, New Zealand. Tel.: 04 586 1862. Fax: 04 586 1890.

Learning Line

17 Logie Mill, Edinburgh EH7 4HG. Tel.: 0131 556 8770.

This is run by the Career Development Edinburgh and Lothians, a registered Scottish charity. It provides information and advice for adults on careers, education and training.

Linking Education and Disability (LEAD)

Free Call: 0800 100 900 (Learning Direct).

Funding of this Group comes from European Social Funds, LECs, colleges, National Lottery Charities, charitable trusts. The main office receives money from SOEID and LAs (social work and community education).

LEAD provides a continuing education gateway. It provides information about education, training and lifelong learning opportunities, guidance and support for adults with disabilities.

LEAD has a regional office in Scotland: 199 Nithsdale Road, Glasgow G41 3RE. Tel.: 0141 423 5710. Free Call: 0800 100 900 (ask for LEAD Scotland). There are a number of offices in Scotland.

London Language and Literacy Unit

South Bank University, 103 Borough Road, London SE1 0AA. Tel.: 0207 928 8989.

The Unit provides a wide range of services, including basic skills, literacy and teaching English to students of other languages. It offers consultancy, training courses for students in FE and HE, and adult learning. It also produces publications.

Medway Dyslexia Centre

1 The Close, Rochester, Kent ME1 1SD. Tel.: 01634 848 232. Fax: 01634 818 787.

The Centre is a registered charity and is a corporate member of the BDA. It provides teaching and assessment for dyslexic children and adults, organises adult support groups, offers RSA training courses and INSET to specialist teachers or other professionals working in the field.

National Bureau for Students with Disabilities (SKILL)

336 Brixton Road, London SW9 7AA. Tel.: 0207 274 0565. Minicom 0207 738 7722 (Information Line). Fax: 0207 274 7840.
E-mail: SkillNatBurDis@Compuserve.com
Website: http://www.skill.org.uk

SKILL is a national organisation which provides an information service for disabled graduates in education, training and employment. It liaises with policy makers and works with universities, employers, other voluntary organisations and publishers to create and promote opportunities for graduates. It organises training events, workshops and conferences. It also produces many publications and is involved in project work and research.

Northern Ireland Dyslexia Association

7 Mount Pleasant, Stranmillis Road, Belfast BT9 5DS. Tel.: 0289 065 9212.

Office for Standards in Education (OFSTED)

Alexandra House, 29–33 Kingsway, London WC2B 6SE. Tel.: 0207 421 6800. Fax: 0207 421 6707. Helpline: 0207 421 6673.

Opportunities for People with Disabilities

1 Bank Buildings, Princess Street, London EC2 8EU. Tel. and Minicom: 0207 726 4963.

People First (Advocacy for People with Learning Disabilities)

207–215 King's Cross Road, London WC1X 9DB. Tel.: 0207 713 6400. Fax: 0207 713 5826.

Polish Dyslexia Association

Marta Bogdanowicz, Dept of Psychology, Gdansk University, Pomorska 68, 80- 343, Gdansk, Poland.

PRODEC

Loretta Giorcelli, Faculty of Education, UWS Macarthur, PO Box 555, Campbelltown, NSW 2560, Australia. Fax: ++61–2–9771 3592
E-mail: l.giorcelli@uws.edu.au

Professional Association of Teachers of Students with Specific Learning Difficulties (PATOSS)

PO Box 66, Cheltenham, Gloucestershire GL53 9YF.

PATOSS has a newsletter, local groups and an annual conference.

Real and Effective Action for Dyslexia

Cloke, 21 Mylady's Mile, Hollywood, Co. Down. N. Ireland BT18 9EW.

Right to Write (UK) Ltd

Head Office, 16 Keirby Walk, Burnley, Lancashire BB11 2DE. Tel.: 01282 412 222.

This company was formed to meet the needs of Employment Service clients who have dyslexic difficulties. They provide the support necessary to help access and maintain employment for dyslexic adults. RTW has established relationships with dyslexia and disability organisations locally and nationally. They suggest that each dyslexic person requires a very individual programme and the different demands of a modern-day workplace training environment, as opposed to academic training, should be reflected in the training.

Royal Association for Disability and Rehabilitation (RADAR)

Tel.: 0207 250 3222. Minicom: 0207 250 4199.

RADAR provides information and advice on many of the areas that affect disabled people on a daily basis, including employment, transport, social security and social services. It also campaigns on behalf of disabled people

Scottish Dyslexia Association

Unit 3, Stirling Business Centre, Wellgreen Place, Stirling, Scotland FK8 2DZ. Tel.: 01786 446 650. Fax: 01786 471 235.
E-mail.: Dyslexia.Scotland@Dial.Pipex.Com

A registered charity, the SDA has branches throughout Scotland and runs helplines, books bus, conferences and engages in consultancy activities to support dyslexic children and adults.

Scottish Dyslexia Forum

Whitelee St, Boswell, Roxburghshire TD6 0SH.

The forum comprises representatives from a number of bodies in Scotland who have contact with dyslexic children and adults. It has supported and advised on research programmes, seminars and teacher and other training programmes.

Self-Help Awareness Programme for Employment (SHAPE)

SHAPE is one of the organisations selected by ES which focuses on individual needs in the provision for practical help to jobseekers with health problems or disabilities. The Group offers flexible and realistic part-time courses, with professional skills and expertise to meet individual needs. The programme is usually provided locally.

Sound Learning Centre

12 The Rise, London N13 5LE. Tel.: 0208 882 1060. Fax: 0208 882 1040.

The Centre provides a range of auditory, visual and sensory learning programmes to help children and adults with learning and sensory difficulties. It also offers assessments and sound therapies.

South Wales Dyslexia Association

4 Dinas Road, Penarn, South Glamorgan CF64 3PL. Tel.: 01222 703 124.

SPELD New South Wales, Australia

129 Greenwich Road, Greenwich 2065, NSW, Australia.

SPELD New Zealand

Box 27–112 Wellington, New Zealand

Watford Dyslexia Institute

47 Little Oxhey Lane, South Oxhey, Watford WD1 5HN. Tel.: 0208 421 4266.

The Institute provides information, tuition, assessments and training. It also operates a flexible payment policy.

Wessex Dyslexia Tutors Group

Tel.: 01202 698 617 or 01929 480 117.

The Group is a corporate member of the BDA. It provides initial assessments and individual specialised tuition for problems with reading, spelling and language skills.

Workable

Head Office, Workable Premier House, 10 Greycoat Place, London SW1P 1SB. Tel.: 0207 222 8866 or 0207 222 1803. Fax: 0207 222 1903. E-mail: WorkableUK@aol.com

There are four regional centres in England. Workable is a charitable organisation which offers placement advice and information about job vacancies to disabled people who are looking for jobs. The Group has links with a number of companies. It campaigns in practical ways to enable employers to offer real work experience to disabled adults, to give direct experience and help to pave the way to job offers. A mentoring scheme is operated by Workable mentors who are trained to work with disabled people to help them to find employment. The Group also runs workshops with regard to the needs of both disabled employees and employers.

Independent adult support groups

An increasing number of adult support groups are offered at local dyslexia associations which are affiliated to the BDA. An up-to-date list can be obtained, if necessary, from the annual BDA *Dyslexia Handbook*.
   There is an Adult Dyslexia Computer Interest Group based in 13 Hurstleigh Drive, Redhill, Surrey RH1 2AA. Tel.: 01737 765 851.

Support groups or centres are also available within universities, for example. Adult guidance is also available from a number of education authorities through a range of adult education, community education, support services, psychological and guidance groups.

Employers Forum on Disability

Nutmeg House, 60 Gainsford Street, London SE1 2NY. Tel.: 0207 403 3020. Fax: 0207 403 0404.

The Forum is concerned with the employment and training of people with disabilities. Founded by a group of members (Barclays Bank plc, BG plc, BT plc, BUPA Camelot Group plc, Centrica, GlaxoWellcome, Kingfisher, LWT, Manpower plc, McDonald's Resturants Ltd, Midland Bank plc, Post Office, Railtrack plc, Rank Xerox, Sainsbury's Supermarkets Ltd), the Forum aims to provide information and practical guidance for employers on specific topics relating to the employment of disabled people. It also aims to improve the job prospects of disabled people by making it easier for employers to recruit, retain and develop disabled employees.

The Forum offers an information and advice service and produces a wide range of briefing papers, guides and factsheets on disability issues for employers. Some of their publications are sponsored by the Defence Evaluation and Research Agency (DERA).

Government agencies (UK)

Department for Education and Employment (DfEE)

Sanctuary Buildings, Great Smith Street, Westminster, London SW1P 3BT. Tel.: 0207 925 5000. Fax: 0207 925 6000.
Website: www.dfee.gov.uk

DfEE provides advice to the government on issues relevant to education and employment. It takes a primary role in generating and developing up-to-date policies in education and employment. For example, in the winter of 1997, DSS and DfEE announced a new £195 million programme, set out to develop ways to help people on disability benefits to obtain or retain work.

Employment Disability Unit

Special working units may be set up within Regional Councils in dealing with supporting dyslexic adults in employment.

Learning Direct

Free helpline: 0800 100 900.

In collaboration with DfEE, Learning Direct offers information about learning and careers to individuals, employers and institutions.

Legal Advice

Disability Law Service: 0207 831 8031.
Employment Rights Service: 0207 713 7616/7583.
Equal Opportunities Commission (EOC): 0161 833 9244.
Commission for Racial Equality (CRE): 0207 828 7022.
Free Representation Unit: 0207 831 0692.
Industrial Tribunal Enquiry Line: 0345 959 775.
Law Centres: 0207 387 8570.
National Association of Citizens Advice Bureaux: 0207 833 2181.

Local Enterprise Councils, Scotland (LECs)

LECs are the English equivalent of TECs in England and Wales. Some of the LECs are subordinated to the government agency. Some of them, funded or contracted by the government, offer a wide range of information, advice and training to help meet the needs of small businesses through many different organisations and employers in local areas. There are 22 offices in different regions throughout Scotland, including the Scottish Enterprise Companies.

Lothian Edinburgh Enterprise Limited (LEEL)

Haymarket Terrace, Edinburgh, Tel.: 0131 313 4000.

LEEL provides Training for Work Programmes for people who have been out of work for some time to get back to work. Their approach emphasises practical training and meeting the needs of the job market. It publicises the names and addresses of a full list of training providers.

Lothian TAP Agency (Training Access Point)

8 St Mary's Street, Edinburgh. Tel.: 0131 557 5822.

TAP provides comprehensive details on training opportunities in Edinburgh and Lothian areas on database. Such a database is available in some Jobcentres, colleges and on the Capital Information System which is linked to every public library in Edinburgh.

Training and Enterprise Councils (TECs), England and Wales

Some of the TECs are subordinated to government agencies. Some of them are funded or contracted by the government to offer a wide range of information, advice and training to help meet the needs of small businesses through many different organisations and employers in local areas. There are 78 offices in different regions throughout England and Wales.

Psychologists

Association of Educational Psychologists (AEP)

26, The Avenue, Durham DH1 4ED.

This is a professional representation of a variety of educational psychologists. A journal, *Educational Psychology in Practice*, is available.

Saville and Holdsworth

3 AC Court, Thames Ditton, Surrey K17 0SR. Tel.: 0208 339 2222.

Occupational psychologists specialising in testing disabled people as part of the recruitment process. They have produced *Guidelines for Testing People with Disabilities*.

The Directory of Chartered Psychologists (BPS)

The British Psychological Society, St Andrews House, 48 Princess Road East, Leicester LE1 7DR.

The *Directory* is the first and only comprehensive reference to services offered by psychologists in the UK. It contains 1,250 entries by individual psychologists giving details about their specialisms under the categories of Clinical Psychology, Clinical Neuropsychology, Counselling Psychology, Educational Psychology, Forensic Psychology, Occupational Psychology, Psychological Services in Social Settings, Services by Teachers of Psychology and other psychological services. The full code of conduct for psychologists is also included in the *Directory*. The BPS also produce a register of Chartered Psychologists which lists 7,800 Chartered Psychologists, including those who have chosen not to appear in the *Directory*.

Careers and counselling services

Chamber of Commerce

There are a total of 200 Chambers of Commerce in the UK providing services to business employers. Some of them are funded by the government and others are independent. The source of income would come from the members' subscription and the sales of their publications (e.g. magazines and journals). Most of them are non-profit-making agencies, but those that are government funded target surplus profit. They are separate bodies and have a clear policy and organisational structure. Some of them have links with TECs and LECs. Their services usually include the following: (i) the networking opportunities for business employers; (ii) the provision of up-to-date information about business legislation and business news; (iii) the publication of magazines and journals; (iv) the provision of relevant training, helplines and databases.

Guidance Enterprises Group

Guidance House, York Road, Thirsk YO7 3BT. Tel.: 01845 526 699.

Lifetime Careers Ltd.

Mexborough Business Centre, College Road, Mexborough, South Yorkshire S64 9JP. Tel.: 01709 572 413.

Sheffield Career Guidance Services (Careers Service for Adults)

42 Union Street, Sheffield S1 2JP. Tel.: 0114 201 2770. Fax: 0114 249 3164.

Other relevant groups

Advisory Centre for Education

18 Victoria Park Square, London E2 9PB. Tel.: 0207 354 8321. OR 1b Aberdeen Studios, 22–24 Highbury Grove, London N5 2EA. Helpline: 0207 354 8321.

It offers advice to parents as to where they stand legally. In particular, their respective roles and the powers of the headteacher, school governors, Local Education Authority (LEA) and central government.

ADHD Family Support Group UK

c/o Director, 1A High Street, Dilton Marsh, Westbury, Wiltshire BA13 4DL. Tel.: 01373 826 045. Fax: 01373 825 158.

British Association for Counselling

1 Regent Place, Rugby CV21 2PJ. Tel.: 01788 578 328.

British Association of Behavioural Optometrists (BADO)

72 High Street, Billericay, Essex CM12 9BS. Tel.: 01227 624 916.

Centre for Accessible Environments

Nutmeg House, 60 Gainsford Street, London SE1 2NY. Tel.: 0207 357 8182. Fax.: 0207 357 8183.
Website:http://www.cae.org.uk

Communication Aids for Language and Learning

Faculty of Education, University of Edinburgh, Paterson's Land, Holyrood Road, Edinburgh EH8 8AQ. Tel.: 0131 651 6236. Fax: 0131 651 6234.
E-mail: CALL.Centre@ed.ac.uk

The Call Centre provides services and carries out research and development projects, working with those involved in meeting the needs of people who require augmentative communications and/or specialised computer technology.

Council for the Registration of Schools Teaching Dyslexic Pupils (CReSTeD)

Greygarth, Littleworth, Winchcombe, Cheltenham GL54 5BT.

CReSTeD is a registered charity which aims to offer guidance and information to parents who are looking for a suitable school for their dyslexic child.

Educational Kinesiology–BrainGym®

Kay McCarroll, Executive International Faculty, Europe Faculty Representative, Vice-Chair US Board, London NW4. Tel.: 0208 202 9747; and David Hubbard, International and UK Faculty, Stroud, Glos. Tel.: 01453 759444.

Teach the BrainGym courses and other professional courses and offer individual consultations.

Independent Panel for Special Education Advice (IPSEA)

4 Ancient House Mews, Woodbridge, Suffolk IP12 1DH. Tel./Fax: 01394 380 518.

IPSEA guides parents through assessment and tribunal procedures and offers advice and help with understanding reports. It will represent parents at special educational needs tribunals.

Multi Sensory Learning Ltd (MSL)

Earlstrees Court, Earlstrees Road, Corby, Northants NN17 4AX. Tel.: 01536 399 003. Fax: 01536 399 012.
E-mail: FirstBest9@aol.com

Parents in Partnership

Top Portakabin, Clare House, St George's Hospital, Blackshaw Road, London SW17 0QT. Tel.: 0208 767 3211.

The Group provides advice on all kinds of special needs.

Scottish Council for Educational Technology (SCET)

74 Victoria Crescent Road, Glasgow G12 9JN. Tel.: 0141 337 5051.

SCET provides general information on aspects of information and communication technology.

Scottish Equal Awareness Trainers in Dyslexia (SEATED)

Old Mill Studios, 187 Old Rutherglen Road, Glasgow G5 0RE. Tel.: 0141 429 2535

Scottish Sensory Centre

Faculty of Education, University of Edinburgh, Holyrood Road, Edinburgh EH8 8AQ.

The centre provides advice, training courses and publications on all aspects of sensory impairments and communication difficulties.

Computing support

British Computer Society Disability Group

Room 216, EASAMS Ltd, West Hanningfield Road, Great Baddow, Chelmsford CM2 8HN. Tel.: 01245 242 950. Fax: 01245 478 317. Website: http://www.bcs.org.uk

This is a membership organisation. It aims to provide information, support and technological assistance to adults with disabilities. It has a quarterly journal, *Ability*, which provides relevant technological information for students with disabilities in higher education.

Computability Centre

PO Box 94, Warwick CV34 5WS. Tel.: 01926 312 847 or 0800 269 545. Fax: 01926 311 345.

Computer Centre for People with Disabilities

University of Westminster, 72 Great Portland Street, London W1N 5AL. Tel.: 0207 911 5000. Fax: 0207 911 5162. Website: http://www.wmin.ac.uk/ccpd/

The Centre is an access centre which provides technological assistance to disabled undergraduates, employed and unemployed adults according to their needs.

Computer Information and Advice Service

98 London Road, Reading RG1 5AU. Tel.: 0118 966 2677. E-mail.: admin@bda-dyslexia

The Service has a good source of information on software and computers suitable for specific learning difficulty individuals of all ages.

Dyslexia Archive

HENSA Computing Laboratory, University of Kent, Canterbury, Kent CT2 7NF. Tel.: 01227 823 784. Fax: 01227 762 811. Website: http://www.hensa.ac.uk/dyslexia.html

Dyslexia Computing Resource Centre

Department of Psychology, University of Hull, Hull HU6 7RX. Tel.: 0148 234 6311.
Website: http://www.hull.ac.uk/psychology/psy.htm

The Centre is affiliated to the BDA. It provides computer information and up-dated guides to software suitable for dyslexic learners, and advice to dyslexic people. The service is free to local dyslexia associations and open to others by subscription. Computer software is available for viewing by arrangements made in advance.

Higher Education National Software Archives (HENSA)

University of Kent, Canterbury, Kent CT2 7NF. Tel.: 01227 823 784.
Fax: 01227762811.
E-mail: dyslexia-admin@unix.hensa.ac.uk
Website: http://www.hensa.ac.uk

Up-to-date materials covering all aspects of dyslexia are stored electronically and can be accessed freely through the internet.

iAnsyst Ltd

The White House, 72 Fen Road, Cambridge CB4 1UN. Tel.: 01223 420 101. Fax: 01223 426 644.
E-mail: sales@dyslexic.com

Lorien Systems

Enkalon Business Centre, 25 Randalstown Road, Antrim BT41 4LJ, Northern Ireland. Tel.: + 44 1849 428 105. Fax. +44 1849 428 574.
E-mail: info@texthelp.com

Markco Publishing

Markco Publishing, Mark College, Mark, Highbridge, Somerset, TA4 9NP.

CD–ROM of 'What to do when you can't learn the times tables' – designed for older and adult learners.

National Council for Educational Technology (NCET)

Milburn Hill Road, Science Park, Coventry CV4 7JJ. Tel.: 01203 416
994. Fax: 01203 411 418.
E-mail: enquiry_desk@ncet.org.uk

The NCET provides information on computers and software; produces
some specialist publications relating to Specific Learning Difficulties.

Pencil Visualising Dyslexia

Mathew Wood, Pencil, 7 Alwyne Road, London N1 2HH.

Pack comprising 14 full colour laminated images to promote
discussion and open up debate on dyslexia.

REM

Great Western House, Langport, Somerset TA10 9YU. Tel.: 01458 253
636. Fax: 01458 253 646.
E-mail.: info@r-e-m.co.uk.

A leading supplier of educational software for the field of special needs.

Rickitt Educational Media Software Directory

Ilton, Ilminster, Somerset TA19 9HS.

Computer software can be purchased.

Special Needs Computing

PO Box 42, St Helens WA10 3BF. Tel./Fax: 01744 24 608.
E-mail.: jeff@box42.com

White Space Ltd

41 Mall Road, London W6 9DG. Tel./Fax: 0208 748 5927.

Provides computer programs for word recognition, spelling, and basic
numeracy to help those with specific learning difficulties.

Xavier Educational Software Ltd

Psychology Department, University College of Wales, Bangor, Gwynedd LL57 2DG. Tel.: 01248 382 616. Fax: 01248 382 599.
E-mail.: xavier@bangor.ac.uk
Website: http:/www.xavier.bangor.ac.uk

Useful contacts (USA)

Equal Employment Opportunity Commission (EEOC)

1801 L Street, NW, Washington DC 20507. Tel.: ++(800) 669–3362.

The EEOC can provide posters, resource information and factsheets on equal opportunities and learning disabilities.

Institute for the Study of Adult Literacy

204 Calder Way, Suite 209, University Park, PA 16801. Tel.: ++(814) 863–3777.

The Institute undertakes research activities in special needs, resources and work-related literacy.

Job Accommodation Network (JAN)

West Virginia University, 809 Allen Hall, PO Box 6123, Morgantown WV 26506. Tel.: ++(800) 526–7234.

JAN provides information to employers on individualised accommodation for people with disabilities.

Learning Disabilities Association of America, Inc. (LDA)

4156 Library Road, Pittsburgh, Pennsylvania 15234. Tel.: ++(412) 341–1515. Fax: ++(412) 344–0224.

Non-profit-making voluntary organisation, runs conferences and provides information for professionals, parents and adults with disabilities.

Learning Disabilities Research and Training Center

The University of Georgia, 534 Aderhold Hall, Athens, Georgia 30602. Tel.: ++(706) 542–1300. Fax: ++(706) 542–4532.

The Center undertakes research and training programmes on assessment, workplace issues and empowering adults with disabilities.

President's Committee on Employment of People with Disabilities

1331 F Street NW, Washington DC 20036. Tel.: ++(202) 376–6200; ++(202) 376–6205. Fax: ++(202) 376–6859.

An independent federal agency which co-ordinates and promotes disabilities in employment. The committee provides information, training to businesses, service providers and individuals with disabilities.

The National Adult Literacy and Learning Disabilities Center

Academy for Education Development, 1875 Connecticut Avenue, NW Suite, 800, Washington DC 20009–1202. Tel.: ++(202) 884–8185; ++(800) 953–2553. Fax: ++(202) 884–8422.

The Center provides a national information exchange on learning disabilities, includes literacy and workplace aspects.

United Way of America

701 North Fairfax Street, Alexandria, VA 22314–2045. Tel.: ++(703) 683–7100.

Supports activities relating to basic literacy, workplace literacy programmes and job training.

Other resources

ABLEC – Keyright

ABLEC Computec Ltd, South Devon House, Newton Abbot, Devon TQ12 2BP. Tel.: 0626 332233. Fax: 0626 331464.

System for developing keyboard skills.

AVP

The Big Black Catalogue, School Hill Centre, Chepstow, Gwent NP6 5PH.

Computer software is available and can be purchased.

Better Books

3 Paganel Drive, Dudley, DY1 4AZ. Tel.: 01384 253276. Fax: 01384 253285

Crossbow Educational

Crossbow Educational, 1 Lichfield Drive, Great Haywood, Stafford, ST18 0SX.

Dyslexia Educational Resources

Broadway Studios, 28 Tooting High Street, London SW17 0RG. Tel.: 01181 682 4522 or 01181 672 4465. Fax: 01181 767 3247.

Hodder and Stoughton Educational Tests and Assessment

Bookpoint Ltd, Hodder and Stoughton Educational, 78 Milton Park, Abingdon, Oxon OX14 4TD.

Full catalogue of educational tests.

Learning Development Aids (LDA)

Duke Street, Wisbech, Cambridgeshire PE13 2AE. Tel.: 01945 463 441.

LDA has a range of multi-sensory teaching materials.

National Adult Literacy and Learning Disabilities Centre

Website: http://novel.nifl.gov/nalld/workplac.htm

Volume 2, No. 1, Spring 1995 contains articles on Workplace Literacy such as 'Making Reading Work for Work' (Esther Minskoff) and 'Tips for Workplace Success for the Adult Learner' (Nancie Payne) and 'Brenda's Tips on Workplace Literacy' (Brenda Sweigart-Guist). There is also a section on Selected Readings.

Next Generation Publisher

17 Medway Close, Taunton, Somerset TA1 2NS. Tel.: 01823 289 559.

NFER–NELSON

Darville House, 2 Oxford Road East, Windsor, Berks SL4 1DF. Tel.: 01753 858 961. Fax: 01753 856 830. E-mail: edu&hsc@nfer-nelson.co.uk Website: http://www.nfer-nelson.co.uk

Psychological Corporation

24–28 Oval Road, London NW1 1YA. Tel.: 0207 424 4456. Fax: 0207 424 4515.
E-mail: cservice@harcourtbrace.com

Read and Write Educational Supplies

Mount Pleasant, Mill Road, Aldington, Ashford, Kent TN25 7AJ. Tel./Fax: 01233 720 618.

Supplies specialised books, games and teaching aids for dyslexic pupils, their teachers and parents.

SEN Marketing

618 Leeds Road, Outwood, Wakefield WF1 2LT. Tel./Fax: 01924 871 697.
E-mail: SEN.Marketing@ukonline.co.uk

John Wiley & Sons Ltd

1 Oldlands Way, Bognor Regis, West Sussex PO22 9SA. Tel.: 0800
243407 (UK) and +44 1243 843294 (overseas). Fax: 01243 843 296
(UK) and +44 1243 843 296 (overseas).
E-mail: cs-books@wiley.co.uk

Has a full catalogue of books and periodicals with specialisms in
psychology and special needs. Also publishes the periodical *Dyslexia*:
An International Journal of Research and Practice (four issues per
year). This journal is also online.
Website: www.interscience.wiley.com

Whurr Publishers Ltd

19b Compton Terrace, London N1 2UN. Tel.: 0207 359 5979. Fax:
0207 226 5290.
E-mail: info@whurr.co.uk

Useful references

- *Adult Dyslexia: Assessment, Counselling and Training* (1994), by
  David McLaughlin, Gary Fitzgibbon and Vivienne Young. Whurr
  Publications.
- *Adult Dyslexia for Employment, Practice and Training (ADEPT) –
  A report on best practice in dyslexia assessment, support and
  training in the Employment Service* (1999), by Gavin Reid and Jane
  Kirk (project leaders) and Dianne Hui and Kirstine Mullin (research
  associates), University of Edinburgh. Report, funded by the
  Employment Service, comments on UK-wide practices in
  assessment and support and makes recommendations within the
  scope of the remit of the Employment Service.

- *Adult Dyslexia Screening Feasibility Study* (1992). Report by the Dept of Psychology, University of Sheffield and the Dyslexia Unit, Bangor. Report available from DfEE, Sheffield.
- *Adult Students and Dyslexia: A Resource book for adult students and staff* (1995), by Vicki Goodwin and Bonita Thomson. Open University.
- *A Guide for Student Nurses and Midwives with Dyslexia* (1996), by David Wright. School of Nursing and Midwifery, University of Sheffield.
- Alm, J. (1996/97) The Dyslexia Project at the Employability Institute of Uppsala, Sweden. Published by the Swedish Market Labour Board AMS Förlagsservice, Box 6, 646 21, Gnesta. Fax: ++0158–100 70. The report describes an integrated diagnostic procedure resulting from over 200 investigations in connection with the project.
- *Arranging a Dyslexia Assessment: A Guide for Adults*, by Sylvia Moody. A paper giving advice on arranging and appraising a psychological assessment for dyslexia. Dyslexia Assessment Service 0207 272 6429.
- *Report on Pilot Survey of Irish Employers in Relation to Knowledge of, and Attitude Towards, Specific Learning Disabilities (Dyslexia)* (1998). Association for Children and Adults with Learning Disabilities (ACLD). Solutions Network funded by the European Commission.
- *Basic Skills Development in Lincolnshire*, published by Lincolnshire TEC and De Montford University, The Gateway, Leicester LE1 9BH. This 31-page booklet charts the progress of Lincolnshire's Basic Skills Policy, mapping the strategies employed during its development and evaluating the outcomes.
- *Basic Skills Quality Mark for Post 16 Programmes* (1999). Available from BSA Commonwealth House, 1–19 New Oxford Street, London WC1A 1NU. Tel.: 0207 405 4017. Fax: 0207 440 6626. Website: www.basic-skills.co.uk
- *Dyslexia: An Unwrapped Gift*. Video which takes a sideways look at dyslexia and asks the question could dyslexia be a gift rather than a disability? Hertfordshire Dyslexia Arts Group (Chris Smart, Project Co-ordinator). Tel.: 01432 341801.

- *Dyslexia Contact – Official magazine of the British Dyslexia Association*. Usually contains a section on Adult Dyslexia and provides news of events in local associations.
- *Dyslexia: A Practitioner's Handbook* (1998), by Gavin Reid, includes a chapter on adult dyslexia and resources for assessment and support.
- *Dyslexia and the Bilingual Learner. Assessing and Teaching Adults and Young People who Speak English as an Additional Language* (1997), by Helen Sunderland, Cynthia Klein, Rosemary Savinson and Tracy Partridge. Published by The London Language and Literacy Unit.
- *Dyslexia and Stress* (1995), by T. Miles and V. Varma. Whurr Publications.
- *Dyslexia – Genius, Criminals and Children.* 20/20 television for Channel 4 (UK), 25 July 1999.
- *Dyslexia: Good Practice Guide (SOLOTEC)* (1998), produced by Cynthia Klein and Helen Sunderland, London Language and Literacy Unit. This is a thorough guide to help training providers identify and support trainees with dyslexia.
- *Dyslexia in Adults – Taking Charge of your Life* (1997), by Kathleen Nosek. Taylor Publishing Company, 1550 West Mockingbird Lane, Dallas, Texas 75235.
- *Dyslexia in Higher Education: Policy, Provision and Practice* (1999). Report of the National Working Party on Dyslexia in Higher Education. This report, funded by the Higher Education Funding Councils of England and Scotland, provides information and recommendations on assessing and supporting students in Higher Education. Published by Dept of Psychology, University of Hull, Hull HU6 7RX. E-mail: dyslexia@hull.ac.uk
- *Dyslexia: Signposts to Success – A Guide for Dyslexic Adults* (1995), compiled by Jo Matty. Available from British Dyslexia Association. This publication is also on tape.
- *Escape from Dyslexia* (1999). How computer-aided programmes are liberating Pentonville prisoners: *Times Educational Supplement*, 19 February 1999.
- *Guidelines for Testing People with Disabilities* (1996). Saville and Holdsworth Ltd, Occupational Psychologists, 3 AC Court, High Street, Thames Ditton, Surrey KT7 0SR.

- *In the Mind's Eye: Visual Thinkers, Gifted People with Learning Difficulties, Computer Images, and the Ironies of Creativity* (1998), by Tom West. This is a landmark book in creativity and visual processing in relation to dyslexic adults. Published by Prometheus Books, 59 John Glenn Drive, New York 14228–2197.
- *Into Teaching – Positive Experiences of Disabled People* (1998), published by Skill: National Bureau for Students with Disabilities, 336 Brixton Road, London SW9 7AA. Contains useful information about choosing a route into teaching, funding courses and getting a job.
- *Learning Disabilities and Employment*, edited by Paul J. Gerber and Dale S. Brown, and published by Pro-Ed 8700 Shoal Creek Boulevard, Austin, Texas 78757-6897, USA. This books provides a comprehensive study of employment issues for people with learning disabilities, including training, workplace issues and experiences.
- *Improving Literacy and Numeracy, A Fresh Start* (1999), by C. Moser. DfEE.
- *Multilingualism, Literacy and Dyslexia: A Challenge for Educators* (2000), edited by Lindsay Peer and Gavin Reid and published by David Fulton Publishers, Ormond House, 26–27 Boswell Street, London, WC1N 3JD, Freecall: 0500 618052.
  E-mail: orders@fultonbooks.co.uk
- *New Thinking for the New Millennium* (1999), by Edward De Bono, Viking Books.
- *Nottingham Dyslexia Association Annual Report* (1999), 5 St Bartholomew's Road, St Ann's Nottingham NG3 3EH. Tel.: 0115 958 8400. Contains information on services and general advice on dyslexia.
- *Options 11: Improving Competency at Work.* Project developed by Park Lane College, Park Lane, Leeds LS3 1AA.
  E-mail: international@mail.parklanecoll.ac.uk
- *Influences on Adult Basic Skills* (1998), by S. Parsons and J. Brynner. Published by Basic Skills Agency, London.
- *Psychological Assessment of Dyslexia* (1997), by Martin Turner. Whurr Publications.
- *Stava Ratt (Spell it Right)*. Specially developed in Sweden specifically for dyslexic people. Developed by Bodil Andersson and Anders Holtsberg and based on research from the University of Gothenberg on spelling errors made by adult dyslexics attending dyslexia courses at AmuGruppen Hadar in Malmo, Sweden.

- *The Dyslexia Handbook*, published annually by the BDA, contains information and articles on adult dyslexia.
- *The Journal of the Application of Occupational Psychology to Employment and Disability*. Journal published by the Employment Service, contains articles on all aspects of employment and disability.
- *The Reality of Dyslexia* (1993), by John Osmond. Cassell Educational.
- *Toe by Toe*, by Keda Cowling. This programme has been beneficial for both children and adults, and has been used successfully in the army and in prisons.

Concluding remarks

This chapter, by providing a fairly extensive range of resources and addresses of support providers for adults with dyslexia, has illustrated how difficult and perhaps how confusing it can be for dyslexic adults to find their way around the available support to get the type of help they need at any particular time. On the positive side, however, it is encouraging that a range of organisations, both voluntary and government sponsored, are in a position to offer such support. This underlines the real concerns that many have for adults with dyslexia. With effective dissemination of useful information, together with training and education of those in a position to help dyslexic adults, the bleak scenario described by some barriers and/or ignorance can be converted to one of fulfilment and success. We hope that this book helps all adults with dyslexia to realise that success.

Appendix 1: Tests for Dyslexia

The following presents a list of standardised instruments used as tests for dyslexia.

Test name	**Basic Skills Test**
Publication date	1988
Supplier and publisher	NFER–NELSON
Test structure	Aims to measure functional literacy skills
Age range (years)	Age 16 to adult
Administrative time	30 minutes

Test name	**British Ability Scales (BAS II) Reading and Spelling Scales**
Publication date	1996
Supplier and publisher	NFER–NELSON
Test structure	Aims to test single oral word reading and spelling
Age range (years)	Age 5–18 (upper limit)
Administrative time	10 minutes per sub-test

Test name	**British Spelling Tests (BST)**
Publication date	1998
Supplier and publisher	NFER–NELSON
Test structure	Contains 5 levels. Aim to assess different areas of spelling ability. Provides screening and monitoring purposes
Age range (years)	Age 5 to adult
Administrative time	Untimed, usually takes 30–40 minutes

Test name	**Spadafore Diagnostic Reading Test**
Publication date	1983
Supplier and publisher	Academic Therapy Publications, USA
Test structure	Tests of single word oral reading, prose reading, reading and listening comprehension.
Age range (years)	School to adult
Administrative time	10 minutes per sub-test

Test name	**Wide Range Achievement Test (WRAT 3)**
Publication date	1993
Supplier and publisher	UK Supplier: Psychological Corporation Delaware
	US Supplier: Jastak Associates
Test structure	Tests of single word oral reading, spelling (and Maths)
Age range (years)	Age 5–75
Administrative time	10 minutes (reading), 10 minutes (spelling)

Test name	**Woodcock Reading Mastery Tests**
Publication date	1987
Supplier and publisher	UK Supplier: Dyslexia Institute Minnesota
	US Supplier: American Guidance Service
Test structure	Tests of non-word reading and single oral word reading with three tests of single word comprehension and one test of passage comprehension
Age range (years)	Age 5–75
Administrative time	30 minutes

Test name	**Wordchains (Research Edn)**
Publication date	1999
Supplier and publisher	NFER–NELSON
Test structure	Aims to screen word reading skills with pupils who have specific learning difficulties. Test on letters and words
Age range (years)	Age 7 to adult
Administrative time	Timed. 90 seconds for Letterchains and 3 minutes for Wordchains

Test name	**Mill Hill Vocabulary Scale (Senior Form)**
Publication date	1943/1994
Supplier and publisher	NFER–NELSON
Test structure	Designed to complement SPM (1958/1979), a test of word definitions and synonyms
Age range (years)	Suitable for adults

Test name	**Raven's Progressive Matrices and Vocabulary Scales**
Publication date	1998
Supplier and publisher	NFER–NELSON
Test structure	Aims to measure both verbal and non-verbal general ability. There are 3 levels (easy, average and difficult)
Age range (years)	Age 5 to adult
Administrative time	Timed and untimed, depending on which levels are being used

Test name	**Bangor Dyslexia Test**
Publication date	1982/1997
Supplier and publisher	LDA
Test structure	10 sub-tests covering the positive signs of dyslexia
Age range (years)	Age 7–18
Administrative time	40 minutes

Test name	**British Ability Scales (2nd Edn) (BAS II)**
Publication date	1996
Supplier and publisher	NFER–NELSON-R
Test structure	A comprehensive set of cognitive and attainment tests. Produces various IQ measures
Age range (years)	Age up to 17

Test name	**Dyslexia Adult Screening Test (DAST)**
Publication date	1998
Supplier and publisher	Psychological Corporation
Test structure	11 sub-tests (1 minute reading, two-minute spelling, verbal and semantic fluency).
Age range (years)	Useful for adult screening purposes
Administrative time	30 minutes

Test name	**QuickScan and StudyScan**
Publication date	1997
Supplier and publisher	PICO Educational Systems Ltd, 11 Steep Hill, London SW16 1UL
Test structure	Computerised assessment
Age range (years)	Adult
Administrative time	20 minutes for QuickScan screening test

Test name	**Wechsler Memory Scale (3rd Edn)**
Publication date	1999
Supplier and publisher	Psychological Corporation
Test structure	Memory test co-normed with the WAIS-III

Test name	**Wechsler Adult Intelligence Test (Revised)**
Publication date	1981
Supplier and publisher	Psychological Corporation
Test structure	An intelligence assessment instrument comprising 11 sub-tests of verbal and non-verbal (performance) IQ
Age range (years)	Widely used for adults (age 16+) in the world
Administrative time	One hour approximately

Test name	**Wechsler Adult Intelligence Scale (WAIS-III)**
Publication date	1999
Supplier and publisher	Psychological Corporation
Test structure	Intelligence test providing a cognitive profile consisting of 14 sub-tests
Age range (years)	Adults
Administrative time	One hour approximately

Appendix 2: Sample Dyslexia Training Evaluation Form

- **How well organised was the session?**

not very well
organised

very well
organised

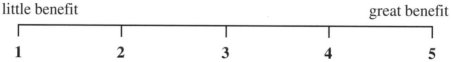

1   2   3   4   5

- **How effective was the session leader in dealing with questions/ queries?**

not effective

very effective

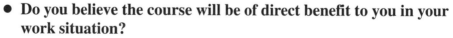

1   2   3   4   5

- **Do you believe the course will be of direct benefit to you in your work situation?**

little benefit

great benefit

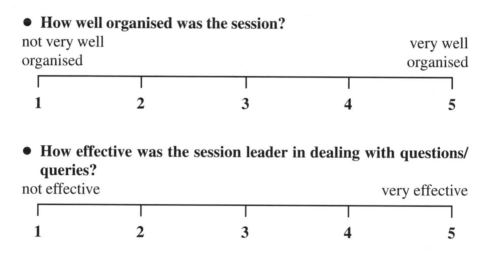

1   2   3   4   5

- **How useful was the course?**

not very useful

very useful

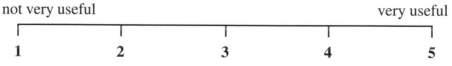

1   2   3   4   5

Any other comments or suggestions for improving the course.

Thank you.

Glossary of acronyms and abbreviations

ABCC	Association of British Chambers of Commerce.
ABE	Adult Basic Education.
AEP	Association of Educational Psychologists.
ACAS	Advisory, Conciliation and Arbitration Service.
ACDET	Advisory Committee for Disabled People in Employment.
ACLD	Association for Children and Adults with Learning Difficulties.
ADA	Americans with Disabilities Act, 1990.
ADDISS	Attention Deficit Disorder Information Services and Support.
ADEPT	Adult Dyslexia for Employment in Practice and Training, an Employment Service project based in the Faculty of Education, University of Edinburgh.
ADHD	Attention Deficit Hyperactivity Disorder.
ADO	Adult Dyslexia Organisation.
ADSDC	Adult Dyslexia and Skills Development Centre
AEB	Associated Examining Board.
AEP	Association of Educational Psychologists.
AIT	Auditory Integration Training.
ALBSU	Adult Literacy and Basic Skills Unit.
ARC	Association for Residential Care.
ASDAN	Award Scheme Development and Accreditation Network.
ASE	A division of NFER-NELSON. ASE provides a range of information on occupational assessments and their training courses.

ATC	Accredited Training Centre.
BADO	British Association of Behavioural Optometrists.
BAS II	British Ability Scales (2nd Edn), 1996.
BDA	British Dyslexia Association.
BMA	British Medical Association.
BPS	British Psychological Society.
BPVS	British Picture Vocabulary Scale, 1982.
BPVS II	British Picture Vocabulary Scale (2nd Edn), 1982.
BST	British Spelling Tests, 1998.
BST	Basic Skills Tests.
BST II	British Ability Scales (2nd Edn), 1996.
CAE	Centre for Accessible Environments.
CAT II	Cognitive Abilities Test, 1986.
CCTE	Chamber of Commerce, Training and Enterprise.
CDL	Career Development Loan.
CPAB	Computer Programmer Aptitude Battery.
CRE	Commission for Racial Equality.
CReSTeD	Council for the Registration of Schools Teaching Dyslexic Pupils.
CSDC	Curriculum and Staff Development Centre.
DARC	Dyslexia Advice and Resource Centre Ltd.
DAST	Dyslexia Adult Screening Test, 1998.
DCD	Developmental Co-ordination Disorder, also known as dyspraxia. It can overlap with dyslexia.
DCP	Division of Clinical Psychology of the BPS.
DDA	Disability Discrimination Act 1995.
DEA	Disability Employment Adviser, ES.
DERA	Defence Evaluation and Research Agency.
DEST	Dyslexia Early Screening Test, 1998.
DfEE	Department for Education and Employment.
DI	Dyslexia Institute.
DILP	Dyslexia Institute Literacy Programme.
DLA	Disability Living Allowance.
DOP	Division of Occupational Psychology of the BPS.
DRC	Disability Rights Commission.
DRTF	Disability Rights Task Force.
DS	Disability Services.
DSA	Disabled Students' Allowances.
DSS	Department of Social Security.

DST	Dyslexia Screening Test, 1998.
DST	Disability Services Team, DS.
DWA	Disability Working Allowance.
EDA	European Dyslexia Association.
EO	Equal Opportunities.
EOC	Equal Opportunities Commission.
EQ	Equal Opportunities.
ES	The Employment Service.
FE	Further Education.
FEATS	Future Education and Training.
FEFC	Further Education Funding Council.
FEU	Further Education Unit.
GNVQ(s)	General National Vocational Qualification(s).
GRT II	NFER–NELSON Group Reading Test 6–14 (2nd Edn), 1997.
GSVQ(s)	General Scottish Vocational Qualification(s).
HADC	Helen Arkell Dyslexia Centre.
HEFCE	Higher Education Funding Council for England.
HENSA	Higher Education National Software Archives.
HE	Higher Education.
HEIs	Higher Educational Institutes.
HKD	Hyperkinetic Disorder.
HMI	Her Majesty's Inspectorate.
IB	Incapacity Benefit.
IDA	International Dyslexia Association.
IE	International Enrichment Programme, developed by Reuven Feuerstein who proposed systematic procedures in teaching thinking skills.
IPSEA	Independent Panel for Special Education Advice.
IQ	Intelligence Quotient.
INSET	In-Service Training.
IT	Information Technology.
JSA	Job Seeker Allowance.
KAIT	Kaufman Adolescent and Adult Intelligence Test, 1993.
LAs	Local Authorities.
LAWTEC	Lancashire Area West TEC.
LBM	Local business managers.
LCCI	London Chamber of Commerce and Industry Training Board.

LDA	Learning Development Aids.
LDs	Learning Disabilities.
LEAs	Local Educational Authorities.
LEAD	Linking Education and Disability.
LECs	Local Enterprise Councils (Scotland). They offer a wide range of information, advice and training to help meet the needs of small businesses.
LEEL	Lothian and Edinburgh Enterprise Ltd.
LGMB	Local Government Management Board.
LOPs	Local Occupational Psychologists.
LRA	Labour Relations Agency.
LTM	Long-Term Memory.
MOST	Modern Occupational Skills Tests.
MSL	Multi-Sensory Learning.
NACEPD	National Committee for the Employment of People with Disabilities.
NARE	National Association of Remedial Education.
NART	National/New Adult Reading Test, 1982.
NCC	National Curriculum Council.
NCET	National Council for Educational Technology.
NCVQ(s)	National Council for Vocational Qualification(s).
NDP	National Development Project.
NDPB	Non-Departmental Public Body.
NI	National Insurance.
NJCLD	National Joint Committee on Learning Disabilities in the USA.
NLTS	National Longitudinal Transition Study (1987–1990), conducted by the Stanford Research Institute International in the USA.
NOCN	National Open College Network.
NVQs	National Vocational Qualifications in England and Wales.
OCR	Oxford Cambridge and RSA Examinations (formerly RSA Examinations).
OPs	Occupational Psychologists.
OT	Occupational Therapist.
PAL	Predictive Writing Aids.
PATOSS	Professional Association of Teachers of Students with Specific Learning Difficulties.
PhAB	Phonological Assessment Battery, 1998.

PWD   People With Disabilities.
QA   Quality Assurance.
RADAR   The Royal Association for Disability and Rehabilitation
            provides information and advice on many of the areas
            that affect disabled people on a daily basis, including
            employment, transport, social security and social
            services. It also campaigns on behalf of disabled
            people.
RSA   Royal Society of Arts, now renamed as OCR.
SCET   Scottish Council for Educational Technology.
SDF   Scottish Dyslexia Forum.
SCOTVEC   Scottish Vocational Educational Council.
SDA   Severe Disablement Allowance.
SDD   Specific Developmental Dyslexia.
SEAC   School Examinations and Assessment Council.
SENs   Special Education Needs.
SENCOs   Special Education Needs Co-Ordinators.
SET   Support Employment and Training.
SHAPE   Self Help Awareness Programme for Employment. A
            flexible and realistic part time course provided by
            selected organisations by the ES, with professional
            skills and expertise to meet individual needs. The
            programme is usually provided locally.
SHEFC   Scottish Higher Education Funding Council.
SKILL   The National Bureau for Students with Disabilities
            provides an information service for disabled graduates.
            It works with universities, employers, other voluntary
            organisations and publishers to create and promote
            opportunities for graduates.
SOEID   Scottish Office Education and Industry Department.
SpLD   Specific Learning Difficulties.
SPM   Standard Progressive Matrices (1958/1979).
STM   Short-Term Memory.
SVQ   Scottish Vocational Qualification.
TAP   Training Access Points, available on database in some
            Jobcentres, colleges and public libraries in Edinburgh
            and Lothian areas.

TECs	Training and Enterprise Councils (England and Wales). They offer a wide range of information, advice and training to help meet the needs of small businesses.
UKRA	United Kingdom Reading Association.
WAIS-R	Wechsler Adult Intelligence Test (Revised), 1981.
WAIS-III	Wechsler Adult Intelligence Test (3rd Edn).
WMS	Wechsler Memory Scales.
WRAT-3	Wide Range Achievement Test, 1993.

Glossary of terms

Access to Work   A programme provided by DS Division within ES which sets out to provide help for people with disabilities to secure/retain employment through practical support such as special aids and equipment, adaptations to premises, support workers and other assistance in meeting personnel needs to work. It will also meet all the approved costs with Travel To Work or Communicator Support at Interview. Details can be discussed with DEA.

Acquired dyslexia   A form of dyslexia is characterised by problems with literacy skills resulting from some form of neurological damage.

Benefit Agency   Located in Jobcentres, it aims to advise on jobseeker benefits (e.g. JSA).

Career Services   Often seen to be linked with the TECs and LECs, they are independent of them, and are often run by private companies contracted by DfEE.

DDA   Disability Discrimination Act 1995. The employment right gives disabled people the right not to be discriminated against in any aspect of employment. This includes: interview arrangements; recruitment; terms and conditions; workplace arrangements; training; promotion; and dismissal. From 2 December 1996, the Act gave disabled people new rights in a number of areas including employment, access to goods and services. Under the Act it is unlawful for employers of 20 or more people to treat a disabled person less favourably than anyone else for a reason connected to their disability, unless there is a good reason. As for HEIs, disability statements illustrating commitment, provisions and future developments for students with disabilities is required.

DEAs   Disability Employment Advisers aim to help and give advice to individuals with severe or complex disabilities on countering barriers to seeking, obtaining or retaining employment. They are mainly based in Jobcentres with administrative support from the PACT teams (supervised by the PACT Managers) or the regional business centre and draw on the professional expertise of OPs. They are under the DS Division (supervised by the DS Managers) and there are over 1,000 trained DEAs.

Developmental dyspraxia   A difficulty with the organisation of movement, perception and co-ordination.

Disability Benefits   A variety of benefits and allowances are available dependent upon the economic status and circumstances of the disabled applicant. Disability benefits are dealt with via the Benefit Agency which is located within the Jobcentre. The Agency aims to advise on jobseeker benefits, for example, JSA, IB, DWA and other benefits. Further information can also be obtained from the regional offices of DSS. The basis of the law concerning the benefits for disabled people is contained within the Social Security Contributions and Benefits Act 1992, the Social Security Administration Act 1992 and the Social Security Act 1992.

Disability Symbol   A way for employers to show their positive attitude towards employing people with disabilities.

Disability Working Allowance   Designed for disabled people who start work and are working for 16 hours or more a week, the amount depends upon net income and savings.

Dyslexia   Described as a syndrome for people with difficulty in one or more of reading, spelling and writing, but the condition is much broader. Some may have problems of auditory and/or visual perception, memory, sequencing and information processing. There are two forms of dyslexia: developmental dyslexia and acquired dyslexia.

Equal Opportunities Principles   Concern for the equality of opportunity across all of the ES' programmes and services regardless of the clients' colour, race, nationality or ethnic origin.

Employment Rehabilitation/Work Preparation   A specialist programme aimed at helping people with disabilities return to work. It is provided by selected local organisations by the ES on either a part-time or full-time basis ranging from a few days to a few weeks dependent upon individual needs. Details can be discussed with the DEA.

Gateway   Part of the New Deal Initiative which can last for up to 16 weeks, this provision aims to get young people into work and includes help with jobsearch, careers advice and guidance, preparation for, and submission to a range of options.

IB   Incapacity Benefits is a benefit for people who are unable to work because of an illness or disability. The beneficiary should be under the pension age (e.g. 65 for both men and women) and who have paid sufficient National Insurance (NI) contributions. The assessment of the application for IB will take account of the advice provided by a qualified doctor via the sick-notes and the results of continuous assessments over time (e.g. the 'own occupation' test and the 'all work' test). There are three different rates of IB and the amount given will depend on individual circumstances.

Job Introduction Scheme   Provides a financial contribution or grant towards the employers' costs for the first six weeks of employment where the employer of a disabled person has some doubts or reservations about whether the job is within their capabilities.

JSA   The Job Seekers Allowance has replaced Unemployment Benefit and Income Support for unemployed people. There are different types of allowances dependent upon the situations and needs of individuals. The basic JSA at present is £50.35 per week under the Job Seeker's Agreement which also sets out what will be done by the individuals to gain work.

LOPs Managers   Local Occupational Psychologists Managers, overall managers supervising the OPs in the region within the Local Occupational Psychologist Service under the Occupational Psychology Division of the ES.

MENCAP's Pathway Employment Service   An organisation set up to help people with learning difficulties and their employers to apply for grants to meet their employment costs.

National Disability Development Initiative   A £0.5 million budget was set aside for the DS to bid for with external organisations to run projects in developing a coherent and focused approach to the development of the ES' services to disabled jobseekers and their employers.

New Deals   A task initiated by the government in May 1997 and taken on by the ES. It aims to help unemployed people (18 to 24 year olds and 25+), lone parents, disabled people and other groups of people (partners, people over 50 and the communities which the government recently announced to provide additional help) in gaining or retaining full employment opportunities. Each New Deal client would work with a New Deal personal adviser throughout the advisory period to work out a suitable New Deal option for the client to prepare and put into action.

New Deals for 18 to 24 year olds   A task was implemented nationally in April 1998. It aims to help unemployed people (18 to 24 year olds) in gaining or retaining full employment opportunities. Each New Deal client would work with a New Deal personal adviser during the Gateway period to work out a suitable New Deal option for the client to prepare and put into action.

New Deals for 25+   Introduced at the end of June 1998 for those people who have been unemployed for two years or more. Early entry is available for those who are particularly disadvantaged in the labour market such as ex-offenders, people with literacy and numeracy problems, people with disabilities and so on. Help can be obtained through a New Deal personal adviser, a range of provision programmes, employer subsidy, full-time education and a follow through period of advice.

New Deals for Disabled People   A £195 million programme taken forward by the DSS, DfEE and ES (partnering some of the bids) aims to develop ways to help people on disability benefits to obtain or retain work. There are four strands: innovative schemes to find new ideas for helping disabled people obtain/regain/stay in work, a personal adviser service to help overcome problems to work, information about existing help available and to campaign to change attitudes of benefit recipients, employers and the public, research and evaluation to understand the client group and determine the effect of the initiative.

New Deal personal advisers   They help the New Deal clients to draw up New Deal action plans throughout the Gateway period (16 weeks).

New Deal Options   A range of options under which the New Deal clients can choose during the Gateway period. There are four options: a subsidised job with an employer, full time education and training, work with a voluntary sector organisation lasting for six months, work with the Environment Task Force lasting six months.

Local Occupational Psychology Service   A sub-division under the Occupational Psychology Division within the ES, works with disability services locally to enable people with disabilities to obtain/retain employment through effective assessment, work preparation and placing action.

OPs   Occupational Psychologists, working under the LOPs Managers in the region. Some of them also work within the PACT teams under DS. They specialise in work with individuals with a disability and offer specialist help and advice to people with disabilities to help them gain or retain employment.

OT   Occupational Therapist assessment tests on technical difficulties with handwriting or evidence of motor inco-ordination or perceptual problems.

Phonological difficulties   General difficulties in pronouncing a number of sounds and/or mispronunciation (place and manner of articulation). These may affect intelligibility and often lead to reading difficulties. There are three relevant terms. 'Phonetic' refers specifically to the acoustic characteristics of speech sounds, the production of these sounds by the vocal organs, and how we perceive them. 'Phonological' is broader and concerns the way how the sounds of speech are arranged. 'Phonic' is the written representation associating the phonetic characteristics of perceived sounds.

Psychometric tests   Test batteries used by the psychologists to measure mental attributes such as attitudes, abilities and intelligence.

Residential training for people with disabilities   A vocational training programme is provided towards employment for disabled individuals at one of four Residential Training Colleges. Training programmes are broad, flexible and most lead to NVQ(s).

SpLD   Special Learning Difficulties, an umbrella term used to describe the more general difficulties resulting from learning disorders (e.g. specific language, development co-ordination disorder, acquired memory, non-verbal learning, autism, dyslexia, etc.). Dyslexia is a sub-category of SpLDs.

Steering Group   A group aiming to monitor progress and efficiency of the ADEPT project and to ensure the focused scope and direction of the project by frequent review.

Supported Employment Programme   A programme designed to help severely disabled people into work through placement in a workshop, factory or, increasingly, within open employment with a host employer and at a pace most suit the individuals. A subsidy is given by the ES to cover the shortfall in productivity levels at the beginning of the programme.

Training for Work   An initiative which helps individuals update or gain new skills. Sponsored by the local government (TECs or LECs), it aims to provide either an in-house training or work placement for a period from 6 weeks up to 6 months dependent upon individual needs. Training for Work was replaced by Work Based Training for Adults in 1998–99.

References

Aaron, P.G. (1989) *Dyslexia and Hyperlexia*. Boston, MA: Kluwer.

Abramson, L.Y., Seligman, M.E.P. and Teasdale, J.D. (1978) Learned helplessness in humans; A critique and reformulation. *Journal of Abnormal Psychology*, **87**, 47–74.

Alm, J. (1997) *The Dyslexia Project at the Employability Institute of Uppsala*. Gnesta, Sweden: Swedish National Labour Board.

Anderson, B. and Holtsberg, A. (1999) Stava Rätt Wordfinder Software, Hadar Amugruppen, Malmö, Sweden.

Anderson, W. (1994) Adult literacy and learning disabilities. In P.J. Gerber and H.B. Reiff, (Eds.) *Learning Disabilities in Adulthood: Persisting Problems and Evolving Issues*. Boston, MA: Andover Medical Publishers.

Ann Arbor (1997a) *Letter Tracking Book 1*. California, Ann Arbor Publications.

Ann Arbor (1997b) *Word Tracking*. California, Ann Arbor Publications.

Ann Arbor (1997c) *Sentence Tracking*. California, Ann Arbor Publications.

Arnold, H. (1992) *Diagnostic Reading Record*. London: Hodder & Stoughton.

Arts Dyslexia Trust (1996) *Arsdyslex One Conference Book*. London: St. Martins College of Art and Design.

BDA (1999) *Achieving Dyslexia Friendly Schools*. Reading: British Dyslexia Association.

Bell, N. (1991) *Visualising and Verbalising for Language Comprehension and Thinking*. Paso Robles, CA: Academy of Reading Publications.

Bertram, M. (1998) *An examination of screening in further education for dyslexia*. Unpublished study, University of Edinburgh.

Biggar, S. and Barr, J. (1993) The emotional world of specific learning difficulties. In G. Reid (Ed.) *Dimensions of Dyslexia*, Vol. 2: *Literacy, Language and Learning*. Edinburgh: Moray House Publications.

Biller, E.F. (1993) Employment testing of persons with specific learning disabilities. *Journal of Rehabilitation*, **59**, 16–23.

Biller, E.F. (1997) Employment testing and the Americans with Disabilities Act of 1990: Court Cases regarding learning disabilities. In P.J. Gerber and D.S. Brown (Eds.) *Learning Disabilities and Employment*. Texas: Pro-ed Publications.

Binder, A. (1988) *Juvenile Deliquency: Historical, Cultural, Legal Perspectives*. New York: Macmillan Publishing Company.

Blackorby, J. and Wagner, M.M. (1997) The employment outcomes of youth with learning disabilities: A review of findings from the NLTS. In P.J. Gerber and D.S. Brown (Eds.) *Learning Disabilities and Employment*. Texas: Pro-ed Publications, pp. 57–77.

Brinckerhoff, L. (1997) Students with learning disabilities in graduate or professional programs: Emerging issues on campus and challenges to employment. In P.J. Gerber and D.S. Brown (Eds.) *Learning Disabilities and Employment*. Texas: Pro-ed Publications.

BPS (1999a) *Dyslexia, Literacy and Psychological Assessment*. Report by a working party of the division of Educational and Child Psychology of the British Psychological Society.

BPS (1999b) *The Directory of Chartered Psychologists*. Leicester, UK: British Psychological Society.

Broadhead, M.R. and Price, G. (1993) The learning styles of artistically talented adolescents in Canada. In R. Milgram, R. Dunn and G. Price (Eds.) *Teaching and Counselling Talented Adolescents : An International Perspective*. Westport, CT: Praeger.

Brown, D.S. (1997) The new economy in the 21st century: Implications for individuals with learning disabilities. In P.J. Gerber and D.S. Brown (Eds.) *Learning Disabilities and Employment*. Texas: Pro-ed Publications, pp. 19–38.

Bruce, I. (1999) *Genius, Criminals and Children*, 20/20 Television for Channel 4, 25 July 1999.

Burns, R.B. (1986) The self concept. In *Theory, Measurement, Development and Behaviour*. London: Longman.

Buzan, T. (1993) *The Mind Map Book – Radiant Thinking*. London: BBC Books.

Carnevale, A.P., Gainer, L.J. and Meltzer, A.S. (1988) *Workplace basics. The skills employers want*. Alexandria, VA: American Society for Training and Development.

Carter, J. and Maher, P. (1999) *Joint Efforts in Training*. http://novel.nifl.gov/nalld/workplac.htm

Congdon, P. (1989) *Dyslexia: A Pattern of Strengths and Weaknesses*. Solihull: Gifted Children's Information Centre.

Cooley, C.H. (1902) *Human Nature and the Social Order*. New York: Scribner.

Critchley, M. (1966) *Developmental Dyslexia*. London: Heinemann.

Critchley, M. and Critchley, E.A. (1978) *Dyslexia Defined*. London: Heinemann.

Davies, K. and Byatt, J. (1998) *Something can be done!* Shrewsbury, Shropshire: STOP Project.

Davis, R.D. (1997) *The Gift of Dyslexia*. London: Souvenir Press.

Dennison, P.E. and Dennison, G.E. (1989) *Brain Gym* (Teacher's edition, revised). Ventura, CA: Edu–Kinesthetics Inc.

Dennison, P.E. and Hargrove, H. (1985) *Personalised Whole Brain integration*. Glendale, CA: Educ. Kinesthetics.

Drew and Bingham, (1997) *The Student Skills Guide*. Aldershot: Gower.

Dunham, J. (1992) *Stress in Teaching* (2nd edition). London: Routledge.

Dunn, J. (1988) *The Beginnings of Social Understanding*. Oxford: Blackwell.

Dunn, R. and Dunn. K. (1993) *Teaching Secondary Students through their Individual Learning Styles. Practical approaches for grades 7–12*. Needham Heights, MA: Allyn & Bacon.

Dunn, R., Bruno, J., Sklar, R., Zenhausern, R. and Beaudry, J. (1990) Effects of matching and mismatching minority developmental college students' hemispheric preferences on mathematics scores. *Educational Research*, **83** (5), 283–288.

Dunn, R., Dunn, K. and Price, G.E. (1996) *Learning Style Inventory (1975–1996)*. Lawrence, KA: Price Systems.

Dunn, R. and Griggs, S.A. (1988) Learning Styles: The Quiet Revolution in American Secondary Schools. Reston, VA: National Association of Secondary Schools Principals.

Edgar, E. (1987) Secondary programs in special education: Are many of them justifiable? *Exceptional Children*, **53**, 555–561.

Everatt, J. (1997) The abilities and disabilities associated with adult developmental dyslexia. *Journal of Research in Reading (Special Issue: Dyslexia in Literate Adults)*, **20** (1), 13–21.

Everatt, J. Steffert, B. and Smythe, I. (1999) An eye for the unusual: Creative thinking in dyslexics. *Dyslexia*, Vol. 5, No. 1. Wiley: Chichester.

Faas, L. A. and D'Alonzo, B.J. (1990) WAIS-R scores as predictors of employment success and failure among adults with learning disabilities. *Journal of Learning Disabilities*, **23** (5), 311–316.

Fairhurst, P. and Pumfrey, P.D. (1992) Secondary school organisation and self-concepts of pupils with relative reading difficulties. *Research in Education*, **47**.

Fawcett, A.J. and Nicolson, R.I. (1996) *The Dyslexia Screening Test*. London: The Psychological Corporation.

Fawcett, A.J. and Nicolson, R.I. (1997) *The Dyslexia Early Screening Test*. London: The Psychological Corporation.

Fawcett, A.J. and Nicolson, R.I. (1998) *Dyslexia Adult Screening Test*. London: The Psychological Corporation.

Frederickson, N. (1999) The ACID test – or is it? *Educational Psychology in Practice*, **15** (1), 2–8.

Fredrickson, N., Frith,V. and Reason, R. (1997) *Phonological Assessment Battery*. Windsor, Berks: NFER–Nelson.

Frey, W. (1990) Schools miss out on dyslexic engineers. *IEEE Spectrum*, 6 December.

Frith, U. (1995) Dyslexia: Can we have a shared theoretical framework? *Educational and Child Psychology,* **12** (1), 6–17.

Gadwa, K. and Griggs, S.A. (1985) The school dropout: Implications for counselors. *School Counselor*, **33**, 9–17.

Galaburda, A. (Ed.) (1993) *Dyslexia and Development: Neurobiological Aspects of Extraordinary Brains*. Cambridge, MA: Harvard University Press.

Gardner, H. (1983) *Frames of Mind: The Theory of Multiple Intelligences*. New York: Basic Books.

Gerber, P.J. (1997) *Life after school: Challenges in the Workplace*. In P. J. Gerber and D.S. Brown (Eds.) *Learning Disabilities and Employment*. Texas: Pro-ed Publications.

Gerber, P.J. and Brown, D.S. (Eds) (1997) *Learning Disabilities and Employment*. Texas: Pro-ed Publications.

Gerber, P.J., Ginsberg, R. and Reiff, H. (1992) Identifying alterable patterns in employment success for highly successful adults with learning disabilities. *Journal of Learning Disabilities,* **25** (8), 475–487.

Giorcelli, L.R. (1995) *An Impulse to Soar: Sanitisation, Silencing and Special Education*. The Des English Memorial Lecture. Australian Association of Special Education Conference, Darwin. Reproduced in SPELD Celebration of Learning Styles, conference proceedings, 1996, New Zealand, Christchurch.

Giorcelli, L.R. (1999) Inclusion and other factors affecting teachers attitudes to literacy programs for students with special needs. In A.J. Watson and L.R. Giorcelli (Eds.) *Accepting the Literacy Challenge*. Australia: Scholastic Publications.

Given, B.K. and Reid. G. (1999) *Learning Styles: A Guide for Teachers and Parents*. Lancashire, Red Rose Publications.

Grainger, J. (1999) *Attention deficit hyperactivity disorders and reading disorders: How are they related?* In A.J. Watson and L.R. Giorcelli (Eds.) *Accepting the Literacy Challenge*. Australia: Scholastic Publications.

Graves, J. (1999) *Tapping into the Dyslexic's Creativity*. Workshop presented at the conference *Dyslexia into the year 2000*. Adult Dyslexia Organisation and the Scottish Dyslexia Association. Dundee, 12 June 1999.

Grayson, T.E., Wermuth, T.R., Holub, T.M. and Anderson, M.L. (1997) Effective practices of transition from school to work for people with learning disabilities. In P.J. Gerber and D.S. Brown (Eds.) *Learning Disabilities and Employment*. Texas: Pro-ed Publications, pp. 77–100.

Hagtvet, B.E. (1997) Phonological and linguistic-cognitive precursors of reading ability. *Dyslexia*, **3** (3), 163–177.

Hales, G. (1994) The human aspects of dyslexia. In G. Hales (Ed.) *Dyslexia Matters*. London: Whurr Publications.

Halpern, A.S. (1992) Transition: Old wine in new bottles. *Exceptional Children*, **58** (3), 202–211.

Healy, J. (1989) *Endangered Minds*. New York: Doubleday.

Healy, J. (1991) *Endangered Minds*. Touchstone: Simon & Schuster.

Healy, J.M. (1998) *Failure to Connect. How Computers Affect Our Children's Minds – for Better and Worse*. New York: Simon & Schuster.

HEFC (1999) *Dyslexia in Higher Education: Policy, Provision and Practice*. Report of the National Working Party on Dyslexia in Higher Education. Hull: Higher Education Funding Councils of England and Scotland.

Hertfordshire Dyslexia Arts Group (1999) *Dyslexia: An Unwrapped Gift* (Video).

Hill, L.E. (1991) Dyslexia: Is it catching? *English in Education,* **25**, 28–38.

Hinton, J. and Burton, R.F. (1992) Clarification of the concept of psychological stress (PSYSTRESS). *International Journal of Psychosomatics*, **39** (1–4), 42–43.

Hoffmann, F.J., Sheldon, K.L., Minskoff, E.H., Sautter, S.W., Steidle, E.F., Baker, D.P., Bailey, M.B and Echols, L.D. (1987) Needs of learning disabled adults. *Journal of Learning Disabilities,* **20** (1), 43–52.

Hopson, B., Anderson, J. and Kibble, D. (1998) *Learn to Learn* Leeds: Lifeskills Publishing Group.

Hopson, B. and Scully M. (1982) *Lifeskills Teaching Programmes*. Leeds: Lifeskills Associates.

Ingham, J. (1991) Matching instruction with employee perceptual preference significantly increases training effectiveness. *Human Resource Development Quarterly*, **2**, (1; Spring).

James, W. (1892) *Psychology: The Briefer Course*. New York. (published in 1961 by Harper & Row).

Jameson, M. (1999) Setting up support groups. Workshop. Presented at *Dyslexia into the Year 2000* conference, 12 June, Dundee, Scotland.

Kaufman, A.S. (1994) *Intelligent Testing with the WISC-III*. New York: Wiley.

Keefe, J.W. (1989) *Learning Style: Theory and Practice*. Reston, VA: National Association of Secondary School Principals.

Keefe, J.W. (1993) *Learning Style: Theory: Practice: Cognitive Skills*. Reston, VA: National Association of Secondary School Principals.

Kirk, J. (1998) *An Assessment Profile*. Disability Office, University of Edinburgh.

Kirk, J. (1999) *Adaptation of QuickScan for different populations of adults.* University of Edinburgh.

Kirk, J. and Reid, G. (1999) *Adult Dyslexia for Employment and Training (ADEPT).* University of Edinburgh.

Klasen, E. (1988) Helping dyslexics – A task for sharing. *Annals of Dyslexia,* **38**, 22–30.

Klein, C. (1993) *Diagnosing Dyslexia: A Guide to the Assessment of Adults with Specific Learning Difficulties.* London: The Basic Skills Agency.

Klein, C. (1998) *Dyslexia and Offending.* London: Dyspel.

Klein, C. and Sunderland, H. (1998) *Dyslexia Good Practice Guide.* London: Language and Literacy Unit.

Lashley, C. (1995) *Improving Study Skills.* London: Cassell.

Latham, P. H. and Latham, P.S. (1997) Legal rights of adults with disabilities in employment. In P.J. Gerber and D.S. Brown (Eds.) *Learning Disabilities and Employment.* Texas: Pro-ed Publications.

Lawrence, D. (1985) Improving self-esteem and reading. *Educational Research,* **27** (3), 194–200.

Lawrence, D. (1996) *Self-esteem in the Classroom.* London: Paul Chapman Publishing.

Lazear, D. (1994) *Multiple Intelligence Approaches to Assessment.* Tucson, AZ: Zephyr Press.

Lewis, M. (1990) Social knowledge and social development. *Merrill- Palmer Quarterly,* **36**, 93–116.

Lewis, I. and Munn, P. (1987) *So you Want to do Research?* Edinburgh: The Scottish Council for Research in Education.

Lloyd, G. and Norris, C. (1999) Including ADHD? *Disability and Society,* **14** (4), 505–517.

LLLU (1990) *Learning Support: A Different Slant on Teaching Adult Dyslexics.* Occasional Paper No. 5. London Language and Literacy Unit.

LLLU (1991) *Setting Up a Learning Programme for Adult Dyslexics.* Occasional Paper No. 6. London Language and Literacy Unit.

LLLU (1995) *Living Literacies: Papers.* London Language and Literacy Unit.

Luecking, R.G. (1997) Persuading employers to hire people with disabilities. In P.J. Gerber and D.S. Brown, (Eds.) *Learning Disabilities and Employment.* Texas: Pro-ed Publications, pp. 215–234.

Lundberg, I. (1985) Longitudinal studies of reading and reading disability in Sweden. In G.E. Mackinnon and T.G. Walker (Eds.) *Reading Research: Advances in Theory and Practice.* London: Academic Press, pp. 65–105.

Mackie, D. (1996) Adult literacy work – Difficulties and needs in reading and writing. In G. Reid (Ed.) *Dimensions of Dyslexia,* Vol. 1: *Assessment, Teaching and the Curriculum.* Edinburgh: Moray House Publications.

MacLaren, L. (1996) *Understanding Depression*. Geddes & Grosset, Children's Leisure Products Ltd, New Lanark, Scotland.

Margulies, N. (1991) *Mapping Inner Space – Learning and Teaching Mind Mapping*. Tucson, AZ: Zephyr Press.

Maston, W.G. (1989) Learning style, repeated stimuli, and originality in intellectually gifted adolescents. *Psychological Reports*, **65**, 751–754

McDowell, A. (1999) Adept Report (personal communication).

McLoughlin, D., Fitzgibbon, G. and Young, V. (1994) *Adult Dyslexia: Assessment Counselling and Training*. London: Whurr Publishers.

Mead, G.H. (1934) *Mind, Self and Society*. Chicago: University of Chicago Press.

Miles, T.R. (1991) *Bangor Dyslexia Test*. Cambridge: Learning Development Aids.

Miles, T.R. (1996) Do dyslexic children have IQs? *Dyslexia*, **2** (3), 175–178.

Milgram, R., Dunn, R. and Price, G. (Eds.) (1993) *Teaching and Counselling Gifted and Talented Adolescents: An International Learning Style Perspective*. Westport, CT: Praeger.

Minskoff, E.H., Sautter, S.W., Hoffmann, F.J. and Hawks, R. (1987) Employer attitudes toward hiring the learning disabled. *Journal of Learning Disabilities,* **20** (1), 53–57.

Moody, S. (1999) *Arranging a Dyslexia Assessment: A Guide for Adults*. London: Dyslexia Assessment Service.

Moody, S. (n.d.) *Dyslexia: An Employer's Guide.* Obtained from the website at http://futurenet.co.uk/charity/ado/employer.html

Morgan, W. (1996) *London Offender Study: Creating criminals – Why are so many criminals dyslexic?* London: Unpublished dissertation.

Moseley, J. (1996) *Quality Circle Time*. Cambridge, UK: LDA.

Muter, V., Hulme, C. and Snowling, M. (1997) *Phonological Abilities Test*. London: The Psychological Corporation.

Nicolson, R.I. (1996) Developmental dyslexia: Past, present and future. *Dyslexia*, **2** (3), 190–207.

Nicolson, R.I. and Fawcett, A.J. (1997) Development of objective procedures for screening and assessment of dyslexic students in higher education. *Journal of Research in Reading* (Special Issue: *Dyslexia in Literate Adults*), **20** (1), 77–83.

NJCLD (1987) Adults with learning disabilities: A call to action. *Journal of Learning Disabilities,* **20** (3), 172–175. (A Position Paper of the National Joint Committee on Learning Disabilities, 10 February 1985. The Orton Dyslexia Society, Baltimore, MD.)

NJCLD (1994) *Secondary to Postsecondary Education Transition Planning for Students.* A technical report prepared by the National Joint Committee on Learning Disabilities. *Perspectives: Orton Dyslexia Society*, Vol. 20 (No.3, Summer).

Nosek, K. (1997) *Dyslexia in Adults: Taking Charge of your Life*. Dallas, TX: Taylor Publishing Company.

NSW Department of School Education (1995) *Talk, Time, Teamwork; Positive and Practical Information for Schools. Collaborative Management of Students with ADHD*. New South Wales Department of Education, Special Education Directorate, Sydney, Australia.

Ohlis, K., Olofsson, A., Leedale, R.C. and Singleton, C.H. (1999) *ReLS Vuxen Test*. Bollnas, Sweden: ReLS.

Osmond, J. (1993) *The Reality of Dyslexia*. London: Cassell (accompanying a video cassette tape).

Ott, P. (1997) *How to Detect and Manage Dyslexia*. Oxford: Heinemann.

Payne, N. (1997) Job accommodations: What works and why. In P.J. Gerber and D.S. Brown, (Eds.) *Learning Disabilities and Employment*. Texas: Pro-ed Publications, pp. 255–276.

Peer, L. (1998) *Winning with Dyslexia: A Guide for Secondary Schools*. Reading: British Dyslexia Association.

Peer, L. (1999) Dyslexia/SpLD: A reappraisal as we move into the next century. In *The Dyslexia Handbook*. Reading: British Dyslexia Association pp. 62–66.

Pellegrini, A.D. and Horvat, M.A. (1995) Developmental contextualist critique of attention deficit disorder. *Educational Researcher*, **24**, 13–19.

Pillarbox Productions (1992) *Public Eye Programme: Dyslexia and Crime*, 21 September.

Plata, M. and Bone, J. (1989) Perceived importance of occupations by adolescents with and without learning disabilities. *Journal of Learning Disabilities*, **22** (1), 64–65 and 71.

Presland, J. (1991) Explaining away dyslexia. *Educational Psychology in Practice*, **6** (4), 215–221.

Price, G. and Milgram, R.M. (1993) The learning styles of gifted adolescents around the world: Difference and similarities. In R.M. Milgram, R. Dunn and G.E. Price (Eds.) *Teaching and Counselling Talented Adolescents : An International Perspective*. Westport, CT: Praeger.

Proctor, J. (1993) *Occupational stress among primary teachers – individuals, organisations*. Unpublished PhD thesis, University of Aberdeen.

Pumfrey, P.D. (1991) Identifying and alleviating specific learning difficulties: Issues and implications for LEAs, professionals and parents. *Educational Psychology in Practice*, **6** (4), 222–228.

Pumfrey, P.D. (1996) Specific developmental dyslexia: Basics to back. The 15th Vernon–Wall Lecture, British Psychological Society.

Pumfrey, P.D. and Reason, R. (Eds.) (1991) *Specific Learning Difficulties: Challenges and Responses.* London: Routledge.

Rack, J. (1997) Issues in the assessment of developmental dyslexia in adults: Theoretical and applied perspectives. *Journal of Research in Reading* (Special Issue: *Dyslexia in Literate Adults*), **20** (1), 66–76.

Rapp, R.H. (1997) Community college programmes: Their role in preparing students with learning disabilities for employment. In P.J. Gerber and D.S. Brown (Eds.) *Learning Disabilities and Employment.* Texas: Pro-ed Publications.

Raskind, M.H., Higgins, E.L. and Herman, K.L. (1997) Technology in the world for persons with disabilities: Views from the inside. In P.J. Gerber and D.S. Brown (Eds.) *Learning Disabilities and Employment.* Texas: Pro-ed Publications.

Raven, J.C. (1993) *Standard Progressive Matrices.* Oxford: Oxford Psychologists' Press.

Reid, G. (1996a) Perspectives on reading. In G. Reid (Ed.) *Dimensions of Dyslexia*, Vol. 2. Edinburgh: Moray House Publications.

Reid, G. (1996b) *Teacher work stress and organisational climate.* Unpublished PhD, University of Glasgow.

Reid, G. (1996c) *Dimensions of Dyslexia*, Vol. 1: *Assessment, Teaching and the Curriculum.* Edinburgh: Moray House Publications.

Reid (1996d) The positive side of dyslexia. In G. Reid (Ed.) *Dimensions of Dyslexia,* Vol. 2. *Literacy, Language and Learning.* Edinburgh: Moray House Publications.

Reid, G. (1998) *Dyslexia: A Practitioner's Handbook.* Chichester: Wiley.

Reid, G (1999a) *Dyslexia, metacognition and learning styles.* Paper presented at the 11th European Conference on Reading. Stavanger, Norway, August 1999.

Reid, G. (1999b) *Dimensions of dyslexia.* Paper presented at the Learning and Behaviour Future Directions Conference, Auckland, New Zealand, 16 July 1999.

Reid, G. (1999c) Research into dyslexia: Developments and dimensions. In I. Smythe (Ed.) *The Dyslexia Handbook 1999.* Reading: British Dyslexia Association.

Reid, K. and Button, L. (1995) Anna's Story: Narratives of personal experience about being labelled disabled. *Journal of Learning Disabilities*, **28**, 602–614.

Reid, G. and Hinton, J.W. (1996) Supporting the system – Dyslexia and teacher stress. In G. Reid (Ed.) *Dimensions of Dyslexia,* Vol. 2. *Literacy, Language and Learning.* Edinburgh: Moray House Publications.

Reid, G. and Hinton, J.W. (1999) Teacher work stress and school organisation: A suitable case for INSET. *Education Today*, **49** (4), 30–37.

Rice, M. (1998) *Dyslexia and Crime: Some Notes on the Dyspel Claim.* University of Cambridge, Institute of Criminology.

Riddock, B., Sterling, C. Farmer, M. and Morgan, S. (1999) Self-esteem and anxiety in the educational histories of adult dyslexic students. In *Dyslexia*, Vol. 5 (No. 4; December). Chichester: Wiley.

Rose, S., Nadin, P. and Bass, A. (1997) *Learning to Succeed.* Birmingham: Ribbon Publications.

Rule, J. (1999) *British Dyslexia Association press release, 29 October 1999.* Reading: British Dyslexia Association.

Runco, M.A. and Sakamoto, O. (1993) Reaching creatively gifted students through their learning styles. In R.M. Milgram, R. Dunn and G.E. Price (Eds.) *Teaching and Counselling Talented Adolescents: An International Perspective.* Westport, CT: Praeger.

Saunders, (1990) Dyslexia as a factor in the young adult offender. in G. Hales (Ed.) *Meeting Points in Dyslexia.* Reading: British Dyslexia Association.

Sauter, D.L. and McPeek, D. (1993) Dyslexia in the workplace: Implications of the Americans with Disabilities Act. *Annals of Dyslexia,* **43**, 271–278.

Scarborough, H.S. (1984) Continuity between childhood dyslexia and adult reading. *British Journal of Psychology*, **75**, 329–348.

Schonell, F.J. and Schonell, F.E. (1950) *Diagnostic and Attainment Testing.* Edinburgh: Oliver & Boyd.

Shaywitz, S.E., Fletcher, J.M. and Shaywitz, B.A. (1997) A conceptual model and definition of dyslexia: Findings from the Connecticut longitudinal study. In J.H. Beitchman, N. Cohen, M.M. Konstantarias, R. Tannock, (Eds.) *Language Learning and Behaviour Disorders.* New York: Cambridge University Press.

Simonton, D.K. (1988) *Scientific Genius.* New York: Cambridge University Press

Singleton, C.H. (Chair) (1999a) *Dyslexia in Higher Education: Policy, Provision and Practice.* Report of the National Working Party on Dyslexia in Higher Education. Hull: University of Hull.

Singleton, C.H. (1999b) *Computerised cognitive profiling and the development of reading and spelling skills.* Paper presented at the 11th European Conference on Reading, Stavanger, Norway, August 1999.

Singleton, C.H., Thomas, K.V. and Horne, J.K. (in press) Computerised cognitive profiling and the development of reading and spelling skills. *Journal of Research in Reading*, **23** (1).

Singleton, C.H., Thomas, K.V. and Leedale R.C. (1996/97) *CoPS Baseline Assessment System.* Beverley, East Yorkshire: Lucid Research Limited.

Singleton, C.H., Thomas, K.V., Plant R.R. and Leedale, R.C. (1997) *Computer-based assessment of reading and spelling.* Paper presented at the Fourth International Conference of the British Dyslexia Association, University of York, April 1997.

Singleton, C. H., Trotter, J.M. and Smart, E. (1998) *Pre-assessment Screening for Dyslexia in Higher Education.* Interim report on a project funded by the Higher Education Funding Council for England. Hull: University of Hull.

Smart, E. and Singleton, C.H. (in preparation) *Screening for dyslexia in higher education.* Final report on a project funded by the Higher Education Funding Council for England. Hull: University of Hull.

Smith, P. and Whetton, C. (1988) *Basic Skills Test.* Windsor, Berks: NFER–Nelson.

Smythe, I. (Ed.) (1999) *The Dyslexia Handbook 1999.* Reading: British Dyslexia Association.

Spadafore Diagnostic Reading Test (1983) Academic Therapy Publications, USA.

Smythe, I. and Salter, R. (1997) *The International Book of Dyslexia.* London: The Dyslexia Network Foundation.

Stanovich, K. (1991) Discrepancy definitions of reading disability: Has intelligence led us astray? *Reading Research Quarterly*, **26**, 7–29.

Stanovich, K.E. (1996) Towards a more inclusive definition of dyslexia. *Dyslexia*, **2** (3), 154–166.

Thomson, W. (1999) *Short Stories and Poetry.* Stirling: Scottish Dyslexia Association.

Treffinger, D.J. (1991) Creative productivity: Understanding its sources and nurture. *Illinois Council for the Gifted Journal*, **10**, 6–8.

Treffinger, D.J. and Selby, E.C. (1993) Giftedness, creativity and learning style: Exploring the connections. In R.M. Milgram, R. Dunn and G. Price (Eds.) *Teaching and Counseling Gifted and Talented Adolescents.* An International Learning Style Perspective. Westport, CT: Praeger.

Turner, M. (1997) *Psychological Assessment of Dyslexia.* London: Whurr Publishers.

Vail, P.L. (1992) *Learning Styles: Food for Thought and 130 Practical Tips for Teachers, K-4.* Rosemount, NJ: Modern Learning Press.

Vinegrad, M. (1994) A revised adult dyslexia checklist. *Educare*, **48**, 21–23.

Ward, C. and Daley, J. (1993) *Learning to Learn. Strategies for Accelerating Learning and Boosting Performance.* Christchurch, New Zealand: Ward & Daley.

Watkins, M.W., Kush, J.C. and Glutting, J.J. (1997) Discriminant and predictive validity of the WISC-III. ACID profile among children with learning disabilities. *Psychology in the Schools*, **34** (4), 309–319.

Wechsler, D. (1981) *Wechsler Adult Intelligence Scale – Revised.* New York: The Psychological Corporation.

Wechsler, D. (1992) *The Wechsler Intelligence scale for Children – Third edition* (WISC-III) New York: The Psychological Corporation.

Wechsler, D. (1999a) *Wechsler Adult Intelligence Test (WAIS-III)*. New York: The Psychological Corporation.

Wechsler, D. (1999b) *Wechsler Memory Scale (WMS-III)*. New York: The Psychological Corporation.

Weedon, C., Reid, G., Ferguson, B. and Mullin, K. (1999) *Listening and Literacy Index* (Pilot Edition). London: Hodder & Stoughton.

Weedon, C. and Reid, G. (2000) *Listening and Literacy Index*. London: Hodder & Stoughton.

Weimer, B.B., Cappotelli, M. and DiCamillo, J. (1994) Self-advocacy: A working proposal for adolescents with special needs. *Intervention in School and Clinic*, **30**, (1; September), 47–52.

West, T.G. (1991) *In the Mind's Eye: Visual Thinkers, Gifted People with Learning Difficulties, Computer Images, and the Ironies of Creativity.* Buffalo, NY: Prometheus Books.

West, T.G. (1997a) Slow Words, Quick Images – Dyslexia as an Advantage in Tomorrow's Workplace. In P.J. Gerber and D.S. Brown (Eds.) *Learning Disabilities and Employment*. Texas: Pro-ed Publications.

West, T.G. (1997b) *In the Mind's Eye: Visual Thinkers, Gifted People with Learning Difficulties, Computer Images and the Ironies of Creativity* (2nd edition). Buffalo, NY: Prometheus Books.

West, T. (1999) *The future is with the dyslexics*. Paper presented at Dyslexia and Employment, Now and the Future Conference, 17 September 1999. London: Adult Dyslexia Organisation.

Wilkinson, G.S. (1993) *Wide Range Achievement Test*. Delaware: Wide Range Inc.

Will, M. (1984) *Keynote address*. Convention of the Association for Children and Adults with Learning Disabilities, New Orleans.

Wood, J.R.A. and Burns, R.B. (1983) Self-concept and reading ability in ESN (M) pupils. *Research in Education*, **29**, 41–55

Woods, K. and Reason, R. (1999) Concentrating in exams. *Educational Psychology in Practice*, **15** (1).

Wright, S.F., Fields, H. and Newman, S.P. (1996) Dyslexia stability of definition over a five-year period. *Journal of Reading*, **19** (1), 46–60.

YHDS (1999) *Quality Assurance of Provision for People with Dyslexia*. Sheffield: York and Humberside Disability Services.

Zdzienski, D. (1997) *Study Scan*. PICO Educational Systems Ltd, London.

Index

Index compiled by Sylvia Potter